Envisioning a Critical and Liberatory Approach to Trans and Queer Center(ed) Diversity Work

Beth Powers and Virginia Stead
Series Editors

Vol. 21

Envisioning a Critical and Liberatory Approach to Trans and Queer Center(ed) Diversity Work

Edited by
D. Chase J. Catalano, Antonio Duran,
T.J. Jourian, and Jonathan T. Pryor

PETER LANG
New York · Berlin · Bruxelles · Chennai · Lausanne · Oxford

Library of Congress Cataloging-in-Publication Control Number
LCCN: 2025004150

Bibliographic information published by the Deutsche Nationalbibliothek.
The German National Library lists this publication in the German
National Bibliography; detailed bibliographic data is available
on the Internet at http://dnb.d-nb.de.

Cover design by Peter Lang Group AG
Cover Image
© iStock, DebraLee Wiseberg (ID:1095981608)

ISSN 2330-4502 (print)
ISBN 9783034350266 (paperback)
ISBN 9783034350242 (ebook)
ISBN 9783034350259 (epub)
DOI 10.3726/b22778

© 2025 Peter Lang Group AG, Lausanne, Switzerland
Published by Peter Lang Publishing Inc., New York, USA

info@peterlang.com – www.peterlang.com

All rights reserved.
All parts of this publication are protected by copyright.
Any utilization outside the strict limits of the copyright law, without the permission of the publisher, is forbidden and liable to prosecution. This applies in particular to reproductions, translations, microfilming, and storage and processing in electronic retrieval systems.

This publication has been peer reviewed.

CONTENTS

List of Tables ix
Acknowledgments xi

Introduction: Conceptualizing a Critical, Liberatory Approach
to TQ Center(ed) Diversity Work 1
*D. Chase J. Catalano, Antonio Duran, T.J. Jourian,
and Jonathan T. Pryor*

Part I Historical and Theoretical Foundations

Chapter 1 Histories, Foundations, and Tensions of TQ Center(ed)
Diversity Work 15
Roman Christiaens

Chapter 2 Frameworks to Guide TQ Center(ed) Diversity
Work: Bridging Critical Theories with Practice 41
Antonio Duran and J. Audra Williams

Part II Present Realities

Chapter 3   Advocating for Equitable Policies for Trans and Queer Communities in Higher Education   57
Em C. Huang and Andy Cofino

Chapter 4   Engaging Institutional Politics through a Power Analysis in TQ Center(ed) Diversity Work   77
Jonathan T. Pryor, Antonio Duran, and Vanessa Aviva González-Siegel

Chapter 5   Beyond Silos: Opportunities for Collaborations Across Student and Academic Affairs with TQ Center(ed) Diversity Workers   87
Chelsea E. Noble and Justin A. Gutzwa

Chapter 6   Rethinking Staffing and Hiring in TQ Center(ed) Diversity Work   105
R.B. Brooks and Tristan Crowell

Chapter 7   From "Safe" to Liberatory: A New Approach to Educating Campus Communities with TQ Center(ed) Diversity Workers   125
Kalyani Kannan and D. Chase J. Catalano

Chapter 8   Serving Trans Students and Addressing Trans Oppression within TQ Center(ed) Diversity Work   143
Alex C. Lange

Chapter 9   Who Said it Was Simple?: Reframing Difficulties and Failures of Supporting Trans and Queer People of Color (TQPOC) Students in TQ Center(ed) Diversity Work   163
Mycall Akeem Riley

Chapter 10   Attending to Ableism in Trans and Queer Center(ed) Diversity Work   175
Ryan A. Miller and Liz Elsen

Part III Visions for the Future

Chapter 11 Senior Leaders as Trans and Queer Advocates
             for TQ Center(ed) Diversity Work   193
             Joshua Moon Johnson

Chapter 12 TQ Center(ed) Diversity Work in Challenging
             Sociopolitical Environments   205
             Kathleen Hobson and T.J. Jourian

Conclusion: Dreaming of Liberation & Solidarity: Notes for How
We Keep Going   225
D. Chase J. Catalano and T.J. Jourian

Notes on Contributors   237

LIST OF TABLES

Table 3.1. Policy Assessment Worksheet   73
Table 8.1. Reflection Questions Based on Love's (2018) Framework 155

ACKNOWLEDGMENTS

This book was our effort to offer a contemporary take on the formative 2002 book, *Our Place on Campus: Lesbian, Gay, Bisexual, Transgender Services and Programs in Higher Education* by Drs. Ronnie Sanlo, Sue Rankin, and Robert Schoenberg. We were (un)surprised and disappointed that in the last 20 years, despite numerous mentions of the need for attention on TQ center(ed) diversity work and workers, a similar text did not emerge. Our motivation was simply to utilize our varying levels and lengths of service in TQ centers and the relationships we had across communities to contribute a book that would enliven conversations about doing and supporting TQ center(ed) work. We thank the Spencer Foundation for the Spencer Conference Grant (*Racial justice and anti-racism work in LGBTQ+ Centers: Creating a shared vision with scholars and practitioners*) that gave us the funding to bring together a collective of practitioners and scholars in the summer of 2022 to dream and discuss about what it means to engage in liberatory TQ center(ed) work. As we endeavored on this book project, in 2023 and 2024, legislative efforts targeted diversity, equity, and inclusion (DEI) in higher education and trans and queer existence and autonomy everywhere, which only increased the necessity for this book. We hope that within these pages TQ center(ed) workers find hope, inspiration, and strategies that will encourage everyone to resist this current iteration of state violence on minoritized communities and advocate for the resurgence of TQ centers shuttered during this time.

On behalf of all the editors, we sincerely appreciate the many individuals whose considerable labor led to the construction and completion of this book. We want to first acknowledge that this book would not be possible without each chapter author who contributed their insights and energies into the pages of this volume. We are grateful to the team at Peter Lang, especially Dr. Alison E. Jefferson, who saw the value in our proposal for practitioners and scholars. We are indebted to our external reviewers who provided important feedback through supportive questions and suggestions to ensure these were the strongest chapters possible: Brian Arao, Asher Burns, Justin A. Gutzwa, Joshua Moon Johnson, Susan Marine, Laila McCloud, Roberto Orozco, Daniel Tillapaugh, Rachel Wagner, Alina Wong. Of course, we also want to take a sentence to recognize each other as editors who approached this project with care and passion in our hopes to provide scholarship that supports TQ center(ed) workers and work. For Chase, Antonio, and Jonathan, we want to express our appreciation to the institutions where we work that encouraged our scholarship: Virginia Tech, Arizona State University, and California State University, Fresno, respectively. Lastly, we want to express our sincerest gratitude to every previous, current, and future TQ center(ed) diversity worker in higher education. We know your work often goes under/unacknowledged and under-resourced, and then pigeonholed as niche, despite the depth and breadth of what you do to cultivate transformative learning environments. We see you and know you are doing tremendous work to support students, staff, administrators, faculty, and our collective diverse communities. Thank you for all of your passion, investment, and fortitude.

INTRODUCTION: CONCEPTUALIZING A CRITICAL, LIBERATORY APPROACH TO TQ CENTER(ED) DIVERSITY WORK

D. Chase J. Catalano, Antonio Duran, T.J. Jourian, and Jonathan T. Pryor

> The diversity worker has a job because diversity and equality are not already given; this obvious fact has some less obvious consequences. When your task is to remove the necessity of your existence, then your existence is necessary for the task.
>
> —Ahmed (2012, p. 23)

Introduction

This chapter provides the overall approach to the edited volume including the language we use, the rationale for its existence, and who should read it. Within this introduction, we name significant bodies of literature that support this practical and scholarly volume, together with theoretical and conceptual ideas that undergird the entire text. Our introduction also provides clarity on what we mean by critical and liberatory approaches to practice. We conclude with providing readers a roadmap to the book that clarifies what they can expect within each chapter.

Initially named the Human Sexuality Office, higher education's first LGBT Center in 1971 was at the University of Michigan (Fine, 2012; Marine, 2011; University of Michigan, n.d.). The decades that followed revealed a slow emergence of campus-based resources for trans and queer (TQ) students, whether through the creation of institutionally supported cultural centers or others through persistent work of grassroots leaders and tempered radicals (Broadhurst & Martin, 2019; Broadhurst et al., 2018). As of the spring of 2024, there are over 260 offices or centers staffed by at least one professional staff member who devotes half or more of their time or a graduate assistant for 20 hours per week whose responsibility officially includes LGBT services (The Consortium of Higher Education LGBT Professionals [Consortium], 2020). Over the next 50 years, an array of scholarship emerged to describe, document, and support those who engage in student-centered work for TQ populations (e.g., Bazarsky et al., 2022; Ritchie & Banning, 2001; Sanlo, 2000).

In a bit of a departure from traditional LGBTQ+ student services language, we intentionally use the language of TQ center(ed) diversity work. We take this approach to begin with trans communities and in recognition that those who engage in supporting, sustaining, and advocating for TQ communities operate both within and outside of the boundaries of a stand-alone TQ center (Oliveira et al., 2025). We also take this approach to resist the use and expansion of LGBTQ+ as an acronym that only seems to engage in additive politics of afterthought that fails to describe the multitudes of our communities. The use of TQ center(ed) diversity worker is a nod to unequal distribution of justice work that is often undervalued by organizational leaders yet expected to project the promise of higher education (Ahmed, 2012). TQ center(ed) diversity work has the arduous (read: impossible) task to solve the problems of injustice and inequality at the college or university, entering from the point of TQ identities. In short, work is an apt description for the tremendous effort required of the role and reflects our intentional language shift to signal our broader approach to this volume: a critical and intersectional exploration of TQ center(ed) work that seeks liberatory futures that benefit all campus communities.

We author this introduction during a time when legislative efforts center TQ antagonism (Branigin & Kirkpatrick, 2022), seek to whitewash U.S. histories, and diminish the funding and aims of diversity, equity, and inclusion work in higher education (The Chronicle of Higher Education, 2023). We do not believe this book is an antidote to the current climate that challenges our existence. We offer this book as one tool of resistance. Resistance to efforts to silence, marginalize, and deny bodily autonomy to our existence. Resistance to the oversimplification that TQ center(ed) work is only about gender and sexuality. Our resistance manifested in this edited volume where we asked authors to critically reflect on the past and present, and to dream of futures that explicate what liberation looks and feels like. Our resistance is also a recognition that this project is a departure from the literature that helped build TQ center(ed) diversity work.

For instance, the edited volume dedicated to LGBT student services work published over 20 years ago by Ronni Sanlo, Sue Rankin, and Robert Schoenberg (The Greenwood Educators' Reference Collection, 2002) was a landmark publication opening the pathway for contemporary TQ center(ed) work. There has not been another comprehensive volume on LGBT student services, nor TQ center(ed) diversity work. Similarly crucial to our project are other tomes such as those about cultural centers (Patton, 2010), multicultural student services (Stewart, 2011), trans people in higher education (Beemyn, 2019; Nicolazzo, 2016), and queer people of color in higher education (Duran, 2021; Johnson & Javier, 2017). These works contributed to policies, practices, and education of TQ center(ed) diversity workers. We offer our volume as building from the foundation of those publications *and* we forge our own pathway forward by taking a more intentionally critical, intersectional, and liberatory approach to TQ center(ed) diversity work.

As editors of *Envisioning a Critical and Liberatory Approach to Trans and Queer Center(ed) Diversity Work*, we had a few audiences in mind for this book. First, to address the paucity of formal educational opportunities for those interested in becoming and those already in the role of practitioner, we invited in and encouraged authorship by TQ center(ed) diversity work practitioners or former practitioners. Second, our chapter topics provide practice-based insights to illuminate the complexity of this work for scholars without formal professional experience or for whom practitioner work was years prior. Finally, we hope that instructors in higher education and student affairs graduate programs, as well as adjacent programs (e.g., women and gender studies, sexuality studies, sociology, American studies), will use this book as course materials to expand career possibilities for TQ center(ed) diversity work.

The Literature and Theories We Build From

TQ center(ed) diversity work literature exists across a vast array of research and scholarship including, but not limited to, educational endeavors (e.g., Draughn et al., 2002; Evans, 2002; Poynter & Tubbs, 2008; Woodford et al., 2014), emergence of TQ centers (e.g., Fine, 2012; Self, 2015), staffing practices and training (e.g., Catalano & Tillapaugh, 2020; Oliveira et al., 2025; Pryor & Hoffman, 2021; Sanlo, 2000), hegemonic whiteness in TQ centers (e.g., Duran & Jourian, 2023; Lange et al., 2022; Ortiz & Mandala, 2021), and programmatic efforts (e.g., Marine & Nicolazzo, 2014). Sadly, there remains insufficient content and conversation within graduate preparation programs of these publications and training for staff in preparation for formal roles tends to be inadequate (Oliveira et al., 2025; Tillapaugh & Catalano, 2019). We find it disconcerting, to say the least, that after over 50 years of existence in higher education and 20 years of scholarship, that TQ center(ed) diversity work remains a niche area of knowledge (see Duran et al., 2023 for a systematic literature review).

The chapters within this volume will cover the terrain of literature that builds the foundation of this work. Threaded throughout each chapter is a reliance on critical theories and liberatory frameworks to encourage more capacious discussions of what TQ center(ed) diversity work should and could be. In Chapter 2, Antonio Duran and J. Audra Williams unpack a variety of critical theories (e.g., queer theory, queer of color critique, critical trans politics) and places them in conversation with National Coming Out Day (NCOD), an annual event on many campuses on October 11 to celebrate awareness of TQ identities. Duran and Williams' approach makes explicit the relationship between theory and enactment, power and privilege, and interpersonal, institutional, and systemic manifestations of oppression. By taking up critical theories as their framework(s), these chapters reveal challenges and opportunities for TQ center(ed) work and workers to transform higher education into hospitable places and spaces. A critical stance invites readers to consider the limitations of characterizing diversity through demographic percentages and assuaging complaints of exclusion through one-off programs or under-funded services (Stewart, 2018).

We offer a liberatory perspective that takes the radical position that liberation is possible. For us, this means instead of responding to the existence of oppression, we imagine a world without oppression and move towards it; we must envision what we hope to transform our campuses into and use that vision as our compass. We take the position that for sustainable, institutional, and systemic justice to occur, we all must contribute to their emergence (Love, 2018). Liberation must include considerations of critical theories (Ryoo & McLaren, 2010), that are anti-oppressive and praxis-based (Freire, 1970), and rely on an intersectional analysis (Crenshaw, 1989, 1991). We envision liberation as resistance to the dehumanization that is the result of oppression, pursued through continuous reflections, and constant pursuit of actions that seek freedom for everyone (Freire, 1970). We offer the development of a liberatory consciousness (Love, 2018), made of four non-linear components of awareness (noticing and content acquisition), analysis (meaning making and theorizing), action (efforts and practices), and accountability (recognition of responsibilities to others), as a framework for humans to operationalize. The four components work simultaneously to draw attention to the dynamics of oppression *and* resist hopelessness that comes from that awareness through analyzing the roles we all play, taking action to interrupt our collusion, and understanding our responsibilities to multiple communities for our actions and inactions (Love, 2018). For instance, in returning to Duran and Williams' chapter, they provide information about critical theories (awareness) and how a reader might consider the necessity of those theories for TQ center(ed) diversity work (analysis). Then, they use NCOD to consider TQ center(ed) diversity work programming (actions) and provide questions for how those events may fall short of critical and intersectional approaches (accountability). Taken in its entirety, this volume coalesces chapters that contribute to various aspects of a liberatory consciousness to inspire readers in their personal and professional development, as well as the development of relationships and mechanisms to transform institutions and systems. To foster reflection, when compelled, authors provided questions that they would ask of readers after engaging with their content at the end of their chapter.

Overview of the Book

We structured the book into three sections: Historical and Theoretical Foundations, Present Realities, and Visions for the Future. In Part I, we begin with Roman Christiaens' Chapter 1: Histories, Foundations and Tensions of TQ Center(ed) Diversity Work. Christiaens' chapter explores the many practices and spaces of TQ center(ed) diversity work as signs of both investment in TQ inclusion and advocacy and mechanisms of absorption and assimilation. Their chapter examines the tensions within the foundation and norms of this work while presenting considerations for its impact on the present and future realities of TQ center(ed) professionals. As previously mentioned, Chapter 2: Frameworks to Guide TQ Center(ed) Diversity Work: Bridging Critical Theories with Practice by Antonio Duran and J. Audra Williams overviews critical theories that are relevant to chapters throughout the book. This chapter is foundational to this edited text in how Duran and Williams introduce readers to the relevant critical theories necessary to TQ center(ed) diversity work. TQ center(ed) diversity workers will find it helpful as a summary of potential frameworks relevant to their work such as queer theory, queer of color critique, and critical whiteness studies. Making the chapter relevant to TQ center(ed) practice is Duran and Williams' use of National Coming Out Day as a case study to showcase how different frameworks accomplish distinct goals in serving TQ communities in higher education.

We transition from the historical and theoretical to Part II: Present Realities where we traverse a range of topics that TQ center(ed) diversity workers might encounter in their campus-based work. Em C. Huang and Andy Cofino's Chapter 3 addresses Advocating for Equitable Policies for Trans and Queer Communities in Higher Education. They argue for the importance of including TQ experiences in decisions about institutional, state, and federal legislation. Their chapter will deepen reader understanding of the complexities of advocating for equitable policies as a core tenet of TQ center(ed) diversity work.

In Chapter 4: Engaging Institutional Politics through a Power Analysis in TQ Center(ed) Diversity Work, Jonathan T. Pryor, Antonio Duran, and Vanessa Aviva González-Siegel offer insights on how to shift the work from student-facing programming to institutional-facing to challenge power structures for inclusion. Pryor, Duran, and González-Siegel elucidates how TQ center(ed) diversity workers can identify their spheres of influence, conduct an accurate and robust power analysis, and shift their focus to develop systems-thinking practices. In a specific look at the location of TQ center(ed) diversity work in relationship to the academic affairs of the institution, Chelsea E. Noble and Justin A. Gutzwa, pen Beyond Silos: Opportunities for Collaborations Across Student and Academic Affairs with TQ Center(ed) Diversity Workers (Chapter 5). Typically, TQ center(ed) diversity work happens within student affairs, siloed from academic affairs (Gutzwa & Owis, 2023). TQ students do not only need support and advocacy in their broader campus life; they experience trans- and queer-antagonism in the classroom and other academic contexts (Gutzwa, 2021). Grounded in scholarship about TQ center(ed) work, TQ students' academic experiences, and faculty attitudes towards identity-based inclusion efforts, this chapter describes current collaborations across student and academic affairs. Additionally, Noble and Gutzwa identify opportunities for student and academic affairs to advance their joint efforts to create conditions in which TQ students can learn and thrive.

Chapter 6: Rethinking Staffing and Hiring in TQ Center(ed) Diversity Work by R.B. Brooks and Tristan Crowell turns our attention specifically to places and spaces devoted to TQ center(ed) diversity work. They begin with the premise that some of the biggest challenges faced by TQ center(ed) diversity workers begin before the person starts their position as hiring decisions may not account for TQ population needs, especially at the intersections of identities. Brooks and Crowell take a critical examination of how hiring practices, using data from The Consortium self-studies, fail to adequately prepare, consider, and address the needs of TQ center(ed) diversity work and workers. They draw attention to how along with the myriad number of responsibilities of TQ center(ed) diversity work includes such as educational efforts to increase campus support for TQ populations (Oliveira et al., 2025), there is also the work of hiring and training staff. Another common responsibility of TQ center(ed) workers are TQ-based social justice educational interventions, often named Safe Zone or Ally Training (e.g., Draughn et al., 2002; Evans, 2002; Woodford et al., 2014) ostensibly aim to develop heterosexual and cisgender allies (DeVita & Anders, 2018), raise awareness, and foster good intentions (Finkel et al., 2003). In Chapter 7: From "Safe" to Liberatory: A New Approach to Educating Campus Communities with TQ Center(ed) Diversity Workers, Kalyani Kannan and D. Chase J. Catalano address how TQ center(ed) diversity practitioners might reimagine these educational workshops to engage attendees in critical self-awareness (Wagner & Catalano, 2021), analysis of power and oppression, actions for change, and establish accountability across and within communities (Love, 2018).

TQ center(ed) diversity work must balance addressing the needs and priorities of the broader communities and those of specific communities. In Chapter 8: Addressing Trans Oppression and Serving Trans Students within TQ Center(ed) Diversity Work, Alex C. Lange recognizes how some campuses seek to support trans students while others circulate trans oppression through their (in)actions. Their chapter first provides a summary of the support trans students need to thrive and persist in college environments, with a focus on the work and advocacy TQ center(ed) diversity work can forward in their roles. Then, they review how trans oppression manifests on college campuses at interpersonal, organizational, and cultural levels while providing ways for educators to address these dynamics. Lange's chapter concludes with reflective questions for practitioners and administrators to consider trans students' needs holistically on campus. In Chapter 9: Who Said it Was Simple?: Reframing Difficulties and Failures of Supporting Trans and Queer People of Color (TQPOC) Students in TQ Center(ed) Diversity Work, Mycall Akeem Riley challenges expectations that inclusion for TQPOC requires only desire for inclusion with minimal efforts. Riley argues that most programs and services in TQ center(ed) diversity work spaces reassert hegemonic systems instead of dismantling them. Riley provides a critical analysis of these supports and uses critical theories to imagine how to create resources that are supportive, affirming, and transformative.

Closing out Part II is Chapter 10: Attending to Ableism in TQ Center(ed) Diversity Work by Ryan Miller and Liz Elsen. Their chapter focuses on disabled TQ people's overlapping forms of oppression (ableism and heterosexism and/or genderism). Within TQ center(ed) work in higher education, disability and ableism are often ignored or treated as an afterthought, at best rendering disability invisible (or potentially rendering people hyper-visible through tokenization) and at worst actively excluding disabled TQ people from physical and online spaces, programming, policies, and practices. Their chapter draws from scholarly literature about disabled TQ collegians and findings from a qualitative study of disabled TQ students and their experiences with TQ centers. They highlight promising practices and conclude with a discussion of how campus-based practitioners and policymakers can create anti-ableist environments for and with disabled TQ people.

In Part III: Visions for the Future we explore what it means to engage in imagining what we hope will be for us all. In Chapter 11: Senior Leaders as Trans and Queer Advocates for TQ Center(ed) Diversity Work, Joshua Moon Johnson offers suggestions on how senior leaders in higher education can offer tangible support for TQ center(ed) workers. Speaking from experience in a variety of roles in and supporting TQ center(ed) work, they offer important insights into what it means to demonstrate the kind of leadership that supports the work of social justice. Kathleen Hobson and T.J. Jourian, in Chapter 12: TQ Center(ed) Diversity Work in Challenging Sociopolitical Environments continue the conversation about how to engage in TQ center(ed) diversity work in precarious socio-political times. Contextualized in the current moment and informed through our collective histories, Hobson and Jourian offer practical and strategic recommendations for practitioners. Their chapter leans on critical hope (Duncan-Andrade, 2009) to instill a queer futurity orientation (Muñoz, 2009) that helps us all dream new worlds into being.

The book's conclusion by D. Chase J. Catalano and T.J. Jourian weave together the collective wisdom and insights from preceding chapters to characterize what it means to engage in critical, intersectional, and liberatory TQ center(ed) diversity work in higher education. They resist the expectation to provide "best practices" because institutions, practitioners, scholars, and communities are too capacious to prescribe any singular action to attend to our needs, desires, and dreams. Instead, they center our critical, intersectional, and liberatory roots to offer reflection questions to inspire thinking and imagining about collectives without boundaries and coalitional relationships to foster sustainable change.

References

Ahmed, S. (2012). *On being included: Racism and diversity in institutional life*. Duke University Press.

Bazarsky, D., Edwards, B. J., Jensen, L., Subbaraman, S., Sugiyama, B., & Travers, S. (2022). Standards of practice: Core competencies for LGBTQIA+ directors and professionals in higher education. *Journal of Diversity in Higher Education*, 15(2), 141–152. https://doi.org/10.1037/dhe0000282

Beemyn, G. (2019). *Trans people in higher education*. SUNY Press.

Branigin, A., & Kirkpatrick, N. (2022, October 14). Anti-trans laws are on the rise. Here's a look at where—and what kind. *The Washington Post*. https://www.washingtonpost.com/lifestyle/2022/10/14/anti-trans-bills/

Broadhurst, C., & Martin, G. (2019). Becoming a tempered radical: Student affairs administrators as advocates for LGBTQ students at eight higher education institutions in the south. *Journal of College and Character*, 20(4), 327–344. https://doi.org/10.1080/2194587X.2019.1669462

Broadhurst, C., Martin, G., Hoffshire, M., & Takewell, W. (2018). "Bumpin' up against people and their beliefs": Narratives of student affairs administrators creating change for LGBTQ students in the south. *Journal of Diversity in Higher Education*, 11(4), 385–401. https://doi.org/10.1037/dhe0000036

Catalano, D. C. J., & Tillapaugh, D. (2020). Identity, role, and oppression: Experiences of LGBTQ resource center graduate assistants. *Journal of Student Affairs Research & Practice*, 57(5), 519–531. https://doi.org/10.1080/19496591.2019.1699104

Crenshaw, K. (1989). Demarginalizing the intersection of race and sex: A Black feminist critique of antidiscrimination doctrine, feminist theory and antiracist politics. *University of Chicago Legal Forum*, 1989(1), 139–168. http://chicagounbound.uchicago.edu/uclf/vol1989/iss1/8

Crenshaw, K. (1991). Mapping the margins: Intersectionality, identity politics, and violence against women of color. *Stanford Law Review*, 43(6), 1241–1299. https://doi.org/10.2307/1229039

DeVita, J., & Anders, A. (2018). LGBTQ faculty and professionals in higher education: Defining allies, identifying support. *College Student Affairs Journal*, 36(2), 63–80. https://doi.org/10.1353/csj.2018.0016

Draughn, T., Elkins, B., & Roy, R. (2002). Allies in the struggle: Eradicating homophobia and heterosexism on campus. *Journal of Lesbian Studies*, 6(3–4), 9–20. https://doi.org/10.1300/J155v06n03_02

Duncan-Andrade, J. M. R. (2009). Note to educators: Hope required when growing roses in concrete. *Harvard Educational Review, 79*(2), 181–194.

Duran, A. (2021). *The experiences of queer students of color at historically white institutions: Navigating intersectional identities on campus*. Routledge.

Duran, A., Catalano, D. C. J., Pryor, J. T., Taylor, J. L., & Jourian, T.J. (2023). Mapping the rise of LGBTQ+ student affairs: A 20 year review. *Journal of Student Affairs Research and Practice, 60*(2), 181–193. https://doi.org/10.1080/19496591.2022.2032112

Duran, A., & Jourian, T.J. (2023). A narrative inquiry study exploring LGBTQ+ center professionals' engagements with anti-racism. *The Journal of Higher Education, 94*(3), 333–356. https://doi.org/10.1080/00221546.2022.2093077

Evans, N. J. (2002). The impact of an LGBT Safe Zone Project on campus climate. *Journal of College Student Development, 43*(4), 522–539.

Fine, L. E. (2012). The context of creating space: Assessing the likelihood of college LGBT center presence. *Journal of College Student Development, 53*(2), 285–299. https://doi.org/10.1353/csd.2012.0017

Finkel, M. J., Storaasli, R. D., Bandele, A., & Schaefer, V. (2003). Diversity training in graduate school: An exploratory evaluation of the Safe Zone Project. *Professional Psychology: Research and Practice, 34*(5), 555–561. https://doi.org/10.1037/0735-7028.34.5.555

Freire, P. (1970). *Pedagogy of the oppressed*. Penguin Books.

Gutzwa, J. A. (2021). "It's not worth me being who I am": Exploring how trans* collegians navigate classroom experiences through a funds of identity lens. *Journal of Women & Gender in Higher Education, 14*(3), 302–323. https://www.tandfonline.com/doi/full/10.1080/26379112.2021.1990077

Gutzwa, J. A., & Owis, B. (2023). Transgressing educational divides: Building bridges between K-12 and postsecondary trans studies. In A. Duran, K. K. Strunk, & R. Schey (Eds.), *Bridging the rainbow gap: Possibilities and tensions in queer and trans studies in education* (pp. 151–171). Brill.

Hooks, B. (1994). *Teaching to transgress: Education as the practice of freedom*. Routledge.

Johnson, J. M., & Javier, G. (Eds.). (2017). *Queer people of color in higher education*. Information Age Publishing.

Lange, A. C., Duran, A., & Jackson, R. (2022). How whiteness werqs in LGBTQ centers. In Z. Foste & T. Tevis (Eds.), *Critical whiteness praxis in higher education & student affairs: Considerations for the pursuit of racial justice on campus* (pp. 155–171). Stylus.

Love, B. J. (2018). Developing a liberatory consciousness. In M. Adams, W. J. Blumenfeld, D. C. J. Catalano, K. DeJong, H. W. Hackman, L. E. Hopkins, B. J. Love, M. L. Peters, D. Shlasko, & X. Zúñiga (Eds.), *Readings for diversity and social justice* (4th ed., pp. 610–615). Routledge.

Marine, S. B. (2011). *Stonewall's legacy: Bisexual, gay, lesbian, and transgender students in higher education* (Vol. 152). John Wiley & Sons.

Marine, S. B., & Nicolazzo, Z. (2014). Names that matter: Exploring the tensions of campus LGBTQ centers and trans* inclusion. *Journal of Diversity in Higher Education, 7*(4), 265–281. https://doi.org/10.1037/a0037990

Muñoz, J. E. (2009). *Cruising utopia: The then and there of queer futurity*. New York University Press.

Nicolazzo, Z. (2016). *Trans* in college: Transgender students' strategies for navigating campus life and the institutional politics of inclusion.* Stylus.

Oliveira, K. A., González-Siegel, V. A., Feldman, S., Kannan, K., Woods, C., Pryor, J. T., Duran, A., Catalano, D. C. J., & Jourian, T.J. (2025). An autoethnographic exploration of the realities of engaging trans and queer center(ed) diversity work. *Journal of Diversity in Higher Education, 18*(2), 111–122. https://doi.org/10.1037/dhe0000501

Ortiz, S. M., & Mandala, C. R. (2021). "There is queer inequity, but I pick to be happy": Racialized feeling rules and diversity regimes in university LGBTQ resource centers. *DuBois Review, 18*(2), 347–364. https://doi.org/10.1017/S1742058X21000096

Patton, L. D. (Eds.). (2010). *Cultural centers in higher education: Perspectives on identity, theory, and practice.* Routledge.

Poynter, K. J., & Tubbs, N. J. (2008). Safe zones: Creating LGBT safe space ally programs. *Journal of LGBT Youth, 5*(1), 121–132. https://www.tandfonline.com/doi/abs/10.1300/J524v05n01_10

Pryor, J. T., & Hoffman, G. D. (2021). "It feels like diversity as usual": Navigating institutional politics as LGBTQ+ professionals. *Journal of Student Affairs Research and Practice, 58*(1), 94–109. https://doi.org/10.1080/19496591.2020.1740717

Ritche, C. A., & Banning, J. H. (2001). Gay, lesbian, bisexual, and transgender campus support offices: A qualitative study of establishment experiences. *NASPA Journal, 38*(4), 482–494. https://doi.org/10.2202/1949-6605.1153

Ryoo, J., & McLaren, P. (2010). Seeking democracy in American schools: Countering epistemic violence through revolutionary critical pedagogy. In R. Hoosain & F. Salili (Eds.), *Democracy and multicultural education* (pp. 99–128). Information Age Publishing.

Sanlo, R. L. (2000). The LGBT campus resource center director: The new professional in student affairs. *Journal of Student Affairs Research & Practice, 37*(3), 485–495. https://doi.org/ https://doi.org/10.2202/1949-6605.1113

Sanlo, R., Rankin, S., & Schoenberg, R. (2002). *Our place on campus: Lesbian, gay, bisexual, transgender services and programs in higher education.* The Greenwood Educator's Reference Collection.

Self, J. M. (2015). Queering center: A critical discourse analysis of University LGBT center theoretical foundations. *Journal of Critical Thought and Praxis, 4*(2), 1–39.

Stewart, D.-L. (Eds.). (2011). *Multicultural student services on campus: Building bridges, re-visioning community.* Routledge.

Stewart, D.-L. (2018). Minding the gap between diversity and institutional transformation: Eight proposals for enacting institutional change. *Teachers College Record, 120*(14), 1–16.

The Chronicle of Higher Education. (2023, July 14). *DEI legislation tracker.* https://www.chronicle.com/article/here-are-the-states-where-lawmakers-are-seeking-to-ban-colleges-dei-efforts

The Consortium of Higher Education LGBT Professionals. (2020). *Find an LGBT center.* https://www.lgbtcampus.org/find-an-lgbtq-campus-center

The University of Michigan. (n.d.). *Our history.* https://spectrumcenter.umich.edu/about/history

Tillapaugh, D., & Catalano, D. C. J. (2019). Structural challenges affecting the experiences of public university LGBT services graduate assistants. *Journal of Diversity in Higher Education, 12*(2), 126–135. https://doi.org/10.1037/dhe0000079

Wagner, R. & Catalano, C. J. (2021). A reflexive self-awareness framework for advising and supporting. In R. Wagner & C. Catalano (Eds.), *Advising and supporting in student affairs* (pp. 3–16). Charles C. Thomas Publisher.

Woodford, M. R., Kolb, C. L., Durocher-Radeka, G., & Javier, G. (2014). Lesbian, gay, bisexual, and transgender ally training programs on campus: Current variations and future directions. *Journal of College Student Development, 55*(3), 317–322. https://doi.org/10.1353/csd.2014.0022

Part I
Historical and Theoretical Foundations

· 1 ·

HISTORIES, FOUNDATIONS, AND TENSIONS OF TQ CENTER(ED) DIVERSITY WORK

Roman Christiaens

Introduction

TQ center(ed) diversity work has a long and varied history within higher education, beginning with its activist origins from the college student protests in the mid 20th century and the development of the first TQ center at the University of Michigan in 1971. Over time, many practices and spaces of TQ center(ed) diversity work have become adopted and incorporated by higher education institutions as signs of their investment in trans and queer inclusion and advocacy. Through these processes of assimilation and integration, TQ center(ed) diversity work has expanded beyond its activist origins while struggling to reach its full liberatory potential within the context of postsecondary institutions. This chapter explores the inherent tension of TQ center(ed) diversity work as a tool for trans and queer equity that grapples with the hegemony of the institution and regulatory norms in its own origins, function and purpose. By tracing the history and professionalization of TQ center(ed) work, this chapter explores the frictions undergirding the work while presenting considerations for its impact on the present and future realities of TQ center(ed) diversity workers.

TQ center(ed) diversity work has an extensive and multilayered history within higher education, beginning with its activist origins of college student protests in the mid 20th century. Many TQ center(ed) spaces and centers arose directly from the organizing efforts of trans and queer campus constituents, who insisted on institutional commitments to trans and queer equity (Duran et al., 2023; Marine, 2011; Oliveira, 2022; Sanlo et al., 2002). For example, one of the first TQ centers in higher education—established at the University of Michigan and named the Lesbian-Gay Male Programs Office—was created in response to direct pressure from students, including members of the campus's Gay Liberation Front (Marine, 2011). These insurgent origins of TQ center(ed) diversity work are a direct extension of the multidimensional beginnings of queer and trans liberation movement (Ferguson, 2019). Inarguably, TQ center(ed) diversity work(ers) today owes its history and existence to the insistence and imaginations of many trans and queer campus communities from decades past.

Since the emergence of institutionally-resourced TQ center(ed) diversity work in the 1970s, there has been an outgrowth of centers, programs and services in higher education intended to address the needs of queer and trans students, staff, and faculty. These centers, programs, and services appear to signal an institutional investment in trans and queer equity, as it has become more commonplace for colleges and universities to have specific TQ centers/offices and/or staff who oversee TQ center(ed) diversity work (Duran et al., 2023; Jeffries & Boyd, 2020; Oliveira, 2022). Yet, these hallmarks of TQ center(ed) diversity work consistently remain understaffed, underfunded and unsupported (Beal, 2024; Catalano & Tillapaugh, 2020; Oliveira et al., 2025). TQ centers/offices only exist at a small percentage of degree granting institutions (Beal, 2024; Catalano & Jourian, 2018; Fine, 2012), and TQ center(ed) diversity work overall is facing a legislative landscape focused on delimiting and defunding its reach, scope and structure (Harper & Associates, 2024; McDaniel, 2024).

These stark realities of TQ center(ed) diversity work indicate that the integration and assimilation of TQ center(ed)-centered diversity work in higher education is not an entirely positive development. The existence of TQ center(ed) diversity work does not prevent the precarity of those tasked with trans and queer equity efforts. In fact, institutionalized TQ center(ed) diversity work often serves as a reason for institutions to avoid and ignore their responsibility to more fully improving trans and queer campus climate (Catalano et al., 2024; Duran et al., 2023; Marine & Nicolazzo, 2014). There is an assumption about the unqualified good of TQ center(ed) diversity work, and that the very existence of TQ spaces, programs and resources inherently benefits trans and queer campus communities (Lange, 2019; Self, 2015). This chapter seeks to trouble the assumptions and realities of TQ center(ed) diversity work by highlighting how its institutionalization over time has come with certain concessions. These concessions may harm multiply marginalized trans and queer communities and support a white cisheteronormative order (Fox & Ore, 2010; Lange et al., 2022; Self & Hudson, 2015).

The institutionalization of TQ center(ed) diversity work in higher education required a reliance on specific mechanisms to legitimize it as deserving of staffing, space and resources. Fox and Ore's (2010) exploration of trans and queer campus safe spaces[1] identified two mechanisms or normalizing devices fundamental to the construction and maintenance of these spaces. These two normalizing devices—dichotomizing and universalizing—constructed and elevated a white gay male subject at the center of TQ center(ed) diversity work. Dichotomizing serves as a binary logic that "constructs 'gayness' as a primary identity and other identities as peripheral and marginal" (Fox & Ore, 2010, p. 632). Universalizing is a logic that suggests all queer people experience heterosexism in similar ways. Dichotomizing and universalizing serve as two ways that regulatory norms around identity, access and privilege are upheld in trans and queer equity efforts.

In a similar way, TQ center(ed) diversity work began with dichotomized focus on sexuality as the driving force for the work. Even as TQ center(ed) diversity work evolved and incorporated gender identity and expression within its mission, the work still utilized universalizing devices in its operationalization (e.g., using the LGBTQ+ acronym to encompass the work in advertising and marketing). Thus, as TQ center(ed) diversity work progresses, it must contend with how its use of normalizing devices still function to minimize difference and principally elevate gender and sexuality, often at the expense of multiply marginalized trans and queer identities and experiences. One only needs to turn to research regarding trans and queer students of color (TQSOC) in TQ centers/offices to see how these spaces may perpetuate dominant norms around race, gender and sexuality and exacerbate feelings of isolation and exclusion for TQSOC populations (Duran, 2021; McCoy, 2018; Simms et al., 2023).

The moves that TQ center(ed) diversity work has made to establish its legitimacy and acceptability in higher education is connected to a broader tension between acceptance, assimilation and self-determination within the mainstream trans and queer movement.[2] The history of the mainstream trans and queer movement was described by Ferguson (2019) as a struggle between one-dimensional queerness and multidimensional queerness. One-dimensional queerness reflects the mainstreaming of sexuality and gender for the "endorsement of state and capital as the satisfiers of queer needs" (Ferguson, 2019, p. 6) while multidimensional queerness recognizes the integral connection between trans and queer collective political struggles for liberation amidst racism, classism, colonization, and capitalism. As the mainstream trans and queer movement grew, there has been a resistance to tell the complexity of their intersectional, multidimensional, and more radical lineage (Ferguson, 2019; Mecca, 2009; Stanley, 2021; Sycamore, 2006); TQ center(ed) diversity work on college campuses reflects a similar struggle in the past few decades as it has advocated for greater acceptance, attention and resources.

A commitment to TQ center(ed) diversity work in higher education necessitates an acknowledgment and understanding of the complicated and often fraught nature of the work. In their efforts towards trans and queer liberation, TQ center(ed) diversity workers should question and reconsider how this work operates in the context of postsecondary institutions. This chapter explores the histories, foundations and tensions of TQ center(ed) diversity work and the negotiations of the past, present and future of this work. It begins with a description of how the author came to TQ center(ed) diversity work and their investment in generative critique of this work, and then discusses tensions of the mainstream trans and queer movement. The chapter subsequently shares an abbreviated history of TQ center(ed) diversity work and investigates the professionalization of the field before highlighting whiteness as an example of a primary tension in TQ center(ed) diversity work. The chapter concludes with reflective considerations for TQ center(ed) diversity workers who seek to understand multidimensional queerness and challenge regulatory norms in their praxis.

Positionality Statement

My entry point to the field of student affairs and higher education was birthed through TQ center(ed) diversity work. As an undergraduate student, I found home in my institution's multicultural office and quickly occupied leadership roles within the office, including serving as a president for the trans and queer student club, participating in a social justice peer dialogue program and advocating for a LGBTQ+ studies minor at the college. My trans and queer campus involvement connected me with student affairs mentors who first introduced me to the field and helped me to conceptualize student affairs as a worthwhile professional career. During this time, I was also exploring opportunities to learn the histories of the trans and queer movements and community organizing. Growing up in a small rural town, I did not initially have access to trans and queer educational materials; once I entered college, I became a voracious reader of all things related to trans and queer identities, experiences and communities.

Through my experiences in the classroom and with my student affairs mentors, I immersed myself in the writing of radical trans and queer thinkers, including the work of Against Equality (Conrad, 2014) and Mattilda Bernstein Sycamore (2004, 2006). These thinkers brought forth various critiques about the mainstream evolution of the trans and queer movement and how this evolution ignored or minimized coalitional struggles against racism, incarceration, capitalism, and colonization. Inspired by these thinkers, I pulled together a panel of local trans and queer activists at my undergraduate college called: *What's Wrong with the Gay Rights' Movement?* The panel of activists discussed the ways that issues and priorities around race, class, ability, and citizenship were sidelined within mainstream trans and queer movement spaces. Thus, my entry into TQ center(ed) diversity work was conjoined with a generative and critical ethic of questioning the role, function, and aims of the work.

As a higher education researcher, I have brought these critiques in conversation and collaboration with many trans and queer scholar-activists. Our work has contested significant functions of TQ center(ed) diversity work including Safe Zone trainings, trans educational programming, and staff development, especially for trans co-curricular educators. Alongside other TQ center(ed) diversity workers, I have also explored how this work should consider the experiences of queer and trans poor and working-class students and the role of homonormative whiteness in TQ centers/offices. With each individual and collaborative exploration, I leveraged my own personal and professional experiences as a white transfemme practitioner to name specific tensions in TQ center(ed) diversity work and examine how this work ignores, minimizes, or avoids the experiences of multiply marginalized trans and queer students. In addition to my scholarly experience, I serve on the board of the Consortium of Higher Education LGBT Resource Professionals, a national non-profit focused on support queer and trans equity work on college campuses. The Consortium is an example of how TQ center(ed) work has become a recognized profession in student affairs with its own professional association, recorded history, standards and competencies (Bazarsky et al., 2022; CAS, 2019; Marine, 2011; Sanlo, 2002). Within this role, I experience firsthand the limitations and challenges of professionalizing TQ center(ed) diversity work while seeking to disrupt hegemonic norms of the profession through our organizational efforts.

My process of questioning TQ center(ed) diversity work comes from a place of seeking to be more generative, creative, thoughtful, and intentional with the work. It is influenced by my own lens as having greater proximity to power and privilege through my whiteness and other dominant subjectivities. Even in times where I have felt isolated as a transfemme practitioner, I recognize the privilege I have as the "only one" in predominantly white spaces. I have questioned whether or not my presence in institutions is used as a justification for higher education's continued trans exclusionary practices (Christiaens, 2024). Are those of us in TQ center(ed) diversity positions merely foils for the institution? Does our very presence allow institutions to avoid large-scale and long-term approaches to TQ center(ed) diversity work? When I worked in a TQ center for four years, there were many times that upper-level administration would refer to our center and its history as proof of the institution's investment in trans and queer equity. However, there was a clear disconnect given that many of our trans and queer students who regularly experienced discrimination, invisibility and neglect on a regular basis at the institution. I bring forth those experiences and questions in my critique of TQ center(ed) diversity work. I acknowledge and honor the passion and labor of TQ center(ed) diversity workers and the vital functioning of our programs and spaces. At the same time, I recognize how our work can also (re)produce norms and narratives of acceptability around who the work truly centers and serves.

Tensions of the Mainstream Trans and Queer Movement

There have long existed debates and dissensions within trans and queer communities about the desire and process for increased representation, access, and rights within society (Conrad, 2014; Ferguson, 2019; Spade, 2015; Stanley, 2021; Sycamore, 2006; Vaid, 2012). While these tensions existed within trans and queer communities throughout the 20th century, emphasis is often placed on the 1969 Stonewall riots in New York City and the trans and queer organizing that followed as the beginning of dissensions within the movement (Ferguson, 2019; Stryker, 2017). A historical example can be found through the experiences of Sylvia Rivera and Marsha P. Johnson, two trans women of color who were key to establishing the gay liberation movement after the Stonewall riots (Gill-Peterson, 2024). Rivera and Johnson were founders of STAR (Street Transvestite Action Revolutionaries), an activist group focused on a coalitional and intersectional politics of queer liberation (STAR, 2013). STAR was often at odds with the Gay Liberation Front (GLF), the primary organizing group following Stonewall, due to GLF's failure to address concerns around sexism, transphobia and racism (Mecca, 2009).

On two separate occasions, one on a college campus and another at a Stonewall commemoration event, the multidimensional politics of STAR would clash with the agendas of GLF and local gay activists (Ferguson, 2019; Giles-Peterson, 2024; Stanley, 2021). The first event was at New York University (NYU) when Rivera and Johnson worked with a student organization, the Gay Activists Alliance, to stage a protest against the university's recent banning of gay social functions on-campus. During the five-day protest and occupation at Weinstein Hall on campus, riot police were deployed to disperse the protestors. When this occurred, most of the college student protestors left, essentially abandoning Rivera, Johnson and other local predominantly trans activists (Gill-Peterson, 2024). In a statement released by STAR about the Weinstein Hall occupation, STAR described the abandonment as a betrayal and the actions of the students as an endorsement of state violence against trans and queer people (STAR, 2013).

The second occasion occurred in 1973 at Christopher Street Liberation Day, an annual commemoration of Stonewall and the progenitor of what we now celebrate as Pride. Rivera had been asked to speak at the event, but several people tried to stop her from speaking (Gill-Peterson, 2024). Rivera essentially scaled the stage and approached the mic, famously saying "y'all better quite down!" During her speech, Rivera called out the crowd for failing to support their trans and queer kin who were experiencing incarceration. She asked crowd members to support the work of STAR, "the people are who trying to do something for all of us, and not men and women that belong to a white middle-class white club" (STAR, 2013, p. 30). The experience of Rivera and Johnson at Weinstein Hall in 1970 and Rivera's speech on Christopher Street Liberation Day in 1973 exemplifies tensions within trans and queer movement organizing and the reality of a long history of racism, transphobia, classism, and ableism and critiques within the broader mainstream movement (Ferguson, 2019; Stanley, 2021; Vaid, 2012).

Despite the efforts of STAR to bring about a more intersectional and coalitional approach to the organizing of the gay liberation movement, the reform focus of the GLF and its offshoot, the Gay Activists Alliance (GAA), would take center stage in the mainstream trans and queer movement (Gill-Peterson, 2024; Stryker, 2017; Mecca, 2009). In fact, the GAA's focus on reform and its orientation around sexuality as a primary driving force would eventually set the tone of single-issue politics for many future gay organizations (Ferguson, 2019). This turn towards reform and assimilation relied on the normalizing functions of dichotomizing and universalizing for organizing and legitimacy, essentially turning away from the multidimensional and intersectional genealogy of the movement (Ferguson, 2019; Mecca, 2009; Stryker, 2017). The evolution of the mainstream trans and queer movement also represented an example of minority absorption (Ferguson, 2012), the way in which divergent marginalized knowledges and practices are subsumed within institutions and the work of a broader mainstream movement.

A retelling of the movement would suggest that its focus on reform and assimilation was "a historical necessity rather than one item on a menu of interventions" (Ferguson, 2012, p. 226). However, to argue that the only method for trans and queer liberation is to reform pre-existing societal structures rather than problematize and challenge those structures in and of themselves, fails to recognize the limitations of the former approach. For example, Spade (2015) explained how focusing on law reform as the primary pathway for improving the lives of trans people is insufficient to address the harm and violence trans people face. These reform-based projects of social inclusion and acceptance rely on visibility and a certain (acceptable) trans subject who has greater access to privilege. Trans and queer individuals who are white, able-bodied, upper class, and with U.S. citizenship are inevitability centered and protected in legal reform-based projects, while those who live further on the margins are least served by these projects. In a similar vein, Stanley (2021) demonstrated that the advancement of trans and queer rights has coincided with a rise in attacks against trans and queer people of color (TQPOC). The expansion of hate-crime legislation, for example, has not necessarily led to decreased rates of harm and violence against those who live at the intersections of race, gender and sexuality.

The work of Spade (2015) and Stanley (2021) are intricately connected with the collective thinking of Against Equality (Conrad, 2014), who developed an online archive in the early 2000s of radical critiques of the mainstream trans and queer movement. Against Equality's focus was on "the holy trinity of mainstream gay and lesbian politics: gay marriage, gays in the military and hate crime legislation" (Conrad, 2014, p. 6). Their work sought to challenge the idea that the trans and queer movements should only focus on assimilation and integration into mainstream society. According to Against Equality, orienting the community's focus on specific legislative sexuality and gender projects that may or may not be aligned with efforts around racial and economic justice ultimately limits trans and queer political imaginations (Conrad, 2014; Ferguson, 2019; Stanley, 2021). Allowing gays to serve openly in the military is a primary example because it demonstrates the idea that gay representation in the military will inherently challenge or transform a deeply flawed system. This theme of visibility and recognition as sufficient to demonstrate inclusion was critiqued within higher education research (Catalano et al., 2024; Christiaens, 2024; Marine & Nicolazzo, 2014; Nicolazzo, 2020). Therefore, TQ center(ed) diversity work is not exempt from these frictions and critiques of the broader mainstream trans and queer movement.

The questions brought forth by STAR (2013) about the future of trans and queer movement building hold profound relevance for those committed to trans and queer equity on college campuses today. Illuminating debates and dissensions within the trans and queer mainstream movement demonstrates what concessions are made when a marginalized community advances a single-issue or one-dimensional agenda around universality, reform, conformity and assimilation. However, this process is not predetermined or inevitable; trans and queer movements have always been connected to other forms of struggle (Ferguson, 2019). As the history of TQ center(ed) diversity work shows, the tensions of the broader trans and queer movement and the forms of struggle that were a part of the movement's genealogy are very much alive in the fabric of higher education institutions.

Our Place on Campus: TQ Center(ed) Spaces on College Campuses

Institutionalized TQ center(ed) diversity work began with the college student activism and protests of the 60s and 70s; during this time period, students mobilized to hold institutions accountable for their failure to fully support students from historically marginalized backgrounds. Student groups were integral to the formation of trans and queer programs, departments, resources and services on college campuses, as well as the broader gay liberation movement within the United States (Beemyn, 2003; Renn, 2010; Marine, 2011). This included the establishment of physical spaces (TQ centers/offices) focused on supporting trans and queer campus populations, and the first TQ center/office opened in 1971 at the University of Michigan.

Though some TQ centers/offices opened in the 1980s, most were founded in the 1990s and early 2000s (Jeffries & Boyd, 2020). For example, during the 1990s, more than 50 colleges and universities established TQ centers/offices with at least a half-time paid director on their college campuses (Beemyn, 2002). While the creation of TQ centers/offices primarily occurred in public institutions, these spaces also cropped up in private institutions (Sanlo et al., 2002) and community colleges (Marine, 2011). As of the spring of 2024, there are 260 centers/offices in operation according to LGBTQ Architect (n.d.), an online resource for campus administrators working with queer and trans campus populations. Despite the presence of TQ centers/offices in higher education, they are relatively sparse compared to the over 4,000 colleges and universities in the United States (Beal, 2024). Additionally, while there has been a steady growth of TQ centers/offices throughout the 2000s, many of these spaces are being threatened by anti-diversity, equity and inclusion (DEI) legislation (Harper & Associates, 2024; McDaniel, 2024). It is highly likely that the number of TQ centers/offices may stagnate or decrease in the coming years.

In the present age, TQ centers/offices contain a complex web of functions that have evolved from their initial focus on providing space and support for gay and lesbian students. These functions exist within four primary areas: support, needs assessment and evaluation, education, and advocacy (Marine, 2011). TQ center(ed) diversity workers in TQ centers/offices provide direct support to queer and trans students, participate in the development of campus climate surveys to measure the perceptions and experience of queer and trans campus populations, facilitate educational outreach to the campus community, and advocate for policy and practice changes, often flowing from direct student experiences and requests (Beal, 2024; Catalano & Tillapaugh, 2019; Oliveira et al., 2025; Pryor & Hoffman, 2021). While TQ center/office functions are typically framed around the experiences and needs of trans and queer students, some TQ center(ed) diversity workers are also responsible for providing support to trans and queer staff and faculty (Oliveira, 2022; Pryor & Hoffman, 2021; Sanlo et al., 2002). Within the four functional areas, there is a wide range of scope, staffing, funding and structure in TQ centers/offices across the country. Although some TQ centers/offices have multiple staff with discrete responsibilities and areas of oversight, other TQ centers/offices exist as an office of one (Consortium, 2024). For example, many institutions still consider undergraduate or graduate students appropriate as the only staff for TQ centers/offices (Catalano & Tillapaugh, 2019). While commonality may exist across the functional areas of many TQ centers/offices, there is much to be researched about the inner workings of these spaces.

One resounding theme across higher education research are the challenges TQ centers/offices and TQ center(ed) diversity workers face in supporting trans and queer campus populations while being overworked, understaffed, underpaid and under-resourced (Beal, 2024; Catalano & Tillapaugh, 2019; Duran et al., 2023; Oliveira et al., 2025; Pryor & Hoffman, 2021). TQ centers/offices and TQ center(ed) diversity workers are expected to navigate these difficult institutional dynamics while attempting to address a wide range of needs and interests of trans and queer campus communities. Relying on normalizing devices is one way that TQ center(ed) diversity work has coped with institutional precarity. In order to advocate for trans and queer equity on a college campus, TQ center(ed) diversity workers have often had to implement a single-issue and universal approach that fits within the DEI expectations and assumptions of the university, such as the idea that trans and queer work should be contained within TQ centers/offices. This means that TQ center(ed) diversity workers are faced with the incredibly difficult task of working towards trans and queer equity within the rules and norms of the institution.

Since its conceptualization, TQ center(ed) diversity work has shifted away from sexuality as its primary mission, incorporated gender identity and expression and tended to various needs of different student generations. However, these moves towards greater inclusion still come with their concessions and are often limited by the institution. For example, since many TQ centers/offices began as Gay and Lesbian Centers, there emerged a need for these spaces to reconsider their naming processes. TQ centers/offices have shifted broader and more generalized names (e.g., pride or rainbow centers), names that explicitly name gender (e.g., gender and sexuality center) or names that have transgender or "T" in their name (Marine & Nicolazzo, 2014). Some institutions merged TQ centers/offices with women's and gender equity centers/offices due the concurring and overlapping work of gender and sexuality in their missions (Jeffries & Boyd, 2020). These shifts around language and mission helped name and center the experiences of transgender and nonbinary individuals who have historically not always been integrated in the work of TQ centers/offices. However, as Marine and Nicolazzo (2014) discovered, these changes do not automatically improve the lived realities of trans and nonbinary students. In fact, their study suggested that TQ center(ed) diversity workers continue to conflate sexualities with gender identities, an example of dichotomizing and universalizing thinking (Fox & Ore, 2010). Tensions and limitations about the role of TQ centers/offices in supporting trans and queer student populations can still exist even through efforts to expand the inclusive capacities of TQ center(ed) diversity work.

A brief overview of the origins, trajectory and expansion of TQ centers/offices in higher education through the late 20th century and early 21st century illuminate several key themes. Firstly, the history of TQ centers/offices is closely connected to the broader mainstream queer and trans movement. Secondly, tensions around the dichotomizing and universalizing aspects of trans and queer movement building also exist within TQ centers/offices. As the mission of TQ centers/offices have shifted and expanded towards sexuality *and* gender, these spaces continue to contend with tensions around their intended purpose, operationalization and function within the hierarchy and constraints of the institution. One of those primary tensions concern the need for TQ center(ed) diversity work to professionalize in order legitimate its place within the field of higher education and student affairs, and how this professionalization establishes boundaries on what TQ center(ed) diversity work is and should look like.

Professionalization of TQ Center(ed) Diversity Work

The evolution of TQ center(ed) diversity work has been a project of legitimacy and visibility as TQ center(ed) diversity workers have insisted not only on the need for their presence on a college campus but also their necessary contribution to the university ecosystem. This project includes the professionalization of TQ center(ed) diversity work within the field of student affairs, driven by TQ center(ed) diversity workers from the 1990s to the present day (Bazarsky et al., 2022; CAS, 2019; Marine, 2011; Sanlo, 2002). Professionalization of TQ center(ed) diversity work encompassed the founding of a national organization called the Consortium of Higher Education LGBT Resource Professionals,[3] the creation of primary guiding documents for TQ center(ed) diversity work, and the development of competencies and standards for TQ center(ed) diversity workers. These components of professionalization have helped establish the legitimacy of TQ center(ed) diversity work within student affairs while promoting specific norms about who does the work and how the work should be implemented on college campuses.

One of the earliest components of professionalization for TQ center(ed) diversity work was the formation of the Consortium. The Consortium was initially borne out the Campus Project at the National Gay and Lesbian Task Force (NGLTF) in 1987. The Campus Project focused on examining campus climate for trans and queer communities on college campuses and served as a liaison to TQ center/office directors. Over time, there became an increased need for additional support for TQ center/offices beyond what the capacity of what the Campus Project and NGLTF could provide. When NGLTF eventually shuttered the Campus Project, three campus directors from the original Creating Change group, known as the Pocono Parents—Ronni Sanlo, Sue Rankin, and Robert Schoenberg—met in the summer of 1997 and developed a proposal for the Consortium. Ronni, Sue and Robert presented the proposal to a group of TQ center/office directors at the Creating Change conference (Sanlo et al., 2002). The organizational proposal was accepted, and over time, the Consortium grew as a separate professional organization and achieved its own non-profit status in 2014 (Consortium, n.d.).

According to the original founders of the Consortium, the organization's purpose was to help foster higher education environments where trans and queer communities "have equity in every respect" (Sanlo et al., 2002, p. 11). The Consortium is a member-based organization focused on (1) providing support to TQ center(ed) diversity workers, (2) consulting with higher education administrations in the interest of improving campus climate and services for trans and queer communities and (3) facilitating education around promising policies and practices (Consortium, n.d.). Because the Consortium has limited funding, it relies on a completely volunteer-led board of TQ center(ed) diversity workers, which impacts the reach and effectiveness of the organization and ostensibly influences the composition of the overall board. While the Consortium is responsible for creating educational materials around TQ center(ed) diversity work, the organization remains relatively under-researched. Internal Consortium documents, including self-studies and self-assessments, indicate challenges around the organization's capacity and how it addresses the professional needs of its members (Consortium, 2018, 2024). For example, respondents from a recent member needs assessment report (2024) highlighted the organization's lack of focus on universities which do not have TQ centers/offices, including MSIs and community colleges. A majority of the respondents in the survey were white, possibly an indication of how the work and the organization struggle to recruit and retain trans and queer professionals of color (TQPOC). In the same report, due to its limitations as a volunteer-led organization, the Consortium (2024) suggests "an alternate model...to meet the needs of its members today" (p. 36). The Consortium as an important dimension of professionalization for TQ center(ed) workers signals a tension of what may be compromised in efforts to establish its legitimacy and authority within the field of student affairs.

In addition to the development of the Consortium, primary texts regarding the foundation of TQ center(ed) diversity work were created in the 1990s and early 2000s. These texts include the NGLTF LGBT campus organizing guide (Outcault, 1995), *Our Place on Campus* (Sanlo et al., 2002), the CAS[4] self-assessment guide for LGBT programs and services (2011), and an Association for the Study of Higher Education (ASHE) commissioned report on LGBT students in higher education (Marine, 2011). Self (2015) conducted a critical discourse analysis of the first three texts and discovered themes relevant to the notion of the one-dimensional queer (Ferguson, 2019). For example, the primary texts acknowledge racial, gender, and ethnic diversity within trans and queer communities but lack theorization around interlocking systems of oppression and a multi-dimensional approach to TQ center(ed) diversity work (Self, 2015).

Though the authors certainly intended the texts as forms of resistance against cisheterosexist conceptualizations of college campuses, the authors still made discursive choices that "reflect an adherence to the singularized experience of the LGBT community" (Self, 2015, p. 30). From my own textual analysis, the comprehensive work of Marine (2011) about the experiences of trans and queer students in higher education operates in similar ways. While there is some attention on LGB students of color, the work assumes whiteness within trans and queer student populations. Additionally, the report highlights the need for TQ centers/offices to address the needs of different queer and trans student subpopulations, but it is limited in its suggestions for policy and practice around various marginalized genders and sexualities. Taken altogether, the foundational texts of TQ center(ed) diversity work further understandings of gender and sexuality campus efforts that may not fully attend to multidimensional and coalitional conceptualizations of trans and queer equity.

Recent developments regarding the professionalization of TQ center(ed) work include the creation of professional standards of practice for TQ center(ed) diversity workers. Commissioned as a workgroup by the Consortium, Bazarsky and colleagues (2022) developed the twelve professional standards of practice as a "navigation tool" for TQ center(ed) diversity workers. The establishment of these professional standards is particularly important in addressing workforce preparation gaps for TQ center(ed) diversity workers. Yet, one's ability to achieve or advance these competencies can often be tied to their institutional location, funding, office/center personnel and scope (Beal, 2024). Additionally, professional standards of practice inevitably enforce specific norms of TQ center(ed) diversity work related to audience, structure, purpose and function. For example, a commitment to intersectionality and racial justice were both outlined in the framework that Bazarsky and colleagues (2022) used in developing standards. However, the ways that intersectionality is specifically connected to power and privilege in trans and queer equity work or the responsibility for TQ center(ed) diversity workers to invest in racial equity are absent from the standards. The standards themselves fall into a similar trap as the foundational texts and the Consortium. In their attempt to legitimate TQ center(ed) diversity work, the standards gloss over the complicated reality of TQ center(ed) diversity workers and the ways that workers have to resist the cisheteronormative logics of the institution while crafting alternative and creative approaches to trans and queer equity efforts.

As the professionalization of TQ center(ed) work develops over time, there exists an intractability of dichotomizing and universalizing thinking across the work. It is not to infer that these steps towards legitimacy are inherently problematic or on their outset compromise the integrity of TQ center(ed) diversity work. In fact, as someone professionally connected to the Consortium, I can recognize the formative role these standards, texts and the organization play in the development of TQ center(ed) diversity work and supporting TQ center(ed) diversity workers across the country and in various institutions. However, in its pursuit of legitimacy through standardization, the professionalization of TQ center(ed) diversity work has often failed to confront the enduring tensions and frictions that undergird the work. In particular, TQ center(ed) diversity work must reckon with the presence, persistence and impact of whiteness in trans and queer movement building on and off college campuses.

The Enduringness of Whiteness in TQ Center(ed) Diversity Work

TQ center(ed) diversity work has progressed with a tremendous of trans and queer visibility, support, and advocacy on college campuses. Still, alongside this progression and expansion exist present-day dynamics around the need for improvement in TQ center(ed) diversity work including center/office (non)presence on more diverse college campuses (Beal, 2024; Beemyn, 2002; Fine, 2012), the whiteness of the TQ center(ed) profession (Duran & Jourian, 2024; Lange et al., 2022; Ortiz & Mandala, 2021), the inability of TQ center(ed) diversity work to actualize institutional transformation (Beal, 2024; Catalano et al. 2024; Duran et al., 2023; Oliveira et al., 2025), and how this work perpetuates regulating norms (Ortiz & Mandala, 2021; Self & Hudson, 2015). For those committed to transformative TQ center(ed) work, it is ever more important to consider how these dynamics influence the functioning of TQ centers/offices and the experiences of TQ center(ed) diversity workers. As a case study, this section will examine whiteness in TQ center(ed) diversity work as a particular embedded tension to be examined, challenged and disrupted. Focusing on whiteness as a pertinent example reflects existing and emerging research on whiteness in TQ center(ed) diversity work and spaces (Duran & Jourian, 2023, 2024; Lange et al., 2022; Ortiz & Mandala, 2021; Self & Hudson, 2015).

Within the context of higher education, whiteness is an unspoken set of behaviors, values, thoughts and actions that are positioned as the center/norm and hold varying degrees of worth, weight and influence within the institution. These normative logics have detrimental effects on people of color and operate in order to maintain whiteness and protect the feelings, experiences and beliefs of white people (Foste & Tevis, 2022). In order to understand whiteness in the context of TQ center(ed) diversity work, the framework of white homonormativity is useful. White homonormativity centers and produces a conceptualization of gayness as being white, middle-class and cisgender and conceives of whiteness and masculinity as static and binary (Self, 2015). Expanding upon this framework, Lange and colleagues (2022) articulate white homonormativity and white transnormativity as being intertwined in TQ center(ed) diversity work. The notion of white transnormativity is one in which "white, straight, trans people who adhere to a binary gender performance are celebrated as the right kind of trans people" (Lange et al., 2022, p. 158). Taken altogether, white homo/transnormativity is a framework to understand the role and function of whiteness in TQ center(ed) diversity work. In particular, the high frequency of TQ centers/offices in predominantly and historically white institutions, the experiences of TQSOC students in these spaces, and the challenges that TQ center(ed) diversity workers face highlight three particular ways that white homo/transnormativity operates in this work.

Within their minor presence on college campuses as a whole, TQ centers/offices predominantly exist at mid-sized and large public institutions (Beal, 2024; Fine, 2012). In the U.S. landscape, these types of institutions are historically and predominantly white (Ortiz & Mandala, 2021). This means that TQ centers/offices are less likely to exist at minority-serving institutions (MSIs) and community colleges, and students at those institutions have differential access to the support that TQ centers/offices have to offer. Since access to and experience with TQ centers/offices is a primary pathway point for individuals who pursue TQ center(ed) diversity work, there are undoubtedly whitening effects regarding these institutional gaps. In two of its most recent self-study reports, the Consortium (2018, 2024) found an under-representation of people of color engaged in TQ center(ed) diversity work. The majority of respondents were also located in predominantly or historically white public institutions. These reports align with qualitative research on perceptions and experiences of TQ offices/centers as often being white and/or white-oriented spaces (Catalano & Tillapaugh, 2020; Duran, 2021; McCoy 2018; Self & Hudson, 2015). Thus, TQ center(ed) diversity work contends not only the predominance of whiteness in the student affairs field but also with the whiteness of institutional spaces, which have historically centered heteronormative and cisnormative people, policies and practices.

Whiteness of TQ centers/offices, spaces and work has a detrimental impact on students with multiply marginalized identities, namely TQSOC students. TQSOC students have to navigate whether or not to seek support from TQ centers/offices or racial/ethnic-based cultural centers, and these spaces can often be inadequate in providing them with holistic, intersectional support (McCoy, 2018). A study by Nicolazzo (2016) of Black trans students' experiences with cultural resource centers found that they felt excluded in both Black cultural centers and TQ centers/offices. TQ centers/offices can often be exclusive, if not directly harmful, to TQSOC, especially if they are located in predominantly white institutions (Duran, 2021; McCoy, 2018; Self & Hudson, 2015; Simms et al., 2023). Thus, TQSOC students are often forced to explore alternative pathways for support and spaces to make meaning of their race, ethnicity, gender and/or sexual identities. For example, Simms and colleagues (2023) found that TQ centers/offices consistently failed to adequately meet the needs of trans students of color, leading these students to craft their own community and peer support networks through digital spaces and networks. On the whole, the exclusion and harm that TQSOC may experience due to the whiteness of TQ center(ed) work is one example of the enduring frames of white homo/transnormativity of this work.

TQ center(ed) diversity workers are uniquely positioned to help address whiteness and white norms, but there are institutional dynamics that pull on their time/capacity and disincentivize work on whiteness and anti-racism. TQ center(ed) diversity workers are consistently contending with under-resourcing and underfunding (Catalano & Tillapaugh, 2020; Duran et al., 2023; Marine & Nicolazzo, 2014; Oliveira et al., 2025; Pryor & Hoffman, 2021), a continual pressure to serve and educate multiple campus constituents, predominantly cisgender and heterosexual campus community members (Beal, 2024; Catalano et al., 2024; Oliveira et al., 2025), and organizational placement on the periphery of the university's diversity work (Beal, 2024; Duran et al., 2023; Oliveira et al., 2025). On top of these challenges is the reality that many TQ center(ed) diversity workers are under-prepared to successfully navigate these competing demands. They are expected to engender positive changes for their queer and trans campus communities while navigating and experiencing exclusive, alienating and harmful campus environments (Catalano & Tillapaugh, 2020; Christiaens, 2024; Hoffman & Pryor, 2021; Oliveira, 2022; Oliveira et al., 2025). By keeping TQ center(ed) diversity workers overworked and underpaid, these dynamics help to maintain whiteness at the institution and by extension whiteness within trans and queer campus equity efforts.

Contending with whiteness in the institution and in TQ centers/offices has differential impacts on white TQ workers and TQ workers of color. Though TQ center(ed) diversity workers are expected to be complicit in expectations of professionalism and collegiality (Hoffman & Pryor, 2023), TQ workers of color have to navigate the compounded effects of racism in their institutional work (Ortiz & Mandala, 2021). Additionally, TQ workers of color are often expected to initiate and/or sustain efforts to support TQSOC and interrogate whiteness in TQ centers/offices (Duran & Jourian, 2023, 2024). Ortiz and Mandala (2021) found that TQ workers of color who advocate for racial equity often experienced consequences (e.g., termination or barriers to advancement) that white TQ workers did not. In their narrative study on TQ center(ed) workers engaged in anti-racism praxis, Duran and Jourian (2024) found three primary themes: (1) white TQ workers may recognize and critique whiteness but they still operated within whiteness, and the racialized nature of TQ centers/offices often meant that there were (2) unequal resources for TQSOC and QTPOC workers, and (3) there were disproportionate effects on agency and labor for TQ center(ed) workers across race. When considering the underrepresentation of TQ workers of color in the field (Consortium, 2018, 2024), the heightened burden and expectation of labor around race and the unequal access they may have to opportunity directly impacts the recruitment, persistence and advancement of TQ workers of color in the field. It also sustains a degree of white homo/transnormativity within TQ center(ed) diversity work.

As it has been highlighted, the persistence of whiteness and white homo/transnormativity in TQ center(ed) diversity work is not solely the fault of TQ center(ed) diversity workers; it is by the design of the institution. Though TQ center(ed) diversity workers should and must address whiteness more comprehensively, the precarity of their roles, the hegemony and the institution and a lack of resourcing and staffing disincentivize the work. The work of Ortiz and Mandala (2021) found that TQ centers/offices were purposely not structurally positioned to shift resources in a way that fully addresses and combats racism. Instead, the expectation to address racial inequity is diverted to other offices and spaces, such as racial/ethnic identity-based resource centers. In fact, a primary finding from Duran and Jourian (2024) study of TQ center(ed) diversity workers highlighted how the racialized nature of TQ centers/offices "restricted their ability to advocate for queer and trans students of color, privileging white queer and trans students" (p. 460). These examples from higher education research demonstrate the complicated nature of whiteness in TQ center(ed) diversity work and the ways this work may fail to fully address interlocking issues of race and racism.

The role of whiteness and white homo/transnormativity in TQ center(ed) work as an example of an imbricated tension demonstrates two key poles of the work. First, TQ center(ed) diversity work is not always set up for success due to the dynamics of oppression within the university; secondly, these machinations are (re)produced within the work and perpetuate regulatory norms around power and privilege, including the persistence and maintenance of whiteness. Thus, as TQ center(ed) diversity workers are navigating cisheteronormative institutions, this navigation is experienced differently for multiply marginalized TQ center(ed) diversity workers. It also informs attrition for those who may experience oppression and bias not only on campus but also within their TQ offices/centers. Those who are dedicated to trans and queer equity in higher education must reckon with how whiteness is a part of the foundation for TQ center(ed) diversity work and continues to influence its history and development. Understanding the persistent tensions within the foundation, histories and operationalization of TQ center(ed) diversity work is an important step that TQ center(ed) diversity workers can take in this process of reckoning.

Conclusion

The history and evolution of TQ center(ed) diversity work has been one in which integration within the today's college and university has not consistently or wholly translated to material change for trans and queer campus communities. As Beal (2024) insisted, TQ center(ed) diversity workers must contend with and hold the tension that their roles and the spaces they work in serve as both counter-spaces to the cisheteronormativity of the institution and symbols of institutional goodness. To understand this tension, TQ center(ed) diversity workers must look to the past and the history of trans and queer movements to understand how challenges around professionalization, assimilation, insurgence and intersectionality influence how trans and queer experiences are currently conceptualized and experienced in higher education.

TQ center(ed) diversity workers should spend time reflecting on how the history and development of the work informs their own approach to TQ center(ed) diversity work, including their outlook and priorities. Engaging in generative critique and reflection about the assumptions one has held onto around TQ center(ed) diversity work is useful and valuable. The reflection questions offered in this chapter can assist TQ center(ed) diversity workers in these acts of discernment and introspection while (re)igniting the passion that inspired many TQ center(ed) diversity workers to enter into the work in the first place. The following chapters in this volume can also offer additional thoughts, reflections and recommendations for wrestling with the persistent frictions of TQ center(ed) diversity work.

One of the core competencies from the work of Bazarsky and colleagues (2022) involved knowledge and utilization of the history of queer and trans movement building in queer and trans equity work. By highlighting past and present examples of contestations and frictions around trans and queer movements and TQ center(ed) diversity work, this chapter sought to problematize how TQ center(ed) diversity workers understand the foundation and professionalization of the work. When considering the history, foundations and critiques of TQ center(ed) diversity work, there have been certainly adverse effects on those who are not primarily centered, uplifted or prioritized in this work. It is primarily crucial that those who are committed to TQ center(ed) diversity work reconcile the fact that their histories and present practices continue to exclude those within trans and queer communities while privileging those who already have a certain modicum of access and positional power in the work. To help further the liberatory aims of TQ center(ed) diversity work, we must continue to honor its insurgent and resistant origins while bringing forth imaginative, critical and generative work through our commitment and praxis.

Reflection Questions

The following questions can guide TQ center(ed) diversity workers in this reflection:

- *Trans and Queer Histories*
    - How does trans and queer movement history, including mainstream and alternative (re)tellings of the history, guide your praxis?
    - What figures and stories of trans and queer history influence your commitments to institutional change work?
- *Normalizing Devices*
    - What are the ways that dichotomizing and universalizing operate within your TQ center(ed) diversity spaces?
    - What other specific normalizing devices, such as white homo/trans-normativity, also play out in your work, and what are key features of these devices?
    - What support and resources do you need in order to challenge and these devices within your capacity and scope?
- *Embracing and Confronting Tensions*
    - How can you attend to the tensions between inclusion, acceptance, self-determination and institutional transformation in your work?
        - Depending on the approach you may take, what type of concessions may be made, and how does that influence your praxis?
    - When you mobilize trans and queer potential for projects that may not be focused on the institution, what challenges will you run into?
        - What do you need in order to envision different creative and imaginative approaches to the work?

Notes

1 In their work, Fox and Ore referred to these spaces as "LGBT safe spaces." The language has been modified from the source in keeping with the style and language of the chapter.
2 Though there are certainly multiple trans and queer movements and movements spaces, the use of "mainstream trans and queer movement" denotes the focus of legal equality (e.g. marriage and other legal benefits) that has been the concentration of large-scale trans and queer organizing within the United States.
3 From this point forward in the book chapter, the Consortium of Higher Education Resource Professionals will be referred to as the Consortium.
4 CAS stands for the Council for the Advancement of Standards in Higher Education. CAS develops and updates functional area standards for higher education programs and services.

References

Bazarsky, D., Edwards, B. J., Jensen, L., Subbaraman, S., Sugiyama, B., & Travers, S. (2022). Standards of practice: Core competencies for LGBTQIA+ directors and professionals in higher education. *Journal of Diversity in Higher Education, 15*(2), 141–152. https://doi.org/10.1037/dhe0000282

Beal, J. (2024). A place for us: Exploring gender and sexuality resource centers within the postsecondary orgscape. In K. Prieto & A. Herridge (Eds.), *LGBTQIA students in higher education: Approaches to student identity and policy* (pp. 198–211). IGI Global Publishing.

Beemyn, B. (2002). The development and administration of campus LGBT centers and offices. In R. Sanlo, S. Rankin, & R. Schoenberg (Eds.), *Our place on campus: Lesbian, gay, bisexual, transgender services, and programs in higher education* (pp. 25–32). Greenwood Press.

Beemyn, B. (2003). The silence is broken: A history of the first lesbian, gay, and bisexual college student groups. *Journal of the History of Sexuality, 12*(2), 205–223. https://doi.org/10.1353/sex.2003.0075

Catalano, D. C. J., & Jourian, T. J. (2018). LGBTQ campus spaces: A queering of gender-aware practice. *New Directions in Student Services, 2018*(164), 41–50. https://doi.org/10.1002/ss.20282

Catalano, D. C., & Tillapaugh, D. (2020). Identity, role, and oppression: Experiences of LGBTQ resource center graduate assistants. *Journal of Student Affairs Research and Practice, 57*(5), 519–531. https://doi.org/10.1080/19496591.2019.1699104

Catalano, C. J., Tillapaugh, D., Christiaens, R., & Simms, S. (2024). 'More than lip service': LGBTQ+ social justice educational interventions as institutional benign neglect. *Review of Higher Education, 47*(3), 373–400. https://doi.org/10.1353/rhe.0.a913752

Christiaens, R. (2024). Desire, refusal, world-making and underworlding: Transfeminist praxis as a transfemme educator in diversity, equity and inclusion (DEI) work. *Journal of Diversity in Higher Education*. Advance online publication. https://doi.org/10.1037/dhe0000572

Conrad, R. (2014). *Against equality: Queer revolution not mere inclusion*. AK Press.

Consortium of Higher Education LGBT Resource Professionals. (2018). *2018 self-study report.* https://lgbtcampus.memberclicks.net/assets/docs/Self%20Study%20Report%202018.pdf

Consortium of Higher Education LGBT Resource Professionals. (2024). *2024 member needs assessment report.* https://lgbtcampus.memberclicks.net/assets/2024%20Consortium%20Member%20Needs%20Assessment%20Report.pdf

Consortium of Higher Education LGBT Resource Professionals. (n.d.). *Vision and mission statement.* https://www.lgbtcampus.org/mission-statement

Council for the Advancement of Standards in Higher Education (2011). *CAS self-assessment guide for lesbian, gay, bisexual, transgender programs and services.* https://store.cas.edu/lgbtq-programs-and-services-self-assessment-guide-sag/

Council for the Advancement of Standards in Higher Education. (2019). *LGBTQ+ programs and services.* https://www.cas.edu/standards.html

Duran, A. (2021). *The experiences of queer students of color at historically white institutions: Navigating intersectional identities on campus.* Routledge.

Duran, A., & Jourian, T. J. (2023) A narrative inquiry study examining gender and sexuality center professionals' engagement with anti-racism. *The Journal of Higher Education, 94*(3), 333–356. https://doi.org/10.1080/00221546.2022.2093077

Duran, A., & Jourian, T. J. (2024). Gender and sexuality center professionals' narrative accounts of racialized institutional resistance in anti-racism work. *Review of Higher Education, 47*(4), 437–465. https://doi.org/10.1353/rhe.0.a914005

Duran, A., Catalano, D. C., Pryor, J. T., Taylor, J. L., & Jourian, T. J. (2023). Mapping the rise of LGBTQ+ student affairs: A 20 year review. *Journal of Student Affairs Research and Practice, 60*(2), 181–193. https://doi.org/10.1080/19496591.2022.2032112

Ferguson, R. A. (2012). *The reorder of things: The university and its pedagogies of minority difference.* University of Minnesota Press.

Ferguson, R. A. (2019) *One-dimensional queer.* Polity Press.

Fine, L. E. (2012). The context of creating space: Assessing the likelihood of college LGBT center presence. *Journal of College Student Development, 53*(2), 285–299. https://doi.org/10.1353/csd.2012.0017

Fox, C. O., & Ore, T. E. (2010). (Un)covering normalized gender and race subjectivities in LGBT "Safe Spaces." *Feminist Studies, 36*(3), 629–649. https://www.jstor.org/stable/27919125

Foste, Z., & Tevis, T. L. (2022). On the enormity of whiteness. In Z. Foste & T. L. Tevis (Eds.), *Critical whiteness praxis in higher education: Considerations for the pursuit of racial justice* (pp. 1–20). Stylus.

Gill-Peterson, J. (2024). *A short history of trans misogyny.* Verso.

Jeffries, M., & Boyd, A. S. (2020). Gender centers in higher education: Spaces for cultivating critical hope. In N. S. Niemi & M. B. Weaver-Hightower (Eds.), *The Wiley handbook of gender equity in higher education* (pp. 359–374). Wiley.

Harper, S., & Associates. (2024). *Truths about DEI on college campuses: Evidence-based expert responses to politicized misinformation.* University of Southern California Race and Equity Center. https://race.usc.edu/wp-content/uploads/2024/03/Harper-and-Associates-DEI-Truths-Report.pdf

Hoffman, G. D., & Pryor, J. T. (2024). Navigating identity and politics as trans gender and sexuality center professionals. *Journal of Diversity in Higher Education, 17*(6), 912–922. https://doi.org/10.1037/dhe0000472

Lange, A. C. (2019). Envisioning new praxis for gender and sexuality resource centers: Place-consciousness in post-secondary education. *Thresholds in Education, 42*(1), 59–73. https://academyforeducationalstudies.org/wp-content/uploads/2019/11/th42_1langefinal.pdf

Lange, A. C., Duran, A., & Jackson, R. (2022). How whiteness werqs in LGBTQ centers. In Z. Foste & T. L. Tevis (Eds.), *Critical whiteness praxis in higher education: Considerations for the pursuit of racial justice* (pp. 155–171). Stylus.

LGBTQ Architect. (n.d.). *Campus LGBTQ centers directory.* https://campuslgbtqcenters.org/

Marine, S. B. (2011). *Stonewall's legacy: Bisexual, gay, lesbian, and transgender students in higher education.* Jossey-Bass.

Marine, S. B., & Nicolazzo, Z. (2014). Names that matter: Exploring the tensions of campus LGBTQ centers and trans* inclusion. *Journal of Diversity in Higher Educationi 7*(4), 265–281. https://doi.org/10.1037/a0037990

McDaniel, J. (2024, June 29). Utah law targeting DEI leads university to close LGBT, women's centers. *The Washington Post.* https://www.washingtonpost.com/nation/2024/06/29/utah-dei-law-university-close-lgbt/

Mecca, T. A. (2009). *Smash the church, smash the state!: the early years of gay liberation.* City Lights Books.

McCoy, S. D. (2018). *Where is my place?: Queer and transgender students of color experiences in cultural centers at a predominantly white university.* (Publication no. 10817628). [Doctoral dissertation, University of Wisconsin-Madison]. UW-Madison Dissertations and Theses.

Nicolazzo, Z. (2016). 'It's a hard line to walk': black non-binary trans* collegians' perspectives on passing, realness, and trans*-normativity. *International Journal of Qualitative Studies in Education, 29*(9), 1173–1188. https://doi.org/10.1080/09518398.2016.1201612

Nicolazzo, Z. (2020). Visibility alone will not save us: Leveraging invisibility and virtual kinship to forward pedagogical progress. In C. Mayo & M. Blackburn (Eds.), *Queer, trans, and intersectional theory to educational practice: Student, teacher, and community experiences* (pp. 120–132). Routledge

Oliveira, K. A. (2022). *Revisiting 'our' place on campus: A queer(ed) and in-depth interview study of QT resource professionals in higher education* (Publication no. 29262001) [Doctoral dissertation, University of South Florida]. ProQuest Dissertations & Theses Global.

Oliveira, K. A., González-Siegel, V. A., Feldman, S., Kannan, K., Woods, C., Pryor, J. T., Duran, A., Catalano, D. C. J., & Jourian, T. J. (2025). An autoethnographic exploration of the realities of engaging trans and queer center(ed) diversity work. *Journal of Diversity in Higher Education, 18*(2), 111–122. https://doi.org/10.1037/dhe0000501

Ortiz, S. M., & Mandala, C. R. (2021). "There is queer inequity, but I pick to be happy": Racialized feeling rules and diversity regimes in university LGBTQ resource centers. *DuBois Review, 18*(2), 347–364. https://doi.org/10.1017/S1742058X21000096

Outcalt, C. (1995). Establishing a LGBT center. In C. F. Shepard, F. Yeskel, & C. Outcalt (Eds.), *Lesbian, gay, bisexual, & transgender campus organizing: A comprehensive manual* (pp. 213–238). National Gay and Lesbian Task Force.

Pryor, J. T., & Hoffman, G. D. (2021). "It feels like diversity as usual": Navigating institutional politics as LGBTQ+ professionals. *Journal of Student Affairs Research and Practice*, 58(1), 94–109. https://doi.org/10.1080/19496591.2020.1740717

Renn, K. A. (2010). LGBT and queer research in higher education: The state and status of the field. *Educational Researcher*, 39(2), 132–141. https://doi.org/10.3102/0013189X10362579

Sanlo, R. Rankin, S., & Schoenberg, R. (2002). *Our place on campus: Lesbian, Gay, Bisexual, Transgender services and programs in higher education*. Information Age Publishing.

Self, J. M. (2015). Queering center: A critical discourse analysis of university LGBT center theoretical foundations. *Journal of Critical Thought and Praxis*, 4(2). https://doi.org/10.31274/jctp-180810-48

Self, J. M., & Hudson, K. D. (2015). Dangerous waters and brave space: A critical feminist inquiry of campus LGBTQ centers. *Journal of Gay & Lesbian Social Services*, 27(2), 216–245. https://doi.org/10.1080/10538720.2015.1021985

Simms, S., Nicolazzo, Z., & Jones, A. (2023). Don't say sorry, do better: Trans students of color, disidentification, and internet futures. *Journal of Diversity in Higher Education*, 16(3), 297–308. https://doi.org/10.1037/dhe0000337

Spade, D. (2015). *Normal life: Administrative violence, critical trans politics, and the limits of law* (Revised and expanded ed.) Duke University Press.

Stanley, E. A. (2021). *Atmospheres of violence: Structuring antagonism and the trans/queer ungovernable*. Duke University Press.

STAR. (2013, March 12). Street transvestites for gay power: Statement on the 1971 NYU occupation. *Street Transvestite Action Revolutionaries: Survival, Revolt and Queer Antagonist Struggle*. https://archive.org/details/untorelli_2013_transvestite/untorelli_2013_transvestite/

Stryker, S. (2017). *Transgender history: The roots of today's revolution*. Seal Press.

Sycamore, M. B. (2004). *Nobody passes: Rejecting the rules of gender and conformity*. Seal Press.

Sycamore, M. B. (2006). *That's revolting: Queer strategies for resisting assimilation*. Seal Press.

Vaid, U. (2012). *Irresistible revolution: Confront race, class and the assumptions of lesbian, gay, bisexual and transgender politics*. Magnus Books.

· 2 ·

FRAMEWORKS TO GUIDE TQ CENTER(ED) DIVERSITY WORK: BRIDGING CRITICAL THEORIES WITH PRACTICE

Antonio Duran and J. Audra Williams

Introduction

Foundational to this edited text is the belief that TQ center(ed) diversity work must take a critical approach to serving TQ students, staff, and faculty on college campuses. This chapter sets the foundation for the chapters to follow by introducing relevant critical theories that TQ center(ed) diversity workers may use in their practice, including but not limited to queer theory, queer of color critique, and critical whiteness studies. Specifically, the chapter describes the potential of various critical theories using programming around National Coming Out Day as a case study to showcase how different frameworks accomplish distinct goals in serving TQ communities in higher education.

As highlighted in the introduction, the programs, services, and resources that TQ center(ed) diversity workers offer on campus are vital in how they support TQ students, staff, and faculty on college campuses, frequently providing them valuable social connections, education, and resources. Specifically, what scholarship does exist about TQ center(ed) diversity workers highlights their potential to facilitate important outcomes for the communities they serve (Duran et al., 2023). And yet, concerns abound about how limited TQ center(ed) diversity workers are in their ability to actualize systemic change that advances equity for TQ students, staff, and faculty (Oliveira et al., 2025). Moreover, certain populations—including those who identify as trans, disabled, and people of color—regularly report feeling as though they are not included within the spaces that these educators create. One does not have to look far to see critiques of TQ center(ed) diversity work of centering whiteness, ableism, and cissexism in programming, advocacy, and resource allocation (Duran & Jourian, 2023; Marine & Nicolazzo, 2014). However, to place the blame solely on TQ center(ed) diversity workers misses the many other factors at play that may be the reason for these patterns.

For instance, scholars have drawn attention to how TQ center(ed) diversity workers often lack the sufficient financial and human capital to execute the various function of their work (Catalano & Tillapaugh, 2020; Marine & Nicolazzo, 2014; Pryor & Hoffman, 2021; Tillapaugh & Catalano, 2019). Others have drawn attention to the very racist, homophobic, and transphobic ways that higher education institutions operate (e.g., Duran & Jourian, 2024; Hoffman & Pryor, 2023), which—among other impacts—contribute to the attrition of multiply marginalized TQ center(ed) diversity workers. These structures further place TQ center(ed) diversity workers under scrutiny when they attempt to enact anti-racist practices (Duran & Jourian, 2023). And importantly, many who do this work do not receive education in their graduate preparation programs about serving TQ students, nor do they often report obtaining sufficient onboarding training in their roles (Oliveira et al., 2025; Tillapaugh & Catalano, 2019). The combination of these factors may then lead to TQ center(ed) initiatives and practices that do not attend to the needs and priorities of the wide diversity of communities found under the TQ umbrella (e.g., those who hold multiple minoritized identities). Scholars such as Ford et al. (2015) made the case that practitioners should use student development theory to undergird the work of serving LGBT students. However, we argue the necessity for more critical theories that do not marginalize subgroups of TQ communities or advance unexamined privilege. As noted in the introductory chapter, the needs of TQ students, staff, and faculty continue to evolve in the shifting sociocultural moment, one that has seen the attacks on TQ communities in education and beyond (Lemerand & Duran, 2024). For this reason, it is ever more so vital for professionals to use lenses that acknowledge and resist systems of power and oppression in their praxis.

Thus, this chapter sets a foundation for the text to come by introducing critical theories that TQ center(ed) diversity workers may employ in their practice. The intention of this chapter is not to be exhaustive in the critical theories highlighted, but rather, to present possibilities that critical theories offer in advancing TQ center(ed) diversity work in higher education, especially for multiply minoritized TQ people. To highlight the potential of critical theories, this chapter uses National Coming Out Day (NCOD) as a case study, as it is a common programming point for TQ center(ed) diversity work. After describing the history and intention behind NCOD, we briefly describe specific critical theories and how they would influence the development of NCOD programming in TQ center(ed) diversity work. Subsequent authors in this edited text will then mobilize critical theories like those named in this chapter to inform their writing.

National Coming Out Day

Beginning outside of educational settings, National Coming Out Day first began in 1988 as a follow up to the National March on Washington for Lesbian and Gay Rights (Cornell University Library, 2006). The aim behind NCOD was to combat the targeting of gay and lesbian populations in the sociopolitical sphere by asserting the visibility of these groups, demonstrating the sheer number of individuals who were affected by legislative bodies in the United States. Five years later, the organization that started NCOD merged with what is presently known as the Human Rights Campaign (n.d.). As documented by Rhoads (1994), NCOD programming quickly came into existence in higher education as soon as 1992. In present times, NCOD occurs on October 11 with many colleges and universities celebrating the day by hosting programming, both in active (e.g., panels, speaker series) and passive (e.g., placing a door on campus for individuals to "come out" through) ways. As a part of LGBTQ+ history month, NCOD quickly became a staple for TQ initiatives in higher education.

However, activists and scholars have lodged complaints against the centrality of NCOD to supporting TQ communities in schools and higher education institutions. For instance, Rasmussen (2004) named how a focus on NCOD can serve to invalidate those who do not disclose their TQ identities, positioning them as not "honest and open" (p. 145). Others have named that the focus on visibility equates coming out with self-actualization, marginalizing communities that may not place a priority on disclosing one's identity (e.g., people of color; Lange et al., 2022) or that may have "layers of negotiation" because of the invisibility associated with the identity (e.g., asexual individuals; Mollet, 2023, p. 22). Coming into one's self may also be more valued by an individual or a community. Using Sekneh Hammoud-Becket's (2007) work with queer Muslims in Australia, Moore (2012) noted how the notion of coming out reifies heteronormativity and rigidity. In the sections that follow, we introduce various critical theories—queer theory, queer of color critique, crip theory, critical trans politics, and critical whiteness studies—and how TQ center(ed) diversity workers may approach NCOD from these different perspectives.

Queer Theory

Queer theory has moved its way into the discipline of higher education and student affairs, as scholars have shown interest in understanding how gender and sexuality operate relative to the collegiate context and broader societal domain (e.g., Abes & Kasch, 2007; Denton, 2019). Situated as a poststructural school of thought, queer theorists seek to expose how identity is not biologically determined, but rather, functions as a social construction that determines what is considered normal/abnormal as a way of structuring dominance. Especially central to the idea of coming out, as well as identity overall, scholars frequently turn to Butler's (1990/2006) concept of performativity. Distinct from ideas of performance which is about artifice, Butler (1990) asserted performativity as how identity construction occurs through iterations of speech acts that are repeated over time, which then create ideas about gender that position people in alignment or divergent from them. Put simply, gender is a copy for which the original category does not exist, but dominant culture uses those categories to dictate gender expression and sexuality (Butler, 1990). Consequently, identity is always shifting and fluid—both when it comes to society's perception of an identity and its performances, but also, a person's own view of themselves.

Queer Theory and NCOD

A central thesis of queer theorists is that identity is inherently unstable and subject to power relations. As a result, it is important to bring a critical eye to how TQ center(ed) diversity workers treat identity within the context of NCOD programming. Scholars like Abes (2008) drew connections between queer theory and the problematic nature of coming out, especially with identities that are constantly in flux and ever evolving. To "come out" as a particular identity may feel constraining to students as they are continuing to question who they are or what others perceive them as. In fact, for those who find value in the notion of coming out, it is frequently said that coming out is an ongoing experience and not one that simply occurs at a singular period of time in one's journey.

Thus, in setting the stage for NCOD, it is crucial that TQ center(ed) diversity workers resist a presentation of identity—and the coming out process, by transitive property—as neat, linear, and coherent. In their work on sexual identity formation, Denton (2016) emphasized the importance of challenging taken-for-granted language or identities relative to helping students in their identity development journeys. As people grow in their understanding of the communities and labels available to them, their view of themselves may similarly shift, representing multiple coming out periods or rejecting coming out altogether. Furthermore, queer theory demands exposing the interplay between identity and power discourses, which means practitioners must reckon with how notions of visibility support oppressive power in the university sphere. For instance, by coming out, people may be made more vulnerable to surveillance by university agents or peers, creating a paradoxical relationship in which NCOD may be harmful instead of helping the communities it professes to assist.

Queer of Color Critique

A central critique of queer theory broadly defined is its inattention to how race and racism operate to determine what society perceives as normal (Barnard, 2004; Cohen, 1997), missing out on the unique challenges that TQ people of color (TQPOC) face. Queer of color critique (QOCC) thus intervened into scholarship by arguing for the need to attend to how racism, capitalism, and heterosexism structure the lives of queers of color (Ferguson, 2004, 2018). Namely, by focusing too much on discourses on conceptual ideas of gender and sexuality, scholars miss out on the material ways in which TQPOC encounter discrimination within and beyond social institutions (e.g., not having access to resources). The focus of QOCC thus provided a notable intervention by amplifying the need to integrate a lens of materialism in thinking through the oppression that TQ communities of color report, challenging scholars to identify policies, economic systems, and other structures that marginalize TQPOC. In education, researchers have mobilized

QOCC to uplift how institutional leaders enact policies and classroom climates that subjugate TQ students of color, while highlighting the agency of these individuals in response to these environments (Brockenbrough, 2013; Duran & Jackson, 2019).

Queer of Color Critique and NCOD

In approaching NCOD from a QOCC lens, it is imperative to acknowledge that individuals have challenged the centrality of coming out for communities of color (e.g., Shulaiba, 2022). It may not be a desire for students to do so or even possible to come out for fear of losing access to important resources (Duran, 2019). In fact, centering trans people of color specifically, Gossett et al. (2022) brought light to the paradoxical nature of claiming visibility, putting at risk individuals who are already vulnerable and also potentially challenging them to acquiesce to particular methods of performing identity. Moreover, coming out extends a surveillance culture that especially harms TQPOC, especially Black trans people (Heberling, 2022). By becoming more visible, TQPOC may face additional consequences tied to this "surveillance culture," one in which they are subject to increased discrimination—whether interpersonal or administrative.

Therefore, to program on NCOD using QOCC as a framework would entail creating space for people to have conversations about the consequences that may result from being visible and inviting community activists to discuss the double-bind that comes with being "counted" within social institutions. This discussions may include conversations about demographic questions on surveys, listing names in "out lists" (a common practice in which an institution's website or newspaper displays the names of TQ people who have consented to being included), and more. In these programming opportunities, it is critical to emphasize the agency of TQ students, staff, and faculty of color (Brockenbrough, 2013), as they make strategic decisions to disclose and/or conceal their identities based on how they perceive the context. Furthermore, TQ center(ed) practitioners could collaborate with other professionals and students to advocate to senior administrations at their college/university that sheer numbers or visibility should not justify action or change. Efforts that focus only on increasing the population of TQ center(ed) professionals, especially TQPOC, is antithetical to a critical approach. Instead, the focus should be on policy, recruitment, and practices that sustain, invite, and promote equity at the institution.

Crip Theory

Resting under the umbrella of poststructuralism, crip theory has its origins tied to queer theory (McRuer, 2006; Kafer, 2013). Specifically, like queer scholarship, crip theory interrogates what is positioned as normal in society, taking a particular look at how members in society construct disability as abnormal. Theorists like McRuer (2006) have argued that compulsory able-bodiedness and able-mindedness are structures of domination that serve to marginalize disabled people especially, but also individuals more broadly, in manners similar to heterosexism. In higher education, Abes (2019) has argued for the usage of crip theory, especially when reflecting upon the subject area of student development. In highlighting the potential of crip theory, Abes (2019) examined topics of cripistemology and claiming crip identity as being central concepts that practitioners can learn about to disrupt ableism in collegiate environments. Cripistemology refers to the idea of embracing the multiplicity of ways that knowledge production occurs, challenging normative ideas of how people should operate temporally (Johnson & McRuer, 2014). Conversely, claiming crip identity emerges as a way to assert the fluidity of disability identity, much like queer theory destabilizes static views of sexuality and gender. In this vein, claiming crip means to assert a disabled identity despite potentially not having a diagnosis declaring them as such. These discourses about what constitutes identity consequently translates well to applying it in the context of NCOD.

Crip Theory and NCOD

Discussions of disability and ableism do not often take center stage in initiatives for NCOD, despite scholars describing how queer disabled students navigate unique concerns pertaining to identity management in higher education (see Miller et al., 2019). In particular, these individuals may have to make considerations of what it means to share about one's identity, especially if they pass as straight, cis, or nondisabled. Thus, TQ center(ed) diversity workers must make a concerted effort to bring attention to ableism and ability within movements around coming out and NCOD especially. This point brings to light the value of cross-movement solidarity that is regularly professed by disability justice scholars. Of note, Abrams and Abes (2021) mobilized crip theory to complicate authenticity in a study of a queer, disabled student. In their work, they emphasize that those at the intersections between queerness and disability can choose to disclose or not these minoritized identities, which is equally valid, and pushes against authenticity as a static concept. TQ center(ed) diversity workers can learn from their research by programming around the practice of radical self-love (Taylor, 2018) or the idea about being queer health rebels (Kafer, 2017)—both highlighted in Abrams and Abes' (2021) research—in contrast to the normative focus on coming out as being revolutionary.

Critical Trans Politics

Critical trans politics (CTP) articulates how administrative structures and legal systems perpetuate forms of violence that disproportionately disenfranchises trans populations (Spade, 2015). These seemingly "neutral" systems actually maintain binaries that place trans people outside of the realm of the social imaginary and consequently cause them to lack access to vital supports and resources that will ensure their livelihood (Namaste, 2000; Valentine, 2008). Higher education scholars have mobilized CTP to understand how higher education institutions themselves also perpetuate administrative violence that others trans students, staff, and faculty—especially when operating within a gender binary (e.g., erasing them in resource creation that targets basic needs; Jourian, 2017; Nicolazzo, 2016). Certain principles undergird CTP, such as understanding those most vulnerable to structures of marginalization by centering an analysis of intersecting structures of domination that shape the lives of trans people, namely Black and brown trans women. Additionally, CTP embraces the practice of trickle-up advocacy that seeks to enact justice and equity from the perspectives of those who are most affected by social institutions.

Critical Trans Politics and NCOD

Colleges and universities are themselves institutions that perpetuate violence toward trans students, staff, and faculty, especially those who hold multiple minoritized identities. Therefore, TQ center(ed) diversity workers must themselves be self-reflexive about how they further this oppression through and beyond their NCOD programming. By foregrounding discourses of coming out, how do TQ center(ed) diversity workers actually place their trans communities more at risk to be affected by administrative violence? This is an important question that practitioners must be able to wrestle with in relation to NCOD. An alternative may be found in CTP's attention to trickle-up social justice advocacy. TQ center(ed) diversity workers should consider collaborating with trans people of color, disabled trans people, and those with other multiple minoritized identities to reimagine a version of NCOD that is rooted in the needs of the community. Doing so must require TQ center(ed) diversity workers finding methods of compensation for the intellectual and physical labor of these individuals.

Critical Whiteness Studies

In recent years, higher education researchers have turned their attention to understanding how ideologies of whiteness have permeated college campuses using the lens of critical whiteness studies (CWS; Foste & Tevis, 2022; Tevis et al., 2023). Crucial to CWS is the idea that "whiteness is the underlying mechanism that maintains a racist system" (Matias et al., 2014, p. 291). To understand how racism operates within education, it is hence vital to take a look at how whiteness upholds various forms of racism (e.g., anti-Blackness). CWS does not have a set list of tenets as its counterpart of critical race theory does, but there are certain constructs that people investigate under the umbrella of CWS. Examples include white normativity, white racial ignorance, and white racial innocence (see Foste & Tevis, 2022). These analyses seek to understand how whiteness functions as the dominant norm; how white people claim ignorance and innocence to their whiteness by discursively minimizing their participation in white norms, or separating themselves as "good white people"; and that people of color may also replicate whiteness when they practice assimilation and regulate others' actions in accordance with this ideology (Tevis et al., 2023). Yet, it is important to note that scholars like Lange et al. (2022) have named that CWS scholarship has rarely engaged with topics of heterosexism and trans oppression in the context of education, meaning that there is an opportunity to further interrogate how structures of whiteness co-constitute TQ antagonism.

Critical Whiteness Studies and NCOD

Leveraging CWS in the context of NCOD would mean that TQ center(ed) diversity workers seek to understand how the very notion of coming out has roots in white norms. In fact, a common critique of TQ center(ed) diversity work is that it privileges whiteness (e.g., white, cisgender, gay and/or lesbian, middle-class; Lange et al., 2022), making it a prime site to use CWS to unpack this reality. One theoretical tool that practitioners can employ in conjunction with CWS is homonormativity, which describes how certain ways of performing sexuality in assimilatory ways is privileged (Duggan, 2002). Homonormativity illustrates how practices of coming out, marriage, and productivity are desirable insofar that it is parallel to heterosexuality. In fact, these practices—what I might argue is a form of disciplining—serve to demonstrate how queer sexuality is not a threat to the norms of white heterosexual pairings. So TQ center(ed) diversity workers must interrogate how coming out is part of a homonormative framework that particularly is beneficial to upholding whiteness and white supremacy. A helpful practice that can be potentially useful is having affinity groups that reflect on the intersections between racism, whiteness, and coming out on college campuses, guided by questions such as: who has the privilege of coming out? How does a politic of coming out serve to prioritize whiteness and homonormative ideals?

Conclusion

Critical theories represent a potentially powerful tool to help move TQ center(ed) diversity work in higher education forward, especially considering the structural and systemic challenges that TQ students, staff, and faculty face on college campuses. Although the theories highlighted in this chapter are only some of many that exist for TQ center(ed) diversity workers to use, it is our hope that they are a starting point for educators to mobilize. Moreover, we encourage TQ center(ed) diversity workers to consider the possibilities that drawing upon multiple critical theories offers in addressing the needs of those who access their services and spaces. In the chapters that follow in this edited text, we will witness how authors draw upon these legacies of critical theorizing to envision liberatory futures for TQ communities in higher education moving forward.

References

Abes, E. S. (2008). Applying queer theory in practice with college students: Transformation of a researcher's and participant's perspectives on identity, a case study. *Journal of LGBT Youth*, 5(1), 57–77. https://www.tandfonline.com/doi/abs/10.1300/J524v05n01_06

Abes, E. S. (2019). Crip theory: Dismantling ableism in student development theory. In E. S. Abes, S. R. Jones, & D.-L Stewart (Eds.), *Rethinking college student development theory using critical frameworks* (pp. 64–72). Stylus.

Abes, E. S., & Kasch, D. (2007). Using queer theory to explore lesbian college students' multiple dimensions of identity. *Journal of College Student Development, 48*(6), 619–636. https://doi.org/10.1353/csd.2007.0069

Abrams, E. J., & Abes, E. S. (2021). "It's finding peace in my body": Crip theory to understand authenticity for a queer, disabled college student. *Journal of College Student Development, 62*(3), 261–275. https://doi.org/10.1353/csd.2021.0021

Barnard, I. (2004). *Queer race: Cultural interventions in the racial politics of queer theory.* Peter Lang.

Brockenbrough, E. (2013). Introduction to the special issue: Queers of color and anti-oppressive knowledge production. *Curriculum Inquiry, 43*(4), 426–440. https://doi.org/10.1111/curi.12023

Butler, J. (2006). *Gender trouble.* Routledge. (Original work published 1990).

Catalano, D. C., & Tillapaugh, D. (2020). Identity, role, and oppression: Experiences of LGBTQ resource center graduate assistants. *Journal of Student Affairs Research and Practice, 57*(5), 519–531. https://doi.org/10.1080/19496591.2019.1699104

Cohen, C. J. (1997). Punks, bulldaggers, and welfare queens: The radical potential of queer politics? *GLQ: A Journal of Lesbian and Gay Studies, 3*(4), 437–465. https://doi.org/10.1215/10642684-3-4-437

Cornell University Library. (2006). *National coming out day.* https://rmc.library.cornell.edu/HRC/exhibition/changingissues/changingissues_1.html

Denton, J. M. (2016). Critical and poststructural perspectives on sexual identity development. *New Directions for Student Services, 2016*(154), 57–69. https://doi.org/10.1002/ss.20175

Denton, J. M. (2019). Queer theory: Deconstructing sexual and gender identity, norms, and developmental assumptions. In E. S. Abes, S. R. Jones, & D.-L. Stewart (Eds.), *Rethinking college student development using critical frameworks* (pp. 64–72). Stylus.

Dugan, L. (2002). *The new homonormativity: The sexual politics of neoliberalism.* Duke University Press.

Duran, A. (2019). Queer and of color: A systematic literature review on queer students of color in higher education. *Journal of Diversity in Higher Education, 12*(4), 390–400. https://doi.org/10.1037/dhe0000084

Duran, A., & Jackson, R. (2019). Thinking theoretically with and beyond intersectionality: Frameworks to center QTPOC experiences. In D. Mitchell Jr., J. Marie, & T. Steele (Eds.), *Intersectionality and higher education: Theory, research, and practice* (2nd ed., pp. 41–50). Peter Lang.

Duran, A., & Jourian, T. J. (2023). A narrative inquiry study exploring LGBTQ+ center professionals' engagements with anti-racism. *The Journal of Higher Education, 94*(3), 333–356. https://doi.org/10.1080/00221546.2022.2093077

Duran, A., & Jourian, T.J. (2024). Gender and sexuality center professionals' narrative accounts of racialized institutional resistance in anti-racism work. *Review of Higher Education, 47*(4), 437–465. https://doi.org/10.1353/rhe.0.a914005.

Duran, A., Catalano, D. C. J., Pryor, J. T., Taylor, J. L., & Jourian, T.J. (2023). Mapping the rise of LGBTQ+ student affairs: A 20 year review. *Journal of Student Affairs Research and Practice*, 60(2), 181–193. https://doi.org/10.1080/19496591.2022.2032112

Ferguson, R. A. (2004). *Aberrations in Black: Toward a queer of color critique*. University of Minnesota Press.

Ferguson, R. A. (2018, March 28). Queer of color critique. *Oxford Research Encyclopedia of Literature*. http://oxfordre.com/literature/view/10.1093/acrefore/9780190201098.001.0001/acrefore-9780190201098-e-33

Ford, M. E., Beighley, C. S., & Sanlo, R. (2015). Student development theory: Theory to practice in LGBT campus work. In J. C. Hawley (Ed.), *Expanding the circle: Creating inclusive environment in higher education for LGBTQ students and studies* (pp. 187–208). State University of New York.

Foste, Z., & Tevis, T. L. (Eds.). (2022). *Critical whiteness praxis in higher education: Considerations for the pursuit of racial justice on campus*. Routledge.

Gossett, R., Stanley, E. A., & Burton, J. (Eds.). (2022). *Trap door: Trans cultural production and the politics of visibility*. The MIT Press.

Hammoud-Beckett, S. (2007). Azima ila Hayati—An invitation in to my life: Narrative conversations about sexual identity. *International Journal of Narrative Therapy and Community Work*, 2007(1). https://dulwichcentre.com.au/product-category/2007/2007-issue-1/

Heberling, W. B. (2022). STOP SURVEILLING MY GENRE!: On the biometric surveillance of (Black trans) people. *Seattle Journal for Social Justice*, 20(3), Article 14. https://digitalcommons.law.seattleu.edu/sjsj/vol20/iss3/14

Hoffman, G. D., & Pryor, J. T. (2023). Navigating identity and politics as trans gender and sexuality center professionals. *Journal of Diversity in Higher Education*. Advance online publication. https://doi.org/10.1037/dhe0000472

Human Rights Campaign. (n.d.). *National coming out day*. https://www.hrc.org/campaigns/national-coming-out-day

Johnson, M. L., & McRuer, R. (2014). Proliferating cripistemologies: A virtual roundtable. *Journal of Literary and Cultural Disability Studies*, 8(2), 149–169. https://www.muse.jhu.edu/article/548848

Jourian, T.J. (2017). Trans*ing constructs: Towards a critical trans* methodology. *Tijdschrift voor Genderstudies*, 20(4), 415–434. https://doi.org/10.5117/TVGN2017.4.JOUR

Kafer, A. (2013). *Feminist, crip, queer*. Indiana University Press.

Kafer, A. (2017, April 6). *Health rebels: A crip manifesto for social justice* [Keynote]. Shepard Symposium on Social Justice, Laramie, WY.

Lange, A. C., Duran, A., & Jackson, R. (2022). How whiteness werqs in LGBTQ centers. In Z. Foste & T. Tevis (Eds.), *Critical whiteness praxis in higher education & student affairs: Considerations for the pursuit of racial justice on campus* (pp. 155–171). Stylus.

Lemerand, S., & Duran, A. (2024). Supporting queer and trans students amidst a rise in anti queer and trans legislation and policies. In K. Prieto & A. Herridge (Eds.), *LGBTQIA students in higher education: Approaches to student identity and policy* (pp. 226–240). IGI Global.

Marine, S. B., & Nicolazzo, Z. (2014). Names that matter: Exploring the tensions of campus LGBTQ centers and trans* inclusion. *Journal of Diversity in Higher Education, 7*(4), 265–281. https://doi.org/10.1037/a0037990

Matias, C. E., Viesca, K. M., Garrison-Wade, D. F., Tandon, M., & Galindo, R. (2014). "What is critical whiteness doing in OUR nice field like critical race theory?" Applying CRT and CWS to understand the white imaginations of white teacher candidates. *Equity & Excellence in Education, 47*(3), 289–304. https://doi.org/10.1080/10665684.2014.933692

McRuer, R. (2006). *Crip theory: Cultural signs of queerness and disability.* New York University Press.

Miller, R. A., Wynn, R. D., & Webb, K. W. (2019). "This really interesting juggling act": How university students manage disability/queer identity disclosure and visibility. *Journal of Diversity in Higher Education, 12*(4), 307–318. https://doi.org/10.1037/dhe0000083

Mollet, A. L. (2023). "It's easier just to say I'm queer": Asexual college students' strategic identity management. *Journal of Diversity in Higher Education, 16*(1), 13–25. https://doi.org/10.1037/dhe0000210

Moore, D. L. (2012, July 13). Coming out or inviting in?: Part II. *The Feminist Wire.* https://thefeministwire.com/2012/07/coming-out-or-inviting-in-part-ii/

Namaste, V. (2000). *Invisible lives: The erasure of transsexual and transgendered people.* University of Chicago Press.

Nicolazzo, Z. (2016). *Trans* in college: Transgender students' strategies for navigating campus life and the institutional politics of inclusion.* Stylus.

Oliveira, K. A., Gonzalez-Siegel, V. A., Feldman, S., Kannan, K., Woods, C., Pryor, J. T., Duran, A., Catalano, D. C. J., & Jourian, T.J. (2025). An autoethnographic exploration of the realities of engaging in TQ center(ed) diversity work. *Journal of Diversity in Higher Education, 18*(2), 111–122. https://doi.org/10.1037/dhe0000501

Pryor, J. T., & Hoffman, G. D. (2021). "It feels like diversity as usual": Navigating institutional politics as LGBTQ+ professionals. *Journal of Student Affairs Research and Practice, 58*(1), 94–109. https://doi.org/10.1080/19496591.2020.1740717

Rasmussen, M. L. (2004). The problem of coming out. *Theory Into Practice, 43*(2), 144–150. https://doi.org/10.1207/s15430421tip4302_8

Rhoads, R. A. (1994). *Coming out in college: The struggle for a queer identity.* Praeger.

Shulaiba, H. (2022, October 12). Coloring outside the lines. *The Michigan Daily.* https://www.michigandaily.com/michigan-in-color/queer-of-color/

Spade, D. (2015). *Normal life: Administrative violence, critical trans politics, & the limits of law* (2nd ed.). Duke University Press.

Taylor, S. R. (2018). *The body is not an apology: The power of radical self-love.* Berrett-Koehler.

Tevis, T. L., Whitehead, M., Foste, Z., & Duran, A. (2023). Whiteness beyond (just) white people: Exploring the interconnections among dimensions of whiteness in higher education. In L. W. Perna (Ed.), *Higher education: Handbook of theory and research* (pp. 95–148). Springer.

Tillapaugh, D., & Catalano, D. C. J. (2019). Structural challenges affecting the experiences of public university LGBT services graduate assistants. *Journal of Diversity in Higher Education, 12*(2), 126–135. https://doi.org/10.1037/dhe0000079

Valentine, D. (2008). *Imagining transgender: An ethnography of a category.* Duke University Press.

Part II
Present Realities

· 3 ·

ADVOCATING FOR EQUITABLE POLICIES FOR TRANS AND QUEER COMMUNITIES IN HIGHER EDUCATION

Em C. Huang and Andy Cofino

Introduction

Policy is a key indicator of institutional commitment, representation, and a driver of change. When TQ experiences are not included in policy, our identities and needs are erased. As practitioners, we must be grounded in an understanding of the landscapes of federal, state, and local legislation and the institutional policies and practices that affect our communities both overtly and covertly. Policies that impact TQ communities range widely; they can be explicitly harmful, ostensibly neutral but have disparate impact, nonexistent, or intentionally inclusive. Some policies may highlight TQ experiences and identities, but as responsible professionals, we must be acutely aware of all policies that impact our communities (e.g., Title IX, FERPA). Policy work encompasses a broad scope which often focuses on advocacy, but also requires development and implementation. We seek to reframe the common conception of policy work as divorced from the people within our institutions, instead as an integration of community work rooted in the experiences of those most impacted. In exploring these dynamics, this chapter aims to deepen practitioners' understanding of the complexities of advocating for equitable policies as a core tenet of TQ center(ed) diversity work.

In higher education, policies are the guiding documents that define the organization's culture and decision-making process by creating clarity, structure, process, and accountability so that all campus community members know what is expected of them. Policies also clarify what is expected of the institution and govern all aspects of campus—from human resources to information technology to community relations. Some policies explicitly apply to all community members, such as those related to nondiscrimination, sexual violence and sexual harassment (SVSH), and Health Insurance Portability and Accountability Act (HIPAA) privacy policies. Others only affect certain groups, such as human resources policies for employees or academic integrity policies for students. Policies can exclude and harm campus community members, whether explicitly or implicitly; yet, they also provide accountability and structure to address discrimination or institutional inequity. Decision makers within institutions often use policy to determine or justify a campus's resource allocations, especially if connected to census data or assessment. Policies can also give name and thought to community issues or needs by defining terms and language within an institutional context[1].

Because of its objective and legalistic language, student affairs professionals may consider institutional policy sterile, an entity divorced and disconnected from the human beings affected by it. Though it is true that policy, like law, can be dry in tone, we challenge the notion that policy *work* is inherently separate from the community that it impacts. Policy is written by people, usually those with institutional power, and thus our ability to collaborate with campus decision makers or be represented within policy development and implementation enables us to render TQ experiences visible and incorporated in the policies impacting our communities. Given the complex and critical impact of policies, it is essential higher education professionals understand what policy requires of them and how they can harness it to ensure all campus community members, including those who are TQ, are treated with dignity and respect. In particular, TQ center(ed) diversity workers must recognize the critical nature of policy advocacy, development, and implementation as a core component of serving TQ communities on campus.

Policy as Community Work

Institutional decision makers have historically harmed TQ communities by creating or maintaining policies that facilitate imbalances of power and barriers to access, participation, or agency of TQ individuals in institutions or public life. In particular, the development and enforcement of these institutional policies often perpetuate inequities that harm TQ communities based on assumptions that set cisgender and heterosexual people's experiences and needs as the norm. Regardless of intent, if policy makers do not hold the perspectives or lived experiences of the communities their work directly impacts, the resulting policy often will not account for the unique needs of TQ individuals. To serve TQ communities, we must instead engage with policy work grounded in centering the experiences of those who are most impacted by the issues at hand, ensuring that we integrate these voices to be reflected in the policies we create. When we reframe policy and understand that it must be rooted in our community work, we learn to utilize it not as a replication of institutional power and harm, but as a tool for improving equity in the structures of the systems we live in.

At its core, community centered policy work starts with a foundational approach of connecting the *who* and the *why* of a policy to influence its *how*. *Who* in our communities is impacted by this issue—what are the needs? *Why* does this matter—what are our values? *How* do we create a policy that addresses these community needs in alignment with our values? These questions are for us to ask ourselves, but also to ask our communities as part of a vital reciprocal process of gathering genuine input and feedback throughout policy development. This method also provides practical and necessary pathways for solidarity and accompliceship from those with decision-making power or influence who may not share identities or experiences with the communities impacted, but seek to engage in meaningful advocacy.

When we understand that policy work is a core tenet of TQ center(ed) diversity work, we can utilize it as one of our tools for addressing inequity. Understanding that institutions of higher education use policy as a language to mandate, regulate, and implement norms and expectations, TQ center(ed) diversity workers can utilize policy work as a key strategy to ensure access to needed resources and protections and make change within organizations. Although policy work is not a magic solution for dismantling all systems of oppression, it can be a critical tactic for reducing institutional harm caused to our communities. Thus, understanding and treating policy work as integral to our work towards equity allows us to become more effective advocates for the communities we serve.

Understanding the Policy Landscape

As practitioners working with policies within our campuses, we must first develop a robust understanding of the policy landscapes of our institutions in order to effectively navigate them. This includes understanding the issues addressed by the policy; identifying who controls the policies, processes, procedures, and practices in place; determining how our communities are affected; interpreting the impacts of federal and state legislation on our campuses; and learning institutional contexts, histories, and cultures.

TQ Issues in Policy

The range of TQ issues impacted by policy is incredibly vast, whether the policies directly address specific TQ experiences or needs, or if they are broader but hold particular implications for TQ communities. Major topics range from legal recognition of identities or relationships, anti-discrimination protections (or lack thereof), access to gender affirming and TQ-competent healthcare, access to facilities that are gender affirming or gender inclusive, access to athletics, social, or other organizational participation that is gender affirming or gender inclusive, censorship of speech and expression relating to TQ experiences, identities, or topics such as drag, and more. These relate to higher education contexts in myriad ways and can depend on what institutions have oversight of, the types of services or resources they provide, what local, state, or federal regulations they are beholden to, among other factors. For example, one institution may have a policy ensuring access to gender inclusive restrooms, while another may not be able to because it is in a state that criminalizes trans and nonbinary people using restrooms in alignment with their gender.

Many policies will have direct and significant impacts on TQ communities even when not directly addressing specific TQ identities or experiences, which necessitates a high level of attention to a wide range of policies and legislation. For example, though legislation protecting the ability to discriminate on the basis of religious belief or a campus policy on free speech may not explicitly name anti-TQ sentiment, how an institution decides to regulate or protect anti-TQ hate speech or discrimination will have significant repercussions on campus TQ communities. In a similar vein, maintaining awareness of the rapidly shifting landscapes of policy and legislation impacting issues such as sexual violence, reproductive rights, and access to related care is crucial due to the disproportionate impacts on TQ communities in these realms.

Policy in Context

Power and Decision Making

Though this chapter focuses on the impact of policies, practitioners must remember that institutional policies exist contextualized by those who hold power. Despite policy being presented as neutral and as speaking on behalf of the institution, it is important to remember that every policy is created by people, typically those who hold power and decision making responsibility in institutions. Even if an institution solicits feedback and input from stakeholders or the campus community, the final product presented in a particular policy must still be approved by institutional decision makers in order for it to exist. This means that all policies are inherently shaped by the perspectives, values, and priorities of those who create, advocate for, or implement them.

Processes, Procedures, and Practices

Even if the impact of a policy may seem straightforward, it can range significantly depending on how the policy is interpreted, implemented, and enforced. This often manifests beyond a policy itself, as the experiences of campus community members will vary depending on what processes and procedures are in place in relation to the policy, and the practices utilized by those at the institution to carry those out. For example, though most higher education institutions must have policies compliant with Title IX, the processes and procedures an institution uses to identify, investigate, adjudicate, and sanction issues of misconduct may differ. Further adding complexity that may lead to different outcomes, the staff members at the institution responsible for implementing these processes will do so with varying practices that may remain undefined by official policies and/or procedures—some may do so using gender inclusive language and a consideration of queer identities and experiences, while others may utilize a cissexist and heterosexist lens that erases or negatively impacts TQ individuals involved. Thus, beyond solely policies themselves, we must be able to identify, analyze, and work with the processes, procedures, and practices that give shape to their impact to effectively navigate the landscape of policy work.

Federal, State, and Cultural Contexts

Institutions of higher education, like for profit businesses, are beholden to federal, state, and local legislation. All institutions receiving federal funding through the U.S. Department of Education, for example, must adhere to the Family Education Rights and Privacy Act of 1974, which protects the privacy of student records (FERPA, 2012). In addition to federal law, administrators must ensure their campus operations abide by local legislation, such as state nondiscrimination laws or those which mandate or prohibit public colleges and universities from engaging in certain activities. For example, at the time of this publication, Alabama Senate Bill 129, prohibits sponsoring "any diversity, equity, and inclusion program or maintain[ing] any office, physical location, or department that promotes diversity, equity, and inclusion programs" (SB129, 2024, para. 68–71). It is also critical that educators are attuned to their specific institution's policies and culture, which are informed by its history, mission, structure, and leadership. For example, being aware of who serves on your institution's governing board or board of trustees can provide helpful cultural context about the people who hold significant power on your campus.

All professionals in TQ center(ed) diversity work must be mindful of federal rules and regulations that influence higher education by learning about the foundational and contemporary laws that affect every institution's policies and how they are implemented on your campus. In addition to FERPA, these include: Title IX of the Education Amendments (1972), which prohibits discrimination based on sex; the Americans with Disabilities Act (ADA, 1990), which provides protections for people with disabilities; and Title VI of the Civil Rights Act (1964), which outlaws discrimination on the basis of race, color, religion, sex, or national origin. The U.S. Supreme Court has also upheld that free speech is protected at colleges and universities under the First Amendment[2]. Though we won't explore each of these in detail in this chapter, it is essential to understand what these laws and regulations require of our campuses, offices, and roles. For example, you may learn you are a "responsible employee" due to federal Title IX policy, requiring you to report to a Title IX office if a student discloses sexual harassment or gender-based discrimination to you.

It is important to note that interpretation and guidance for laws may change as the federal administration does and that new legislation may be introduced. For example, the landmark Supreme Court decision *Bostock v. Clayton County* (2020) clarified that sexuality and gender identity are considered protected classes in relation to employment discrimination under the Civil Rights Act of 1964. In turn, the U.S. Department of Justice released a memo clarifying that gender identity and sexual orientation are also to be considered protected classes under Title IX, explicitly providing these protections for any education program or activity that receives federal funding (U.S. Department of Justice, 2021). Because the law can change and dramatically impact our work, it is imperative to keep up with these updates by following news from the federal government and reputable higher education resources, attending national conferences, and being connected to professional networks such as NASPA: Student Affairs Administrators in Higher Education and ACPA–College Student Educators International.

In addition to the federal landscape, it is equally as important to pay attention to local and state politics to ensure you are acting in compliance and to understand how local protections or explicit barriers may affect your work. For example, knowing if your state offers nondiscrimination protections or the legal ability to update name or gender markers on state issued documentation is critical. Similarly, it is vitally important to know if a state bill has passed that limits your institution's ability to, for example, provide direct support to TQ people or bans mandatory training on topics related to diversity and inclusion, such as North Dakota Senate Bill 2247 [2023].

Though policy is often straightforward, a college or university's history, campus-specific politics, and "unwritten curriculum" can be hard to discern and often takes significant time to learn (Jackson, 1990). Some elements of the institution, such as institutional type, can provide helpful cultural context (e.g., if it is a historically Black college or university, a Hispanic-serving institution, public or private, an Ivy League school, a religious institution, or a small community college). A school's organizational chart also provides critical information on campus demographics and clarifies where power lies in key decision making and influence. In consideration of this and the changing legal landscape, it is helpful to develop a strategic relationship with legal counsel, whose advice and support may be necessary to interpret evolving law and its impact on institutional risk to develop an appropriate approach to your work.

Lastly, the organization's history—which can be accessed from the campus website, library, or archives—can provide detailed information on historical policy changes and indicate the institution's level of openness to change over time. For example, one might note from files found in the UCLA Special Collections Archive that the Chancellor's Advisory Committee on

Lesbian and Gay Community was first established in 1990 (Online Archive of California). This committee was created in part to provide recommendations to senior leadership on policy concerns of TQ community members, suggesting that the administration was not only open to institutional change in the early 1990s, but created a clear structure to seek feedback from stakeholders (UCLA Office of Equity, Diversity and Inclusion, n.d.).

How Policies Impact TQ Communities

When analyzing institutional policy landscapes, it is valuable to understand the different ways that they may interact with TQ communities. Distinguishing among these different iterations equips practitioners with a more complete understanding of how policies have been developed and implemented, as well as how this shapes their impact on TQ communities. In relation to an issue impacting TQ communities, a policy can be explicitly harmful or discriminatory, ostensibly neutral but have disparate impact, intentionally inclusive, or it may not exist at all.

For any particular issue, policies may or may not exist to address the issue itself, how an institution should respond to the issue, or what should be done if campus constituents do or do not align with policies related to the issue. These may exist in alignment or contrast with federal, state, and local legislation. For example, in relation to restroom access for trans and nonbinary communities, an institution might have a policy that states that all community members can access restrooms in alignment with their gender identity. Another institution might have a policy addressing the creation of more gender inclusive restrooms on campus. Still another might have a policy holding campus community members accountable for gender-based discrimination if they prohibit trans and nonbinary people from accessing restrooms. Yet, another institution may not address restroom access for trans and nonbinary individuals in any of their policies at all, especially if there is state or local legislation either codifying or criminalizing access that is in alignment with gender.

Policies that are explicitly harmful target, exclude, or discriminate against people on the basis of their sexual orientation or gender identity. Examples of this include policies that bar trans or nonbinary people from receiving institutional recognition, accessing restrooms, or participating in activities in alignment with their gender identity. These policies may exclude either based on the designation of a group, identity, or experience as the "correct" way to exist or navigate (e.g., a policy that requires individuals to utilize restrooms based on their sex assigned at birth) or conversely, by explicitly designating queer or trans people to be excluded (e.g., a policy that bans all transgender athletes from women's sports).

Policies that are ostensibly neutral but have disparate impact are often not immediately thought of as discriminatory. A policy may have been developed without intention of inequity, but due to historical factors or contexts, still result in outcomes that continue to adversely affect particular marginalized groups. For example, an institution may have a survivor benefits policy that allows the spouse of a retired employee to receive their benefits upon the former employee's death regardless of the spouse's gender, as long as they had been married at least one year prior to the former employee's retirement. This may seem like an inclusive policy as it has the same requirements for establishing an existing relationship between the spouses prior to retirement whether they are of the same or different gender. However, as same-sex marriage was not legalized in many U.S. states until 2015, many queer partnerships would not have been able to fulfill this requirement, creating a disparate impact on queer employees.

As another example, several institutions offer paid time off as an incentive or benefit to employees who choose to donate blood. However, not all employees have had the same opportunities to donate blood; until 2015, the U.S. Food and Drug Administration (FDA) had a blanket ban in place that prevented all gay and bisexual men from donating blood, as well as women who had sex with men who had sex with men. Even after the blanket ban was repealed, men who had sex with men still faced additional restrictions to donation, including a required period of abstinence—first set at one year in 2015, later changed to 90 days in 2020. Though restrictions specific to men who have sex with men were replaced in 2023 by a new risk assessment tool utilized for all donors regardless of identity, the current regulations defer potential donors who are on PrEP, again creating an outsized impact on men who have sex with men.

Although institutions may apply policies like these consistently to all of their constituents, their lack of awareness of and responsiveness to relevant historical and structural barriers that shape TQ community experiences lead to disparate impacts. By engaging with campus communities as a monolith and failing to recognize the need for a critical analysis of structural inequality, these policies continue to perpetuate discriminatory effects regardless of intent.

In contrast to these, policies that are intentionally inclusive recognize the multiple communities that may be impacted by a particular issue and the policies developed in response. The diversity of communities is recognized instead of treating them as a monolithic entity, and there is active engagement with those that are most marginalized in policy creation, development, and implementation. These policies utilize a critical lens that understands and incorporates the contexts of relevant historical and structural inequities and seeks to rectify them.

Foundational Approaches to Engaging in Policy Work

There are a few foundational aspects of policy work that are core to affecting change in TQ center(ed) diversity work. Below, we cover these aspects, but we also provide a worksheet in Appendix A that will be helpful in working through these questions. For example, it is essential to constantly work in conversation with TQ students, staff, faculty, and alumni who are most impacted by the policy at hand to ensure your efforts align with the actual community's needs, especially if it is outside of your own personal lived experience. For example, if a policy is being drafted to systemize the collection of student sexual orientation and gender identity data, it is critical to ensure the voices of students of different genders and sexualities are reflected in policy decisions. By consulting with students on what specific terms resonate with them, not only will the institution reflect the language with which students actually identify, but the policy will be more precise, and the institution's data more accurate.

Another important aspect in engaging in policy work is to take into account how varying communities and the intersections of identities are affected. For example, when considering a policy change that will allow for the creation of gender inclusive facilities, it is necessary to identify a solution that accounts not only for transgender and nonbinary community members' concerns, but also those of religiously orthodox students, survivors of sexual assault and violence, and students with disabilities. Of course, in doing so, you will ensure students who identify with all of these communities have their needs met holistically.

Another critical element of policy work is to identify and understand existing (or nonexistent) relevant policies and practices. We have discussed this already with regards to federal and state legislation, but what other relevant policies or practices might you consider at the institutional level? For example, if the outcome you are hoping to achieve is addressing over surveillance of Black and Brown students by campus police at your institution, have you researched to see if there is a community safety plan that is of particular relevance, such as the one in place at the University of California system (ACLU, 2023; University of California Office of the President, 2021)?

Practitioners often perceive policy work as synonymous with its implementation, a narrow scope focused on executing a set of new or modified rules or regulations. While implementation is a key aspect, before a new or changing policy can be administered, a need or goal must first be identified along with a strategic plan to create such a change. Let us now turn to these three foundations of policy work so we can understand how to apply them in TQ center(ed) diversity work: advocacy, development, and implementation.

Advocacy

Before recommending a specific policy change, one must first identify and articulate: (a) the defined need(s) for the policy proposal; (b) relevant stakeholders to consult in its design; (c) clearly established goals, strategies, and outcomes to track progress; and (d) key decision-makers with influence over the matter. Let's explore each of these aspects of advocating for policy change.

Though it may seem obvious, the critical first step in advocating for a policy change is to identify a specific (set of) need(s) and confirm if policy can address it. Policy cannot solve every institutional issue, so it is critical to ask the question: will changing or introducing a policy result in the intended outcome we are hoping to achieve or the problem we are aiming to solve? The answer should be informed by institutional data or evidence-based research. Campus climate and/or demographic data can indicate unmet institutional needs that policies can often address in combination with other campus inventions. For example, if data indicates that transgender and nonbinary students have a demonstrated lower sense of belonging due to experiences of being referred to by their deadname, a policy change allowing students to indicate their lived name within academic systems (and hide their deadname) will assist faculty and staff in correctly utilizing their students' proper names. This change would then hopefully result in more positive outcomes for transgender and nonbinary students' sense of belonging. If such data does not exist on your campus and the concern has been brought to your attention anecdotally, consider developing a method of collecting such data to bolster your argument. Focus groups and surveys that illustrate community members' experience and concerns in their own words are often powerful testimonials to inspire policy change.

With a need identified and data to support it, it is time to gather relevant stakeholders to consult on the potential policy. As noted, stakeholders should engage community members most impacted along with those with overlapping needs, but must also include key personnel who have expertise in the subject matter connected to the proposed policy. For example, if you are attempting to change an aspect of your campus' information systems, it is critical to include a campus partner from your IT department. Other stakeholders to consider partnering with may include legal counsel, the chief diversity officer, representatives from the Title IX office and communications, and staff from the multicultural and/or TQ center spaces. This consultative group can provide additional insights on the identified need, anticipate potential challenges or barriers, and provide resources to make progress towards shared goals.

Once your coalition of stakeholders are in conversation, it is essential to establish clear goals, strategies, and intended outcomes to track progress towards achieving them. SMART goals that are specific, measurable, achievable, relevant, and time bound are particularly helpful in this process (Doran, 1981). For example, imagine the outcome you hope to achieve is for a new policy that would allow for students' lived names[3] (versus their legal names) to be permitted on eligible academic documents, such as university-issued diplomas. Working backwards from this goal, the group would want to assess whether or not it is achievable (are there state laws that currently prohibit this practice?) and if so, outline a specific course of action noting milestones towards completion. In this example, these could include: meet with relevant stakeholders by the end of summer, research similar policy language from peer institutions in the fall, and present a proposal to senior leadership by the following spring.

Another essential component of successful advocacy is understanding who has the ultimate authority and decision-making power over your proposed policy change, and determining how to secure their buy-in. The practice of power mapping can be particularly helpful in this process—enabling you to identify critical decision-makers and what resources they are connected to, how decisions are made, and how to effectively communicate to achieve your goals (Boyles, 2022; National Education Association, 2023). Using the earlier example of a policy change to allow the usage of lived names on academic documents, a critical campus leader who would have authority in this process is the campus registrar. Not only may they have the power to approve the ultimate policy change, they are a powerful resource to advocate for it, help identify potential roadblocks, and move the project along in an efficient and timely manner.

Development

Once a need has been identified and relevant stakeholders and senior leaders have been brought into conversation, the focus turns towards the development of the policy. As noted, it is critical the group is clear on its desired impacts and results and has established clear goals and milestones. The development process should include opportunities to gather input and feedback from a wide range of stakeholders at differing levels, positions, and interaction points with the proposed policy. For example, for a policy that would mandate university information systems to allow for three equally recognized gender options (nonbinary, woman, and man), it would be critical to engage students and staff who will input this data, along with data information systems colleagues who can share challenges and concerns with campus systems that may limit their ability to allow for such a change.

Part of the development process will also include understanding where consistency versus flexibility is important, impractical, or impossible. It may be the case that a policy change you want to implement may simply not be possible to complete in a timely fashion or at all due to legal, political, budgetary, or staffing constraints, or a lack of buy-in from senior leadership. As such, it is important to continue to build a case for the need, but to know where your time and energy may be better spent in the short term. Anticipating trends in language, terminology, law, and culture can also help to plan a more realistic timeline to achieve your goals as you begin identifying needs.

Implementation

Upon completion of policy development comes the actual implementation of the policy itself, which is the process of translating the goals and objectives of a policy into action. Creating a robust implementation plan that identifies, defines, and communicates the path forward to all partners, stakeholders, and relevant campus constituents is essential and should be done prior to policy enactment. This plan should not be limited just to the enactment of the specific policy, as there are multiple key components that must be considered and addressed in creating viable pathways for successful policy implementation.

The foundation of a strong implementation plan rests on clearly identifying goals, outcomes, intended impacts, and how these all fit into the bigger picture for the organization, all crucial aspects of the policy development process. When clarity for those has been determined, policy implementers can construct a plan in collaboration with key partners that incorporates the multiple components of preparing your institution to successfully navigate organizational change, which include institutional investment, communication, change management, education, and compliance. Some of these components help ascertain the readiness of the institution to move forward with implementation, while others guide and support implementation in ways that increase the likelihood of achieving the policy's desired outcomes.

As previously addressed, institutional investment and buy-in from senior leadership are critical for a strong foundation in policy advocacy, development, and similarly, implementation. These help to clarify accountability to implementation at an institutional level, which includes defining policy governance by answering the question of who is responsible for, or "owns," the policy and its implementation. Along with determining governance, institutional investment should also be reflected by prioritizing the provision of appropriate resources that are needed for successful implementation. These resources may include funding, staffing, inventories of assets, necessary systems or infrastructure, and more. Institutional support in these forms will help you develop your plan both for the initial implementation along with setting up the policy for ongoing sustainability.

Though the hope is that institutional leadership will be supportive or collaborative partners, practitioners may encounter reluctance, resistance, or sometimes, outright opposition. Each of these responses requires a distinct approach to navigate, which may involve different strategies of working with, or perhaps around, leadership who are hesitant to advance policy work supporting TQ communities. For example, reluctance to prioritize the development and implementation of an equitable policy due to concerns about limited resources may be alleviated by developing a plan that outlines achievable deliverables based on available resources. This may be paired with data and storytelling to indicate needs that would be addressed in alignment with institutional mission and values to clearly demonstrate why the institution should invest in the policy. When resistance is encountered, practitioners can work to identify areas of concern and help leadership understand the impacts and risks to campus community members and the institution if the issue is not addressed. A strategy to navigate direct opposition might be to utilize a long-term approach, identifying upcoming opportunities when the landscape of the institution or its leadership may change and advancing policy work may become more feasible.

Communication about the policy implementation itself is a key component, especially so that all relevant stakeholders and partners are aware of their roles and responsibilities in the implementation process. Information that is necessary to provide includes, at minimum, what the policy entails, why it exists, what the goals and desired outcomes are, what steps and timeline are necessary for successful implementation, and what its impacts on partners and stakeholders are. As an implementation plan is developed, ensuring that all parties involved are clearly aware of (and ideally in alignment with) these aspects create clarity for the implementation plan and allows you to identify and anticipate possible areas of concern or challenge to address.

Change management is another major component of policy implementation and has multiple aspects to consider when developing the implementation plan. At its core, understanding change management involved in the implementation of a policy requires identifying (a) what changes to operations, processes, or systems are needed, (b) how different partners, stakeholders, or constituents will be affected by these changes, and (c) how to set up all constituents for success to operationalize these changes. To understand the range and scope of changes that the implementation of a policy will entail, it is important to inventory all systems, processes, and operations that will be affected, how they will change, and what needs to happen for those changes to be made. Policy makers should identify the various constituents that interface with these systems, processes, and operations who will be impacted by these operational changes in the inventory—this can be determined based on roles, departments, individuals, and/or communities, and is important to do in collaboration with your campus partners and stakeholders. Once you have identified these constituents, it is crucial to work with your partners to ascertain and anticipate as best as possible how these impacts will occur to build a robust understanding of how each constituent group will experience changes related to the policy. Your implementation team can then develop specific strategies to address each constituent group's particular needs, which will often incorporate aspects such as obtaining resources, communicating clear expectations and timelines, and providing necessary education and training.

Education is another crucial component of policy implementation that may vary widely in scope and audience. Some questions to consider when identifying potential needs or opportunities for education might include: what do campus community members need to know to understand that this policy exists and why? How does this policy and any related changes impact TQ campus community members? What pertinent changes to job functions or practices will exist as a result of this policy, and what training do staff members need to successfully enact these changes? Exploring questions such as these should also be paired with a consideration for how necessary information should be conveyed. For example, methods of education might range from providing key partners or stakeholders with specific operational training about implementing certain new business processes to launching an educational campaign raising awareness within the campus community about a new policy's existence and implications.

Finally, addressing compliance is a necessary component for policy implementation, particularly in setting and maintaining institutional accountability. Some questions to explore may include: what does accountability entail in terms of policy implementation and successful change management? Who is responsible for holding individuals, units, or the institution accountable in relation to the policy? What are the procedures and consequences when addressing any failures to comply with the policy once it has been implemented? Unless compliance procedures and the entities responsible for them are clearly identified, structured, and set up for success, the impact and sustainability of the policy will be limited.

Strategically developing a holistic implementation plan that understands and addresses the various needs of all impacted campus constituents is key to successful policy work. Once a robust and collaborative plan has been developed and implementation has begun, tracking progress, assessing effectiveness, and being adaptive to new or shifting needs that arise will guide your course. As organizational change takes place, documenting knowledge and processes as changes are being solidified will set the institution up for sustained success and contribute to the longevity of the policy and its impact.

Conclusion

Though policy can and has been used to harm, exclude, and even erase queer and trans people from institutional settings, it can also enable us to give voice, rationale, and resources to TQ community members, who continue to experience significant marginalization on college campuses. When we understand that policy can be a powerful tool to invite TQ community members into conversation with our institutions to create impactful change, we can appreciate it as an essential element of TQ center(ed) diversity work. As higher education professionals, it is imperative we understand the social, political, and cultural landscapes of our institutions and utilize policy work as a tool to create greater equity within higher education.

Appendix A

Below, we offer a policy assessment worksheet to aid your work in advocating for equitable policies.

Table 3.1. Policy Assessment Worksheet

Advocacy	
What is the issue/concern that your proposed or revised policy will address?	
What communities are affected and how are they experiencing the impact of this issue/concern?	
How is policy the right solution (versus changes to practices or procedures)? *i.e. Would an educational campaign to change campus practices be more effective than a change to policy to meet stated goals?*	
How does the suggested policy/change align with the values and/or mission of the institution? *Communicating the connection between a proposed policy and institutional mission and/or values can bolster the proposal.*	
What feedback has been gathered from stakeholders? *Who are the stakeholders? How have they provided feedback on the issue/concern and policy proposal at hand? Are key stakeholders part of the decision making process?*	

(continued)

Table 3.1. *Continued*

What is my institution's current legal and political landscape as it relates to the specified need? *Do federal, state, or local laws prohibit or support this policy/change?*	
What relevant institutional policies or practices might impact or inform this policy? *Is there a similar or related policy to take into consideration? (i.e. if the policy is about allowing systems to use lived name, is there a relevant IT or data privacy policy to be mindful of?)*	
What existing data or evidence-based research exists to support this policy/change? *If not, is there a way to gather this data through analyzing existing data sets, distributing a survey or facilitating focus groups?*	
What are the intended outcome(s) of the proposed policy? *What are the clear, specific, and measurable goals this policy aims to achieve? Be as specific as possible (i.e. this policy change will allow asexual students, staff, and faculty to share their identity in University systems where sexual orientation is collected.)*	
Which potential accomplices, collaborators, and detractors have been identified through a power mapping exercise? *If so, how will you work with these colleagues or community members to garner support or address concerns?*	
What considerations have been identified by legal counsel to ensure the proposed policy is compliant?	

Table 3.1. *Continued*

Development	
What stakeholders are represented in the development process of the policy? *i.e. If the policy is affecting TQ communities, has the TQ director been included?*	
How are the intended outcomes and goals clearly identified in the policy?	
How does the policy proposal address potential barriers, objections or concerns?	
Implementation	
What resources have been identified to successfully implement this policy change? *e.g. funding, staffing, inventories of assets, necessary systems or infrastructure, etc.*	
How will the policy change be communicated? What education will be required? Who needs to learn about this policy change?	
Who is responsible for upholding policy?	
What metrics to assess and track progress are included in the proposal?	
What key milestones and deadlines to implement the policy have been identified? *This helps ensure accountability has time bound markers to assess progress.*	
What opportunities for continual feedback and input from community members exist?	

Notes

1. For example, see page 2 of the University of California Gender Recognition and Lived Name Policy (2020), which provides definitions for gender and sexuality terminology.
2. See Lake (2021) for more information on First Amendment rights and free speech in higher education.
3. Lived name: A self-chosen or preferred personal and/or professional name used instead of a legal name (University of California, 2020).

References

American Civil Liberties Union. (2023, February 27). *Colleges and universities have a racial profiling problem.* https://www.aclu.org/news/racial-justice/colleges-and-universities-have-racial-profiling

Americans With Disabilities Act of 1990, 42 U.S.C. § 12101 et seq. (1990). https://www.ada.gov/pubs/adastatute08.htm

Bostock v. Clayton Cty., 140 S. Ct. 1731. (2020). https://www.supremecourt.gov/opinions/19pdf/17-1618_hfci.pdf

Boyles, M. (2022, July 7). *Power mapping: What it is & how to use it.* Harvard Business School Online. https://online.hbs.edu/blog/post/power-mapping-what-it-is-and-how-to-use-it

Civil Rights Act of 1964, Pub. L. No. 88-352, 78 Stat. 241. (1964). https://www.govinfo.gov/content/pkg/STATUTE-78/pdf/STATUTE-78-Pg241.pdf

Doran, G. T. (1981). There's a S.M.A.R.T. way to write management's goals and objectives. *Management Review, 70,* 35–36.

Education Amendments Act of 1972, 20 U.S.C. §§1681–1688. (1972). https://www.govinfo.gov/content/pkg/USCODE-2021-title20/pdf/USCODE-2021-title20-chap38.pdf

Family Educational Rights and Privacy Act (FERPA). 20 U.S.C. § 1232g. (2012). https://www.govinfo.gov/app/details/USCODE-2011-title20/USCODE-2011-title20-chap31-subchapIII-part4-sec1232g

Jackson, P. W. (1990). *Life in classrooms.* Teachers College Press.

Lake, P. F. (2011). *Foundations of higher education law & policy: Basic legal rules, concepts, and principles for student affairs.* NASPA.

National Education Association. (2023, May 17). *Power mapping 101.* https://www.nea.org/professional-excellence/student-engagement/tools-tips/power-mapping-101

Online Archive of California. (n.d.). *Finding aid for the lesbian gay bisexual transgender resource center. Administrative files 1974–2011.* https://oac.cdlib.org/findaid/ark:/13030/c8v69m23/admin

Senate Bill 129, 2024 Reg. Sess. (Ala. 2024). https://legiscan.com/AL/bill/SB129/2024

Senate Bill 2247 | 2023-2024 | 67th Legislative Assembly. (Nd. 2023). https://ndlegis.gov/assembly/68-2023/regular/documents/23-0417-02000.pdf

UCLA Office of Equity, Diversity and Inclusion. (n.d.). *Mission of the UCLA committee on LGBTQ affairs.* https://equity.ucla.edu/lgbtq/mission/

University of California. (2020). *Gender recognition and lived name.* https://policy.ucop.edu/doc/2700693/GRLN

University of California Office of the President. (2021). *Systemwide community safety.* https://www.ucop.edu/uc-operations/systemwide-community-safety/index.html

U.S. Department of Justice. (2021, March 26). *Memorandum: Application of Bostock v. Clayton County to Title IX of the Education Amendments of 1972.* https://www.justice.gov/crt/page/file/1383026/dl

· 4 ·

ENGAGING INSTITUTIONAL POLITICS THROUGH A POWER ANALYSIS IN TQ CENTER(ED) DIVERSITY WORK

Jonathan T. Pryor, Antonio Duran, & Vanessa Aviva González-Siegel

Introduction

Higher education institutions exist as complex and bureaucratic systems of organization and administration. Each level of administration is broken down into units, departments, offices, and teams which comprise staff and other workers. TQ center(ed) diversity workers are situated as student-facing staff within larger departments and offices tasked with supporting students and creating more inclusive campuses. TQ center(ed) diversity work is not only investing in community development via programming, education, and student organizational advising, but is also changing organizational practices. When TQ center(ed) diversity workers attempt to elevate or shift the work from student-facing to institutional-facing, there are often barriers within organizational structures as well as a lack of training on how to navigate institutional politics. In order to do this, TQ center(ed) diversity workers must be able to engage in an evaluation of their spheres of influence via a power analysis. This chapter will illustrate how TQ center(ed) diversity workers and other practitioners can identify their spheres of influence, conduct an accurate and robust power analysis, and shift their focus to begin to develop systems-thinking practices to understand how to navigate ambiguous and ever-changing institutional politics and leverage coalitions to enact institutional change.

Higher education institutions are complex organizations with intricate structures. TQ center(ed) diversity workers typically operate within Divisions of Student Affairs, Diversity, Equity, and Inclusion (DEI), or other student-facing departments. Although their primary focus is on supporting TQ students, it is essential for these workers to analyze and understand the organizational context in which they operate. By comprehending the organizational complexities and their place within the larger power structure, TQ center(ed) diversity workers must elevate their work to encompass systems, institutions, and the organization as a whole. Moreover, understanding power dynamics in organizational settings is crucial for grasping how decisions are made, how resources are allocated, and how to transform institutions (Capper, 2018).

What Is Power?

Power is defined as a social production of an effect that determines the capacities, actions, beliefs, or conduct of actors. Power does not exclusively refer to the threat or use of force by one individual against another, but may also be exerted through diffused means or filtered through institutions (Barrett et al., 2005; Finnemore et al., 2013). For example, in a higher education context, this may surface in how institutions structurally locate TQ center(ed) spaces, which may subsequently hinder TQ center(ed) leaders' autonomy to enact meaningful change. Power relies on the ignorance of its agents and survives by being dispersed through an apparatus that is both efficient and silent. It is because of this action that power is unlikely to be detected and remains elusive (Foucault, 1995).

Power within organizations is the ability or capacity of individuals or groups to influence, control, or command resources, decisions, and actions of others within the organizational structure. This influence can appear in various forms, including positional power, expert power, reward power, coercive power, referent power, and informational power (Anderson & Brion, 2014). Positional power is authority that is derived from an individual's position or role within an organization. This is the job or function that one is charged with and the inherent power and influence that comes with it. Expert power is influence based on the skill, expertise, knowledge, or previous work experience that a worker possesses. Reward power is the ability to provide or withhold rewards (resources) such as promotions, budget increases, salary adjustments, etc. Coercive power is the ability to enforce or enact discipline or penalties for actions that are deemed unfit. Referent power refers to the influence an individual has based on their personal traits such as their personality, charisma, or the respect that they receive from others. Informational power is having oversight of how information is shared with others, particularly information that others need or want.

Colleges and universities are hierarchical organizations where titles carry significant weight. TQ center(ed) diversity workers know this reality well as they navigate ambiguity and competing institutional priorities (Oliveira et al., 2025). Formal authority stems from official positions within the organizational hierarchy (Anderson & Brion, 2014). This type of authority allows individuals with specific titles (e.g., director, dean, assistant vice president) to make decisions and allocate resources based on their position alone. TQ center(ed) diversity workers, even if they rise to the level of director, often lack direct power over organizational resources. Here, the roles of referent and expert power become crucial. Building coalitions and networks of support is standard practice for diversity work within higher education and forms the foundation of referent power[1]. Additionally, TQ center(ed) diversity workers often need to understand various functional areas of their institutions more comprehensively than their colleagues, positioning them uniquely to build referent power, and by extension model expert power. This unique positioning can lead to the development of soft power on campus.

Soft power is the ability to shape the preferences of others through appeal and attraction rather than coercion or payment (Vuving, 2009). It is cultivated through positive interactions, expertise, charisma, and a commitment to kindness. Soft power operates subtly and indirectly, making it difficult to measure but evident through influence. Vuving (2009) explained that soft power manifests through power currencies: attraction, persuasion, and agenda-setting. Attraction involves drawing others through cultural appeal, values, and policies, relying on qualities like kindness, competence, and commitment. Persuasion changes others' preferences through communication, while agenda-setting shapes priorities by controlling discourse topics. Although Vuving (2009) discussed soft power in the context of international relations, this conceptual framework is also valuable for TQ center(ed) diversity workers. By leveraging their unique positions and developing both referent and expert power, TQ-center(ed) diversity workers can effectively utilize soft power to influence their institutions. These forms of power, built through relationships and recognized expertise, enhance their ability to navigate institutional complexities and drive meaningful change. By being aware of these forms of power and adopting these relational approaches, TQ-center(ed) diversity workers can subtly but powerfully shape their institutions and foster a more inclusive and supportive environment for TQ students.

For Your Consideration

Understanding and developing power is crucial for TQ center(ed) diversity workers to be effective in transforming institutions. However, leveraging power within an institution comes with unintended consequences and ethical considerations that must be carefully managed. As a TQ center(ed) diversity worker, it is essential to navigate these dynamics thoughtfully to effectively advocate for TQ students while maintaining ethical integrity.

Lorde and Freire emphasized that true liberation cannot be achieved through oppressive frameworks. Lorde (1984) argued that the existing societal structures and methods, which uphold systems of oppression, cannot be used to achieve true liberation and justice. Lorde emphasized that relying on the same tools and frameworks created by oppressors will only perpetuate inequality. Instead, marginalized groups must develop new strategies and ways of thinking that challenge and transcend the existing power dynamics to create genuine and lasting change. Similarly, Freire (1970) cautioned that using oppressive methods to achieve liberation only perpetuates the cycle of oppression. He stressed the importance of developing a pedagogy that promotes critical consciousness, where the oppressed are active participants in their liberation. Freire warned that if the oppressed adopt the oppressors' tactics, they risk becoming oppressors themselves. True liberation requires a break from oppressive practices and the adoption of new, transformative approaches that empower and humanize all individuals. This consciousness raising necessitates TQ center(ed) workers to thoughtfully engage their practice to uphold these principles, which may necessitate fearless vulnerability given the form of power the TQ center(ed) worker may (or may not) yield.

Both Lorde and Freire advocated for new strategies and methods for liberation. Lorde (1984) promoted reimagining power dynamics through marginalized perspectives and emphasizes intersectionality, while Freire (1970) encouraged critical thinking and active participation. The synergy between Lorde's and Freire's ideas lies in their shared belief that true liberation requires a fundamental transformation of power relations. They advocate for approaches that empower the oppressed to reclaim their agency and reshape societal structures. Connecting Lorde's (1984) and Freire's (1970) writings to TQ center(ed) diversity work, TQ center(ed) diversity workers must understand and develop their own power not to become institutional agents or gain control, but to transform institutions. They must use their referent and soft power to establish new structures that deviate from traditional operations, aiming for genuine and lasting change within the organization. Imploring stakeholders and accomplices to hold institutional leadership and colleagues accountable for their oppressive acts; actively championing support for oppressed communities on campus; advancing equity through institutional policy, expansive programming, and access to life saving resources and programs are just some strategies TQ center(ed) leaders may seek to champion within their (limited) power structures.

There is not a single playbook or guide for identifying and leveraging power to transform institutions, as each institution is unique, and every TQ center(ed) diversity worker faces a distinct context. Understanding power within these specific contexts is crucial for TQ center(ed) diversity workers to effectively identify decision-making processes, resource distribution, and conflict resolution mechanisms. Although power can seem elusive and theoretical, it becomes tangible through physical resources, institutional roles, and direct influence. When new to their role, TQ center(ed) workers should identify accomplices who can help contextualize their institutions campus climate for TQ work, and understand the political realities they have entered. This assessment will be necessary to fully contextualize their environment and better understand the oppressive histories and contemporary challenges before them when advocating for TQ center(ed) policy and practices. Whether leading a space at an institution with multiple TQ focused positions, or as a sole provider of TQ center(ed) leadership (Pryor & Hoffman, 2021; Tillapaugh & Catalano, 2019), TQ center(ed) diversity workers are tasked with leading liberation efforts that challenge the oppressive structures of higher education institutions. While this will certainly look different dependent on institutional context, the work must be intersectional and aligned with transformative efforts.

Depending on TQ center(ed) leaders' institutional context, power is clearly evident in the formal authority granted by organizational roles. Positions like directors, deans, or senior leaders come with specific powers to make decisions, allocate resources, and direct actions (Anderson & Brion, 2014). This authority is embedded in hierarchical structures, where titles confer actionable power. Additionally, power manifests in the control and distribution of resources. Those who manage financial resources, physical assets, or critical information wield considerable influence. In international politics, states with significant economic resources or military capabilities can exert substantial influence over other nations (Barnett & Duvall, 2005). Similarly, within organizations, individuals or departments that control budgets or access to key information hold tangible power. Navigating contexts where budgets are limited, TQ center(ed) leaders may have to leverage partnerships with affirming departments or divisions who can help champion their efforts. Collaborating, with a true emphasis on liberation, can help thwart status quo approaches to TQ center(ed) practices, by offering additional resources or programs that advocate student success given often limited budget constraints. Additionally, partnering with Institutional Research divisions to develop structures for understanding student success progress and support can help illuminate the experiences and persistence of TQ student success. Thus, leveraging relationships and elements of soft power will be useful for TQ center(ed) leaders seeking to create change.

Furthermore, power is physically manifested through symbols, infrastructure, and the presence of authority figures. Foucault (1995) discussed how institutions like prisons, schools, and hospitals use architecture and spatial arrangements to exert control and influence behavior. The physical presence of these institutions and their representatives serves as a tangible reminder of power. Legal systems and regulatory frameworks also embody power concretely, and are evident in the recent legislative attacks on DEI efforts in conservative states (Lemerand & Duran, 2024). Laws, regulations, and policies enacted by governments or organizations create binding rules that influence behavior and ensure compliance (Finnemore & Goldstein, 2013). These elements demonstrate that power is deeply rooted in tangible, observable aspects within institutions. Specifically, these efforts can hinder TQ center(ed) work, thus by actively challenging them through campus support efforts (e.g., policy advancement, student scholarships, supporting student activism, robust programming), TQ center(ed) leaders can actively subvert actions of resistance imposed by state and institutional policy actors. By recognizing these forms of power, TQ center(ed) diversity workers can strategically navigate and influence their institutions to foster more inclusive and equitable environments.

Now What?

Lorde's (1984) assertion that "the master's tools will never dismantle the master's house" and Freire's (1970) emphasis on developing a pedagogy that promotes critical consciousness underscore the necessity of transformative approaches to power and change. For TQ center(ed) diversity workers, this means fundamentally rethinking and queering how they engage with power within institutions. TQ center(ed) leaders must adopt critical frameworks to challenge oppressive forms of power that inhibit their work of advancing liberatory goals for TQ communities. Traditional methods and frameworks, which often perpetuate systems of oppression, are insufficient for achieving true liberation and equity. By adopting innovative, intersectional strategies that challenge and subvert existing power dynamics, TQ center(ed) diversity workers can foster environments that are genuinely inclusive and supportive of all identities. Intersectional strategies necessitate an understanding of TQ communities' needs across identity (e.g., race, ability, class) and offer support that affirms intersectional realities. This approach, advocated by Oliveira et al. (2025), is essential for transforming higher education institutions into spaces where diversity is not only recognized but actively celebrated and empowered.

Msibi's (2013) "Queering Transformation in Higher Education" provided an insightful and empowering model for TQ center(ed) diversity workers looking to foster genuine and equitable change within their institutions. Msibi highlighted the need to recognize and address the intersectionality and multiplicity of social identities, advocating for a comprehensive approach that moves beyond traditional focuses on race and gender (Msibi, 2013). For TQ center(ed) diversity workers, this means understanding the unique challenges and experiences of TQ individuals and ensuring their voices are integral to the transformation process. By leveraging their referent power, which is built on relationships and trust within the institution, diversity workers can effectively advocate for policies and practices that support all marginalized groups.

Msibi also stressed the importance of creating inclusive environments that validate and support diverse identities. TQ center(ed) diversity workers can follow Msibi's approach by using their soft power to influence institutional culture in subtle yet effective ways. This involves fostering positive interactions, demonstrating expertise, and building coalitions that prioritize inclusivity and equity (Msibi, 2013). By doing so, they can create a supportive network that challenges homophobia and other forms of oppression, aligning with Freire's emphasis on critical consciousness and active participation (Freire, 1970). This participatory model is essential for empowering marginalized individuals to take an active role in their liberation and the broader transformation of their institutions.

Moreover, Msibi's model underscored the need for adopting new frameworks that challenge existing power structures. TQ center(ed) diversity workers can implement this by developing innovative strategies that disrupt traditional hierarchies and promote equity. This aligns with Audre Lorde's (1984) assertion that the tools of the oppressor cannot bring about true liberation. By queering their approach to power and change, TQ center(ed) diversity workers can create new, inclusive structures that genuinely reflect the diverse experiences and identities within their institutions. This transformative approach not only addresses immediate issues of discrimination but also establishes a foundation for sustainable, long-term change.

Conclusion

TQ center(ed) diversity workers must engage in a thorough power analysis and develop their own power to transform institutions effectively. This transformation requires learning and adopting a nuanced understanding of how power operates within organizational structures (Anderson & Brion, 2014). TQ center(ed) diversity workers must develop and leverage their referent and soft power to advocate for and implement policies that uplift TQ individuals. By queering their institutional work, TQ center(ed) diversity workers challenge traditional power dynamics and promote inclusivity. Drawing on Foucault's (1995) concepts of how institutions exert control through physical and symbolic means, they can subvert these mechanisms to create spaces that honor diverse identities. Freire's (1970) emphasis on critical consciousness underscores the need for TQ center(ed) diversity workers to foster environments where marginalized voices are not only heard but are also integral to the decision-making process. This aligns with Audre Lorde's (1984) assertion that new, transformative approaches are necessary to dismantle oppressive structures.

However, institutional change is a gradual process that requires sustained effort and intention and can be burdensome to one or just a couple of people often charged with TQ center(ed) leadership. Developing and utilizing soft power, as discussed by Vuving (2009), involves building relationships and influencing through attraction and persuasion rather than coercion. This approach enables TQ center(ed) diversity workers to create a lasting impact by embedding equity and justice into the fabric of institutional culture. Drawing from Msibi's (2013) model, TQ center(ed) diversity workers can adopt intersectional strategies that reflect the complexity of social identities, ensuring that transformation is comprehensive and genuine. Ultimately, while the path to institutional change is complex and time-consuming, the intentional and ethical use of power by TQ center(ed) diversity workers can lead to meaningful, equitable transformation.

Note

1 Coalition building has historic significance for TQ center(ed) diversity work (Marine, 2011; Pryor, 2021). However, it is important to note the necessity for TQ center(ed) workers to engage in coalition development is often in addition to the responsibilities of TQ center functions. Yet, the systemic oppression higher education institutions perpetuate requires TQ center(ed) leaders to be nimble and frequently organize support to sustain TQ center(ed) work. This additional labor can lead to burnout and overwork of TQ center(ed) leaders, impacting their retention in the field.

References

Anderson, C., & Brion, S. (2014). Perspectives on power in organizations. *Annual Review of Organizational Psychology and Organizational Behavior, 1*(1), 67–97. https://doi.org/10.1146/annurev-orgpsych-031413-091259

Barnett, M., & Duvall, R. (2005). Power in international politics. *International Organization, 59*(1), 39–75. https://www.cambridge.org/core/journals/international-organization/article/power-in-international-politics/F5F3C74D30A12A5C4CC9B4EFEA152967

Capper, C. A. (2018). *Organizational theory for equity and diversity: Leading integrated, socially just education*. Routledge.

Finnemore, M., & Goldstein, J. (2013). Puzzles about power. In *Back to basics: State power in a contemporary world* (pp. 1–17). Oxford University Press. https://doi.org/10.1093/acprof:oso/9780199970087.003.0001

Foucault, M. (1995). *Discipline and punish: The birth of the prison* (2nd ed.). Vintage Books.

Freire, P. (1970). *Pedagogy of the oppressed*. Herder and Herder.

Lemerand, S., & Duran, A. (2024). Supporting queer and trans students amidst a rise in anti queer and trans legislation and policies. In K. Prieto & A. Herridge (Eds.), *LGBTQIA students in higher education: Approaches to student identity and policy* (pp. 226–240). IGI Global.

Lorde, A. (1984). The master's tools will never dismantle the master's house. In *Sister outsider: Essays and speeches* (pp. 110–114). Crossing Press.

Marine, S. B. (2011). *Stonewall's legacy: Bisexual, gay, lesbian, and transgender students in higher education*. John Wiley & Sons.

Msibi, T. (2013). Queering transformation in higher education. *Perspectives in Education, 31*(2), 65–73. https://journals.co.za/doi/abs/10.10520/EJC145499

Oliveira, K. A., González-Siegel, V. A., Feldman, S., Kannan, K., Woods, C., Pryor, J. T., Duran, A., Catalano, D. C. J., & Jourian, T.J. (2025). An autoethnographic exploration of the realities of engaging in trans and queer center(ed) diversity work. *Journal of Diversity in Higher Education, 18*(2), 111–122. https://doi.org/10.1037/dhe0000501

Pryor, J. T. (2021). Queer activist leadership: An exploration of queer leadership in higher education. *Journal of Diversity in Higher Education, 14*(3), 303–315. https://doi.org/10.1037/dhe0000160

Pryor, J. T., & Hoffman, G. D. (2021). "It feels like diversity as usual": Navigating institutional politics as LGBTQ+ professionals. *Journal of Student Affairs Research and Practice, 58*(1), 94–109. https://doi.org/10.1080/19496591.2020.1740717

Tillapaugh, D., & Catalano, D. C. J. (2019). Structural challenges affecting the experiences of public university LGBT services graduate assistants. *Journal of Diversity in Higher Education, 12*(2), 126–135. https://doi.org/10.1037/dhe0000079

Vuving, A. (2009). How soft power works. *SSRN Electronic Journal*. https://doi.org/10.2139/ssrn.1466220

· 5 ·

BEYOND SILOS: OPPORTUNITIES FOR COLLABORATIONS ACROSS STUDENT AND ACADEMIC AFFAIRS WITH TQ CENTER(ED) DIVERSITY WORKERS

Chelsea E. Noble and Justin A. Gutzwa

Introduction

Faculty and staff are often quick to refer trans and queer (TQ) students to their campus' TQ center. Yet, TQ center(ed) diversity work is often constrained by the institutions' positioning, including divisional structures as well as limited financial and human resources. Typically, TQ center(ed) diversity work is housed within student affairs, which is often siloed from academic affairs. TQ students require support and advocacy not only in their broader campus life but also in the classroom and other academic contexts, where they encounter trans and queer antagonism. TQ-centered diversity practitioners are often tasked to bridge student and academic affairs. Grounded in scholarship about TQ center(ed) diversity work, TQ student's academic experiences, and faculty attitudes towards identity-based inclusion efforts, this chapter describes the present state of collaborations across student and academic affairs. Further, we identify opportunities for student and academic affairs to advance their joint efforts to create conditions in which trans and queer students can learn and thrive.

So much of the need for TQ center(ed) diversity work comes from the animating location of higher education: the classroom and curricula. Yet, due to structural, resource, and mindset challenges, TQ center(ed) diversity work is lacking in academic affairs spaces. Faculty and staff may refer TQ students to their campus's TQ center(ed) diversity workers, often housed within a gender and sexuality campus center (GSCC). Yet, TQ center(ed) work is often constrained by its positioning within the institution. Typically, TQ center(ed) work is housed within an institution's division of student affairs, often siloed from academic affairs and subject to the persistent disconnects between academic and student affairs' functions, theories, and cultures (Gutzwa & Owis, 2023; Torres & Renn, 2021). The constraints of this positioning can include limited financial and human resources as well as reputation, though certainly these limitations can be true of TQ center(ed) diversity work regardless of its organizational location within the institution (Oliveira et al., 2025; Tillapaugh & Catalano, 2019). TQ students not only need support and advocacy in their broader campus life, but also experience trans and queer antagonism in the classroom and other academic contexts (Gutzwa, 2021). Accordingly, TQ center(ed) practitioners are often obligated to bridge student and academic affairs by institutional expectations. Responsive to their institutional contexts, their efforts might include educational offerings (e.g., trainings for academic departments and units) and policy changes (e.g., names and pronouns on rosters, student records, and facilities access), which seek to create structures for greater inclusion in academic spaces.

In the midst of current precarious and restrictive contexts wherein TQ campus spaces are closing because of legislative mandates or the specter of such mandates (e.g., Casper, 2024; Field, 2024), TQ center(ed) diversity work remains vital. Correspondingly, it is also essential to fortify institutions against legislative shifts through embedding TQ center(ed) work across institutional contexts, including deepening collaborations between student and academic affairs. Grounded in scholarship about TQ center(ed) work, TQ students' academic experiences, and faculty's attitudes towards identity-based inclusion efforts, this chapter describes the present state of collaborations across student and academic affairs. Further, we identify opportunities for student and academic affairs to advance their joint efforts to create conditions in which trans and queer students can learn and thrive.

TQ Center(ed) Diversity Work

Often, TQ center(ed) diversity work on U.S. college and university campuses occurs in LGBTQ+ resource centers, now increasingly referred to as gender and sexuality campus centers (GSCCs). Although professionals who engage in TQ center(ed) work outside of GSCCs certainly exist and have for decades, the majority of scholarly attention has focused on GSCCs (Duran et al., 2023; Oliveira et al., 2025). The first GSCC was founded in 1971 at the University of Michigan (Marine, 2011). Today, there are approximately 260 centers across the U.S. (Consortium of Higher Education LGBT Resource Professionals [Consortium], 2024a), although the numbers are shifting due to recent anti-diversity, equity, and inclusion (DEI) legislation causing some public institutions to shutter GSCCs (e.g., Casper, 2024; Field, 2024).

The purpose of GSCCs is to promote the thriving and success of LGBTQ+ students at their college or university (Marine, 2011). Each center pursues this purpose in their own particular way, responsive to evolving campus contexts, resources, student needs, and a host of other factors. Yet, across GSCCs, there are four common areas of work: assessment and evaluation of campus climate and community needs, counseling and support for students, education about gender and sexuality, and advocacy for policy and practice changes to reduce bias and oppression (Bazarsky et al., 2022). Of most direct relevance to colleagues in academic affairs, GSCCs typically offer educational resources and trainings, such as ally trainings and speakers, for individuals, departments, and classes (Woodford et al., 2014). GSCCs also engage in advocacy and change work across campus, such as supporting chosen name and pronoun policies (Noble, 2022). Chosen name and pronoun policies often mean that course rosters and online learning platforms reflect a student's correct name, minimally giving faculty no excuse for misgendering a student because they did not have accurate information.

According to a recent self-study by the Consortium of Higher Education LGBT Resource Professionals (2024b), approximately 80 % of GSCCs report to their student affairs or student life division. Student affairs divisions typically center the holistic development of and support for students. Thus, consistent with their organization as part of student affairs, GSCCs' purpose and scope are focused on serving students and attending broadly to campus climate, culture, practices, and policies. Yet, GSCCs are often tapped for trainings, consultations, and other activities beyond their official scope and mission (Beal, 2024; Oliviera et al., 2023). For example, trainings for non-learner units and spaces such as human resources or campus-affiliated health systems are likely well outside of a GSCC's scope and capacity.

TQ center(ed) diversity workers are often caught between the significant needs and demands from across campus—from students seeking housing resources to faculty requesting LGBTQ+ speakers for their classes to meetings about bathrooms for the newest campus building—and the chronic underfunding of TQ center(ed) work. This underfunding not only limits the programs and resources that GSCCs can offer, but also inhibits adequate staffing for this work (Oliviera et al., 2023; Pryor & Hoffman, 2021; Tillapaugh & Catalano, 2019). A number of GSCCs are staffed exclusively by half-time graduate assistants, which leads to significant structural challenges and constrained capacity to respond to student needs as well as faculty and staff educational opportunities (Tillapaugh & Catalano, 2019). As Beal (2024) so succinctly summarized, "[gender and sexuality resource center] practitioners are hired to play a rigged game" (p. 198). In many centers, the sole staff person simply cannot meet all of the needs on campus, which limits their capacity to engage with academic affairs. Further, a number of TQ center(ed) diversity workers are hired into a purportedly entry-level position. An entry-level title may cause faculty and administrators to assume TQ center(ed) diversity workers lack experience, thereby undermining their credibility and by extension their ability to advance TQ-focused work in academic affairs (Pryor & Hoffman, 2021).

One of the tensions of TQ center(ed) work is that campus members often default to sending all LGBTQ+ students and any LGBTQ+-related issue to the TQ center(ed) office or practitioner. Yet, there is a clear need for all units at the institution to develop competency serving TQ communities as well as inclusive policies (Bazarsky et al., 2015). Certainly, centers and professionals have specialized knowledge about gender and sexuality, and skills to serve LGBTQ+ populations. However, they are not the only people who are or should be equipped to support students and promote equitable, affirming policies supporting TQ communities. Unfortunately, this dynamic is prevalent in identity and cultural center(ed) work. For example, many faculty, staff, and administrators assume that "the concerns of ethnic/racial minority students should be the sole responsibility of the [multicultural affairs and cultural center] professional... [which in turn] releases other campus administrators from their responsibility to work closely with ethnic/racial minority students" (Sutton & McCluskey-Titus, 2010, p. 161). Relatedly, TQ students, and particularly TQ Students of Color, have expressed confusion regarding the happenings of GSCCs and a lack of understanding regarding the resources that they provide. They also express frustrations that the work of GSCCs too often prioritizes a certain type of TQ student—one that is white and able to fit into a whitened "queer aesthetic"—erecting GSCCs as spaces that are, in perception as much as in reality, unable to support the full range of TQ students on college campuses (Velázquez et al., 2024).

In qualitative work with TQ Students of Color imagining a more inclusive and anti-racist future for the University of Michigan's Spectrum Center, one hope student co-researchers shared was for the Spectrum Center to collaborate and partner with other entities on campus in ways that "de-center[ed] the center" (Velázquez et al., 2024, p. 259) as the only place where TQ center(ed) work, especially work centering TQ Students of Color, can/should happen. In sitting with these recommendations offered by Velázquez and colleagues' (2024) co-researchers, we come to this chapter with the desire to "de-center the center" by imagining possibilities for student and academic affairs to collaborate in ways that prioritize supporting TQ students in all of the strata they engage within higher education, including the collegiate classroom. In what follows, we explore the limited ways scholars have explored the experiences of TQ students in academic affairs contexts.

Academic Affairs

Despite decades of scholarship contributing to collective understandings of TQ student experiences in higher education, scholarship specifically locating student experiences in the academic strata of the university is still burgeoning (Gutzwa, 2021; Lange et al., 2019). The collegiate classroom is one of many places where TQ students experience identity-based oppressive dynamics. Scholars (e.g., Duran & Nicolazzo, 2017; Ehlinger & Ropers, 2020; Gutzwa, 2021; Linley & Nguyen, 2015; Pryor, 2015) have long identified classrooms as sites of cisheterogenderist exclusion, highlighting "how academic environments isolate, target, or render LGBTQ students invisible" (Lange et al., 2019, p. 517). For many TQ students, particularly trans students, curricular exclusion comes at the hands of faculty, who students feel are at best unequipped and at worst are actively oppressive in working to create classroom environments that support their abilities to embody their identities and to learn about TQ issues (Gutzwa, 2021; Linley & Nguyen, 2015). Some TQ students perceive faculty as adhering to neoliberal ideals of identity neutrality and career preparedness in curricular design, therein contributing to students' internalized understandings that their queer and trans identities "do not belong" in the collegiate classroom (Friedensen et al., 2021; Gutzwa & Marx, 2025), while others recall times where faculty actively told them who they are as people "does not matter" in the classroom context, particularly in STEM disciplines (Gutzwa et al., 2024). Conversely, faculty also have the power to radically transform students' experiences when intentionally and carefully integrating queer and trans perspectives, voices, epistemologies, topics, and considerations into their course design (Gutzwa, 2024; Linley & Nguyen, 2015).

Said differently: collegiate academic environments can become spaces with powerful liberatory potential for TQ students when they are constructed with the existence and lived realities of TQ people in mind (Gutzwa, 2024). Increased attention to TQ perspectives, pedagogies, and practices are needed in higher education and student affairs research, practice, and curricula (Lange et al., 2019). As we unpacked earlier, however, such reimagination is often relegated only to spaces at colleges and universities that are created to serve TQ students—namely, GSCCs.

Individual actors within universities, ranging from faculty to administrators, and campus conglomerates like academic affairs units, departments, and degree programs, all have much to learn from incorporating TQ epistemologies in their work (Lange et al., 2019). Despite scholars calling for such inclusion of TQ perspectives in praxis and pedagogy, individual and collective institutional agents have historically avoided doing so. This evasion is reflected by the relative dearth of scholarship centering the intersection of university academic affairs and queer and trans identities at an organizational, administrative, or any other level that does not directly engage the collegiate classroom. What is troubling about such evasion is that it persists despite the well-documented knowledge that faculty are often perceived as being ill-equipped at engaging with TQ students (Linley & Nguyen, 2015). Recent research, for example, demonstrates that how TQ undergraduate students engage in the process of selecting their majors is directly informed by homophobia, transphobia, and cisheteronormativity that they experience from faculty, career counselors, academic advisors, and other institutional agents (Hoffshire, 2024). Further, and as we unpack in greater detail later in this chapter, faculty who *are* seen as being able to support TQ students, as well as other students from minoritized backgrounds, are themselves minoritized (e.g., Black women faculty; TQ faculty). Their labor of supporting minoritized students is often invisible, uncompensated fiscally, and unrecognized by the university in tenure and promotion (White-Lewis et al., 2022). These nuanced tensions in concert underscore the power that identity affirming praxis can have in supporting TQ students, demonstrating the need for the thoughtful and intentional integration of TQ-centered approaches to teaching, mentorship, and support across the myriad strata of a university—not just within a campus' TQ center.

To illustrate this duality, we use the example of literature on collegiate-level TQ ally training programs. Scholars have long argued that ally training programs have "potential positive impact" (Woodford et al., 2014, p. 319) on college campuses that adopt them, particularly when they are constructed in ways that construct one's allyship as a part of adopting a liberatory consciousness as opposed to being a title one receives through attending to a "checklist" of responsibilities and actions (Catalano & Christiaens, 2022). Scholars exploring TQ students' classroom experiences, however, have shared that students express frustrations regarding how, or even if, faculty engage in these trainings. In González's (2024) qualitative study of TQ visibility and sense of belonging in community colleges, several of their student cocreators problematized faculty for displaying signals of having completed ally training (such as a sticker in their office's window declaring the room a "safe space" for TQ students—a common token often given to faculty following the completion of an ally training) while continuing to engage in behaviors that demonstrate "the misalignment between a faculty member's actions and/or words and usage of PRIDE and safe zone images" (p. 8). Similarly, some participants in Gutzwa and Marx's (2025) exploration of trans college students' experiences in classrooms at a public university in the United States expressed their perceptions that faculty were at best unaware that TQ ally trainings specifically designed for faculty were offered by their campus' queer student center, and at worst, were wholly disinterested in attending. Despite the existence of such programming through the campus queer student center, Gutzwa and Marx's participants perceived that individual professors and the university's administration more broadly treated the labor of faculty and academic affairs as separate from the work of the campus' TQ center. We offer these examples not to decry or delegitimize the work of TQ centers, but instead to assert that this work cannot remain the *only* work being done to support TQ students on college campuses. TQ student frustrations with faculty and campus administrators demonstrate the necessity of shared educational and support work between academic affairs professionals and the campus stakeholders who are currently, by job title, "designated" to perform TQ center(ed) labor.

While extant and emerging literature questions the efficacy of ally trainings through the vantage of TQ students, who continue to overwhelmingly report experiences of hostility and isolation in their collegiate classrooms, this inquiry has not fully extended to the vantage of university faculty, administrators, and other stakeholders—the individuals who, in principle, many such trainings are designed for. In writing this chapter, we reflected on our own lived experiences as people who have worked at institutions of higher education in a variety of capacities. Justin, for example, reflected on a TQ pedagogy training workshop they attended while serving as a teaching assistant during their doctoral program: although the training was open to instructors of all levels, the audience was overwhelmingly fellow TQ graduate student instructors. These tensions we and others have experienced are reflective of the tensions raised by scholars exploring culturally relevant mentorship trainings that extend beyond centering gender and sexuality. Scholars have noted, for example, that some faculty are reluctant to attend race-based pedagogical and mentoring trainings due to their perceptions that such trainings provide little benefit or incentive for attending (Griffin, 2013; White-Lewis et al., 2022). In particular, Griffin's (2013) work also demonstrated the reality that those most likely to support students holding minoritized identities (in her work's case, Black students), either through continued professional development or through invisible labor, are faculty who share those minoritized identities (namely, Black women faculty).

These tensions remind that it is unsurprising that faculty, who are bound by the neoliberal machinations of the academy that push faculty to prioritize modalities of research and teaching that is "commodifiable," "competitive," and therefore often identity-neutral (Gutzwa & Marx, 2025), have the propensity to devalue participating in identity-centered professional development opportunities such as ally trainings and race-based pedagogy/mentoring trainings due to a perceived lack of fiscal or temporal benefit. While faculty reticence to participate in professional development regarding TQ-affirming pedagogical and advising practices may, in some cases, be a reflection of an individual faculty member's desires, politics, or perceived "need" for improvement, it is important to not solely place the burden of competency training prioritization on the shoulders of faculty. Rather, cross-institutional reform is needed to place greater value on the dire importance of acquiring TQ center(ed) competency skills. Such importance can be institutionalized campus-wide in a variety of ways, whether through fiscally compensating faculty and administrators for participating in such training, or by positively rewarding faculty for participation in professional development opportunities in the promotion and tenure process.

Again, we focus on allyship trainings here not to suggest that they are (or even that they can be) a panacea for addressing TQ oppression within higher education, but rather to emphasize that such trainings are one of the only areas where academic and student affairs currently coalesce with regards to supporting TQ students in colleges and universities. Still, these trainings are almost exclusively located within the seemingly never-ending portfolio of responsibilities TQ-serving centers are tasked with, rarely offered or even co-sponsored by academic affairs offices writ-large, or even by individual departments and academic programs. In order for the wellbeing and liberation of TQ students to be prioritized as a goal of higher education, TQ center(ed) work needs to not be siloed to being the sole responsibility of TQ-serving centers on college campuses. In the next section, we imagine what a future for TQ center(ed) work might look like if partnerships between academic and student affairs targeted towards TQ students were prioritized.

Liberatory Opportunities

We envision a world where much of TQ center(ed) diversity work is no longer necessary because oppression of all kinds has been eradicated from society. Instead of focusing on creating safe havens and combating oppression, this work could shift to intra- and inter-community connections. To be clear, we are not lauding the recent closure of campus centers under state DEI bans; those are instead an indicator of how much work remains to be done. Until this utopian future vision is a reality (and we are far, far away from it), there is much campus colleagues can do to partner with and advance liberation in educational spaces and well beyond.

Structural Change

Silos are a notable challenge across higher education. Certainly, as we have outlined, siloing TQ center(ed) work within monolithic understandings of who is capable or suitable to carry out such work constrains current policies, practices, resources, and formal responsibilities affecting TQ lives across colleges and universities, but especially TQ students (Oliveira et al., 2025). Recalling Torres and Renn's (2021) wise counsel to prioritize deep, structural changes to support student success, we call for continued work to break down silos and to create more integrated, mutually supportive organizational structures. Such structures should prioritize collaboration with the goal of creating educational environments that facilitate the holistic learning and growth of all students.

It is possible to begin to work toward this integrated structure now, and we see multiple areas requiring attention to better support TQ lives. First, institutions need to consider the missions and resources of different units. GSCCs, as part of student affairs, have primary responsibility for attending to students and the institutional contexts that support student learning and development. Their scope is typically limited to life outside of the classroom. Academic affairs stewards the academic, curricular, and scholarly mission of the institution. In contrast to student affairs' co-curricular scope, academic affairs work that directly engages students centers their curricular learning experiences. Even when this work takes the shape of professional development opportunities for faculty, these events are usually marketed as ways for faculty to develop better teaching practices that can impact student learning. Each of them has their own budget and associated strategy for distributing resources. Academic affairs must reflect on their reliance on GSCCs funded by student affairs and invest their own resources of time, money, and personnel towards collaborative TQ center(ed) diversity work.

Torres and Renn (2021) detailed the emergence of two additional silos: faculty and student success services. Their analysis is particularly compelling because it describes the further splintering of higher education into silos rather than integration and collaboration among its many actors. We view the project of creating liberatory spaces as everyone's work, with each area of the institution holding primary (but not sole) responsibility for particular areas of focus. We advocate for a shift in perspective and approach from silos to a unified mission with interdependent areas of work, expertise, and responsibility.

For example, gender studies departments, as well as cultural and disability studies programs, seem to be logical partners with TQ center(ed) diversity work to increase the visibility of TQ lives and to combat homophobia and transphobia as they manifest on campuses. Although one might assume that shared topic areas and concern for oppressed peoples would lead these academic departments and GSCCs to commonly work together, our anecdotal evidence suggests that such collaborations are rarer and more informal than expected. A note of caution: we do not intend for GSCCs and gender or cultural studies departments to serve as the main or indeed only units attending to gender and sexuality. This work is undoubtedly vital to the functioning of the university, and thus should be prioritized and institutionalized at a university level through compensation, fiscal and spatial resource allocation, and codifying the protection of such work in institutional policies. In future recommendations, we continue to emphasize the responsibility of all units and individuals on campus to engage in anti-oppression work.

Such responsibility also reminds us that existing TQ center(ed) work in higher education has often been critiqued for advancing the understanding of an aggregate TQ student "monolith" by treating all TQ students as having the same needs, ultimately erasing the voices and needs of multiply minoritized TQ students, particularly TQ Students of Color (Simms et al., 2023; Velázquez et al., 2024). The sadly common "whitewashing" of TQ center(ed) work parallels both the whitewashing of other campus resource centers that silences Students of Color, such as disability support services (Karpicz, 2020), and the frequent evasion of engaging TQ identities in campus racial and ethnic affinity centers that displaces TQ Students of Color (Martinez & Jackson, 2018). In each of these cases, a normalized avoidance of intersecting identities undoubtedly impacts what little collaboration exists between the work of these student-serving centers and academic affairs units. These shortcomings of equity-minded work across campus present an additional avenue for partnership and collaboration. To truly view (and thus support) students holistically, the academic TQ center(ed) work carried out by GSCCs must be carried out not only with a university's academic affairs divisions, but also in community with other support services on campus (e.g., disability support services; racial and ethnic affinity centers) and academic departments that center identity-based experiences in their course offerings (e.g., Disability Studies; Africana Studies; Chicanx Studies; Race & Ethnic Studies).

Finally, TQ center(ed) work (whether curricular or otherwise) often falls under the purview of broader campus-wide "diversity" initiatives. The outcome of "diversity" work is often the same—regardless of whether such initiatives are specifically geared towards TQ issues, designed to center other minoritized communities, or created as broader, amorphous "equity for all" programs, and no matter if such work is located within GSCCs, other "multicultural" affairs centers, or in broader college- or university-wide settings. Campus "diversity" work is rarely designed to fully meet the needs of minoritized students, but rather to "educate," "engage," and ultimately preserve the hegemonic power of white, cisgender, heterosexual, able-bodied, and otherwise majoritarian university stakeholders (Baldwin, 2022; Marine & Nicolazzo, 2014). This troubling reality notably extends to the TQ center(ed) work that GSCCs provide their campuses daily, which in many ways is designed with the white, cisgender, heterosexual gaze in mind as opposed to the particular and nuanced needs of TQ students (Marine & Nicolazzo, 2014; Simms et al., 2023).

So long as the primary beneficiaries of any DEI initiative on campus remain the overarching institution and the institution's white, cisgender, heterosexual stakeholders, this work will never truly redress the power dynamics that exacerbate oppression within colleges and universities (Baldwin, 2022). As such, advancing TQ center(ed) work that truly centers TQ students mandates the transformation of how institutions perceive, prioritize, and carry out DEI work broadly. Moves towards collective justice for TQ communities are needed throughout the university–not just within GSCCs, and not just within academic affairs. While some of these moves can be accomplished through a prioritization of DEI work through compensation and resource management, the mere expansion of DEI work without reimagining the purpose *of* such work can never fully disrupt how power and oppression manifest within the university.

Development of Common Knowledge

To foster a more integrated and collaborative future, institutions need to invest in sustained capacity building across former silos. Campus staff and faculty should know how to demonstrate basic cultural awareness and engage with all in respectful, non-oppressive ways. We do not expect someone in the Registrar's Office to know if the university health insurance covers transition-related care, but they should be able to direct someone to the proper resource without asking invasive questions or misgendering them.

Yet, we previously critiqued the common occurrence of the GSCC being tapped for all gender- and sexuality-related trainings on campus and the challenges reaching people who would benefit from ally development or similar trainings. Human resources and the center for learning and teaching have both significant access to campus constituencies and experience with holding large-scale and ongoing trainings. For example, human resources should host general trainings (e.g., ally training, pronouns 101) while the center for learning and teaching should take the lead on inclusive pedagogy resources. In addition to distributing the responsibility for trainings and resource sharing, it is important to reach the people who need this information. We advocate for making ongoing learning about different identities and communities part of the expectation and criteria for job success. Faculty, staff, and administrators should have this expectation baked into their annual evaluation and promotion requirements.

Curriculum and Teaching

We would be remiss if we did not also address the need for anti-oppressive coursework and pedagogy across the curriculum. Faculty have an incredible opportunity to offer important educational materials while also affirming the TQ members of their courses by intentionally integrating TQ-related history, perspectives, epistemologies and methodologies, and more, as scholars have long argued (e.g., Gutzwa, 2021; Nicolazzo, 2017). Said differently, "in addition to modeling inclusive language, faculty can also challenge queer and trans oppression in their classrooms through their curricula and pedagogy" (Prieto & Duran, 2024, p. 155). For example, an English course might deconstruct the gender norms in a given novel while a biology course might discuss the vast naturally-occurring variation in "biological" sex rather than unthinkingly reifying the gender binary. There are scores of TQ writers, thinkers, activists, villains, etc. that an instructor might highlight. Representation is not everything, but positive acknowledgment of TQ communities and topics can significantly and positively influence students' college experiences.

Similarly, finding ways to incorporate TQ perspectives and lived realities into STEM curricula has the potential to dispel the normative understanding that who someone "is" has no place in STEM learning spaces (Gutzwa et al., 2024), as well as to disrupt the hetero- and homonormativity latent in STEM fields that "impacts the ways that [TQ] students imagine their futures as [TQ people] in STEM" (Friedensen et al., 2021, p. 348). Compulsory cisheterosexism in STEM spaces permeates into how TQ students who operate within STEM majors speak about and make sense of their identities, presenting the transformation of STEM curricula through TQ-liberatory praxis as one place where disciplinary norms of identity neutrality and cisheterosexism can be disrupted (Stephens-Peace et al., 2024). It is important to remember that many doctoral programs, for example, do not include formalized pedagogical training for students, particularly and especially those who aim to enter a career in the academy by way of teaching and instruction. To this aim, departments should work with academic affairs and those performing TQ center(ed) work to incorporate and incentivize professional development on TQ issues and perspectives for not just faculty, but graduate students and other instructors as well.

Academic affairs professionals are uniquely well-suited to provide pedagogical training for faculty working to revise curricula and teaching strategies in ways that affirm all students lives and experiences, but especially TQ students. As such work is often relegated to the never-ending responsibility lists of GSCCs, we argue this trend demonstrates one possible avenue for academic and student affairs to collaborate in ways that "de-center the center" (Velázquez et al., 2024). Accomplishing some of the above end goals can be facilitated through such intentional collaboration between academic and student affairs. As argued earlier, this work must also be carried out in conjunction not just with academic affairs, but also with other minoritized student-serving centers and a range of academic departments and programs in order to advance holistic student support that pushes TQ center(ed) work to truly address the needs of *all* TQ students–not just those who are white, able-bodied, and cisgender.

Conclusion

TQ center(ed) work remains vital to the flourishing of TQ students in higher education. Supporting TQ students across campus contexts requires a broad scope of work beyond what is reasonable for any one office (such as a GSCC) to orchestrate and fund. The challenges faced by TQ students are not isolated to one sphere of the university, and thus require deep, collaborative efforts from across the institution. We advocate for creating intentional structural and financial collaborations between academic affairs and student affairs to advance TQ center(ed) diversity work.

Reflection Questions

- Where is TQ center(ed) work located in your campus context?
- What collaborations have you observed between TQ center(ed) work and academic affairs?
- Where have you noticed potential opportunities for such collaborations?
- How can TQ center(ed) work involve other units beyond academic affairs to support students, faculty, and other stakeholders in their curricular pursuits?

References

Baldwin, A. (2022). *A decolonial Black feminist theory of reading and shade: Feeling the university.* Routledge.

Bazarsky, D., Edwards, B. J., Jensen, L., Subbaraman, S., Sugiyama, B., & Travers, S. (2022). Standards of practice: Core competencies for LGBTQIA+ directors and professionals in higher education. *Journal of Diversity in Higher Education, 15*(2), 141–152. https://doi.org/10.1037/dhe0000282

Bazarsky, D., Morrow, L., & Javier, G. (2015). Co-curricular and campus life contexts. *New Directions for Student Services, 2015*(152), 55–71. https://doi.org/10.1002/ss.20145

Beal, J. (2024). A place for us: Exploring gender and sexuality resource centers within the postsecondary orgscape. In K. Prieto & A. Herridge (Eds.), *LGBTQIA students in higher education: Approaches to student identity and policy* (pp. 198–211). IGI Global.

Casper, C. (2024, July 2). In a valley with few resources for LGBTQ Utahns, a key center closes its doors. *The Salt Lake Tribune.* https://www.sltrib.com/news/2024/07/02/they-dont-want-me-fit-key-lgbtq/

Catalano, C. J., & Christiaens, R. (2022). Reimagining allyship: Commodification, resistance, and liberatory potentials. *College Student Affairs Journal, 40*(2), 87–99. https://doi.org/10.1353/csj.2022.0017

Consortium of Higher Education LGBT Resource Professionals. (2024a). *Find an LGBTQ center.* https://lgbtcampus.memberclicks.net/find-an-lgbtq-campus-center

Consortium of Higher Education LGBT Resource Professionals. (2024b). *2024 member needs assessment report.* https://lgbtcampus.memberclicks.net/assets/2024%20Consortium%20Member%20Needs%20Assessment%20Report.pdf

Duran, A., & Nicolazzo, Z. (2017). Exploring the ways trans* collegians navigate academic, romantic, and social relationships. *Journal of College Student Development, 58*(4), 526–544. https://doi.org/10.1353/csd.2017.0041

Duran, A., Catalano, D. C., Pryor, J. T., Taylor, J. L., & Jourian, T.J. (2023). Mapping the rise of LGBTQ+ student affairs: A 20 year review. *Journal of Student Affairs Research and Practice, 60*(2), 181–193. https://doi.org/10.1080/19496591.2022.2032112

Ehlinger, E., & Ropers, R. (2020). "It's all about learning as a community": Facilitating the learning of students with disabilities in higher education classrooms. *Journal of College Student Development, 61*(3), 333–349. https://doi.org/10.1353/csd.2020.0031

Field, K. (2024, February 12). What's in a name? after Texas banned DEI, a campus space for LGBTQ students got an overhaul. *The Chronicle of Higher Education.* https://www.chronicle.com/article/the-misnomer

Friedensen, R. E., Kimball, E., Vaccaro, A., Miller, R. A., & Forester, R. (2021). Queer science: Temporality and futurity for queer students in STEM. *Time & Society, 30*(3), 332–354. https://doi.org/10.1177/0961463X211008138

Griffin, K. A. (2013). Voices of the "othermothers": Reconsidering Black professors' relationships with Black students as a form of social exchange. *Journal of Negro Education, 82*(2), 169–183. https://doi.org/10.7709/jnegroeducation.82.2.0169

González, Á. D. J. (2024). "Whenever I see those little rainbow stickers, I know that there is a place you can go": Visibility and sense of belonging for queer and/or trans community college students. *Journal of Diversity in Higher Education.* Advance online publication. https://doi.org/10.1037/dhe0000584

Gutzwa, J. A. (2021). "It's not worth me being who I am": Exploring how trans* collegians navigate classroom experiences through a funds of identity lens. *Journal of Women & Gender in Higher Education, 14*(3), 302–323. https://www.tandfonline.com/doi/abs/10.1080/26379112.2021.1990077?casa_token=eay6zkNwT8wAAAAA:rEkAlBrnLBqzmciL1UXjZni2GTJXUB6YojyPo3vPOCMGG7eJpn6YwMTkaMedklosMrDHx2lnIBRow

Gutzwa, J. A. (2024). "It's survival mode": Exploring how an indigenous trans* student of color (per)forms identity while transgressing space. *Journal of Diversity in Higher Education*, 17(2), 243–255. https://doi.org/10.1037/dhe0000410

Gutzwa, J. A., & Marx, R. A. (2025). "I Need This Person's Support to Have a Career" The Material and Emotional Impacts of Neoliberalism on Trans Collegians' Classroom Experiences at a Public University. Critical Education, 16(1), 155–181. https://ices.library.ubc.ca/index.php/criticaled/article/view/186961

Gutzwa, J. A., & Owis, B. (2023). Transgressing educational divides: Building bridges between K-12 and postsecondary trans studies. In A. Duran, K. K. Strunk, & R. Schey (Eds.), *Bridging the rainbow gap: Possibilities and tensions in queer and trans studies in education* (pp. 151–171). Brill.

Gutzwa, J. A., Barthelemy, R. S., Amaral, C., Swirtz, M., Traxler, A., & Henderson, C. (2024). How women and lesbian, gay, bisexual, transgender, and queer physics doctoral students navigate graduate education: The roles of professional environments and social networks. *Physical Review Physics Education Research*, 20, 020115. https://doi.org/10.1103/PhysRevPhysEducRes.20.020115

Hoffshire, M. (2024). "It's uncomfortable being closeted": Exploring the impact of sexual orientation on major/career selection. In In A. Herridge & K. Prieto (Eds.), *Perspectives on transforming higher education and the LGBTQIA student experience* (pp. 91–112). IGI Global.

Karpicz, J. R. (2020). "Just my being here is self-advocacy": Exploring the self-advocacy experiences of disabled graduate Students of Color. *Journal Committed to Social Change on Race and Ethnicity*, 6(1), 138–163. https://doi.org/10.15763/issn.2642-2387.2020.6.1.137-163

Lange, A. C., Duran, A., & Jackson, R. (2019). The state of LGBT and queer research in higher education revisited: Current academic houses and future possibilities. *Journal of College Student Development*, 60(5), 511–526. https://doi.org/10.1353/csd.2019.0047

Linley, J. L., & Nguyen, D. J. (2015). LGBTQ experiences in curricular contexts. *New Directions for Student Services*, 2015(154), 41–53. https://doi.org/10.1002/ss.20144

Marine, S. B. (2011). Stonewall's legacy: Bisexual, gay, lesbian, and transgender students in higher education. *ASHE Higher Education Report*, 37(4). https://doi.org/10.1002/aehe.3704

Marine, S. B., & Nicolazzo, Z. (2014). Names that matter: Exploring the tensions of campus LGBTQ centers and trans* inclusion. *Journal of Diversity in Higher Education*, 7(4), 265–281. https://doi.org/10.1037/a0037990

Martinez, K., & Jackson, R. (2018). Am I this or that? Supporting queer and trans Students of Color. In S. Thompson (Ed.), *Campus diversity triumphs* (pp. 87–93). Emerald Publishing.

Nicolazzo, Z. (2017). *Trans* in college: Transgender students' strategies for navigating campus life and the institutional politics of inclusion*. Stylus.

Noble, C. E. (2022). *Students' conceptions of their campus LGBTQ+ center* (Publication No. 29262101) [Doctoral dissertation, Michigan State University]. ProQuest Dissertations Publishing. https://www.proquest.com/openview/9a29feb36b3e4442dfdcb6c0f6e06774/1

Oliveira, K. A., González-Siegel, V. A., Feldman, S., Kannan, K., Woods, C., Pryor, J. T., Duran, A., Catalano, D. C. J., & Jourian, T. J. (2025). An autoethnographic exploration of the realities of engaging in trans and queer center(ed) diversity work. *Journal of Diversity in Higher Education*, 18(2), 111–122. https://doi.org/10.1037/dhe0000501

Prieto, K., & Duran, A. (2024). Engaging LGBTQIA+ identities in teaching: Considerations for graduate student instructors and those teaching graduate students. In A. Herridge & K. Preito (Eds.), *Perspectives on transforming higher education and the LGBTQIA student experience* (pp. 146–163). IGI Global.

Pryor, J. T. (2015). Out in the classroom: Transgender student experiences at a large public university. *Journal of College Student Development, 56*(5), 440–455. https://doi.org/10.1353/csd.2015.0044

Pryor, J. T., & Hoffman, G. D. (2020). "It feels like diversity as usual": Navigating institutional politics as LGBTQ+ professionals. *Journal of Student Affairs Research and Practice, 58*(1), 94–109. https://doi.org/10.1080/19496591.2020.1740717

Simms, S., Nicolazzo, Z., & Jones, A. (2023). Don't say sorry, do better: Trans students of color, disidentification, and internet futures. *Journal of Diversity in Higher Education, 16*(3), 297–308. https://doi.org/10.1037/dhe0000337

Stephens-Pearce, K., Friedensen, R., Kimball, E., Forester, R., Miller, R., Vacarro, A., Forsythe, D., & Jones, M. C. (2024). "You assumed that everybody was...": Hermeneutic injustice and cisheteronormativity in STEM coursework. In A. Herridge & K. Prieto (Eds.), *Perspectives on transforming higher education and the LGBTQIA student experience* (pp. 73–90). IGI Global.

Sutton, E. M., & McCluskey-Titus, P. (2010). Campus culture center directors' perspectives on advancement, current issues, and future directions. In L. D. Patton (Ed.), *Culture centers in higher education: Perspectives on identity, theory, and practice* (pp. 157–177). Stylus.

Tillapaugh, D., & Catalano, D. C. J. (2019). Structural challenges affecting the experiences of public university LGBT services graduate assistants. *Journal of Diversity in Higher Education, 12*(2), 126–135. https://doi.org/10.1037/dhe0000079

Torres, V., & Renn, K. A. (2021). Is metric-centered leadership generating new silos? *Change: The Magazine of Higher Learning, 53*(2), 49–56. https://doi.org/10.1080/00091383.2021.1883982

Velázquez, D., Beal, J., & Perez, R. (2024). Reclaiming imagination: Exploring QTBIPOC students' perceptions of and hopes for UM's Spectrum Center. In A. Herridge & K. Prieto (Eds.), *Perspectives on transforming higher education and the LGBTQIA student experience* (pp. 241–264). IGI Global.

White-Lewis, D. K., Romero, A. L., Gutzwa, J. A., & Hurtado, S. (2022). "Moving the science forward": Mentor training outcomes of faculty working with racially/ethnically diverse students in the biomedical sciences. *CBE–Life Sciences in Education, 21*(2). https://doi.org/10.1187/cbe.21-08-0217

Woodford, M. R., Kolb, C. L., Durocher-Radeka, G., & Javier, G. (2014). Lesbian, gay, bisexual, and transgender ally training programs on campus: Current variations and future directions. *Journal of College Student Development, 55*(3), 317–322. https://doi.org/10.1353/csd.2014.0022

· 6 ·

RETHINKING STAFFING AND HIRING IN TQ CENTER(ED) DIVERSITY WORK

R.B. Brooks and Tristan Crowell

Introduction

This chapter seeks to illuminate the multiple challenges and opportunities TQ center(ed) diversity workers navigate in their roles. Specifically, we provide considerations for staffing and hiring of TQ center(ed) roles from the perspective of two TQ center(ed) professionals. Woven throughout the chapter, we offer personal reflections and critical questions for TQ center(ed) workers and their institutional leaders to consider as they approach hiring, staffing, and supervision of these invaluable roles. Within the chapter, we also present the pitfalls TQ center(ed) workers may navigate when operating as the sole professional for their campus, the systemic conditions that perpetuate identity taxation and burn through, the impact of fit and anti-DEI legislation, and the opportunities for TQ center(ed) roles to improve campus climates for TQ communities in higher education. We boldly proclaim that though the TQ center(ed) diversity worker is under brutal attack, we will persist beyond this precarious moment.

Meet the TQ center(ed) diversity worker. There is no one pathway that leads to a position as a TQ center(ed) diversity worker. Perhaps s/he/ze/they earned a degree in counseling, student affairs, or social work. Maybe she was an active student leader, resident assistant, or intern in a campus office. Maybe he had a mentor who *taught him about a career path in higher education and student affairs. Maybe ze came to college with dreams of teaching and decided zir wanted to work with college-age students instead. Regardless of what pathway a TQ center(ed) diversity worker took to end up at an institution of higher education, a campus functions as both sites of liberatory promise and as complex working conditions. TQ center(ed) diversity workers must endure the tides that push against and for diversity, equity, and inclusion (DEI). For example, in the early 2000s, there were significant efforts to create and grow positions that focused on supporting TQ students, staff, and faculty followed by backlashes against DEI in higher education in 2024 that sought to disband and/or defund their offices and/or reorganize or eliminate positions. TQ center(ed) diversity workers must find ways to navigate shifts in politics as they imagine what it means to engage in contested political work sometimes against the institution itself that, at the end of the day, signs their paychecks.*

In this chapter, we, two TQ center(ed) diversity workers, explore areas of staffing that influence our work. We begin with an exploration of job descriptions as the entry point of the work, as they ostensibly proffer all aspects of the role. Next, we explore the processes of recruitment and retention and how dynamics of burn out and burn through (Anderson, 2020) impact persistence of TQ center(ed) workers. Then we explore how TQ center(ed) diversity workers must navigate legislative changes in their work, including advocating for their continued existence in higher education. Finally, we offer insights into the interplay of campus climate and working conditions. We intersperse our own voices and experiences throughout the chapter and provide reflection questions for readers to invite thinking that will expand how TQ center(ed) diversity work can truly provide liberatory futures for higher education.

What's in a [TQ Center] Name?

Before TQ center(ed) diversity workers enter campus, a job description defines our roles. How employers write job descriptions can be early signs of whether a candidate will be successful in their role or whether they will be set up for failure. Job descriptions help potential employees determine interest in the job by giving them a clear outline of the scope of their responsibilities and expectations for their performance (Janosik et al., 2004). They can also identify the institution's mission and values, allowing employers to envision potential fit along those lines. For example, Mehta et al. (2023) and Gaucher (2011) showed how gendered language in job descriptions has the passive effect of discouraging individuals (particularly women) from applying. Job descriptions serve as the primary foundation for any job, creating clear guidelines for effective performance (Adhikari, 2015). However, when the reality of the work does not match the job description, satisfaction levels drop, and the work suffers (Ramhit, 2019).

A major challenge for TQ center(ed) diversity workers are when job descriptions do not align with holistic and intentional practices, intersectional cultural and identity experiences, and embodied knowledge about how to actualize their work on college campuses (Ellingson, 2008). Misalignments can result in tensions between worker and supervisor(s), between worker and students, and between worker and self.

> **Tristan:** *Over the very short amount of time I've held my position, the number of responsibilities I held quickly went beyond the scope outlined by my job description. Because our department was without a director at the time (and I happened to be the most senior person on our team) I was tasked with managing student workers, taking the lead on department-wide projects, and answering requests from other departments on campus. After about a year and a few months of this work, I had a check-in with my supervisor about potentially updating my job description (as I was still facilitating some of these responsibilities) to better reflect the scope of work I was taking on and to use as a negotiating tool for a salary increase. This process has yet to happen and it has been about two years (almost the entire length of time I have been employed) since I first started taking on extra tasks. It seems that these updates are not a priority for the institution, especially after finding out that there is currently no formal mechanism to make these and similar updates to job descriptions.*

The level of knowledge and experience supervisors have with TQ center(ed) diversity work can impact the experiences of a TQ center(ed) diversity worker, especially when the supervisor is not (or was never) a TQ center(ed) diversity worker. Supervisors are usually involved in creating job descriptions, posting job announcements, and contributing to final decisions about hiring a candidate. Yet, we know TQ center(ed) diversity workers experience a lack of awareness from their supervisors on the extent of what their responsibilities entail (Catalano & Tillapaugh, 2020; Oliveira et al., 2025; Pryor & Hoffman, 2021). When supervisors of TQ center(ed) diversity workers—direct supervisors and those higher up the reporting line—do not hold themselves accountable for understanding the unique experiences of these employees, patterns emerge that emphasize the key pitfalls this chapter identifies in terms of hiring and staffing practices.

While the institutional context may necessitate varied responsibilities for managing TQ center(ed) spaces, there is well-established guidance for the basic foundations of TQ center(ed) work. Bazarsky et al. (2022) outlined "standards of practice" for LGBTQIA+ directors and professionals in higher education. These standards introduced twelve "core competencies" to "establish [the] direction of the profession" (p. 141). Bazarsky and colleagues (2022) worked with the Consortium of Higher Education Lesbian, Gay, Bisexual, Transgender (LGBT) Resource Professionals (The Consortium) and offered 12 competencies that provide insights for those in the roles, guidance for institutions to support those in the roles, and pathways for new professionals into these roles. Even with the existence of these core competencies, TQ center(ed) diversity workers may still experience unreceptive or unprepared supervisors. In turn, there may not be any clear processes available to address misalignments between job descriptions, personal philosophies, and liberatory frameworks. In other words, informed guidance on how to create a well-crafted TQ center(ed) diversity worker job description is only useful when applied. Instead, TQ center(ed) diversity workers may be left with the burden of initiating conversations about mismatched job descriptions and duties because no one in leadership truly understands their role. This creates another form of invisible labor for the already overworked TQ center(ed) diversity worker.

We offer some critical reflective questions for TQ center(ed) diversity workers and their supervisors to consider as they support the staffing and hiring of these invaluable roles:

- Why do TQ center(ed) diversity workers fear or hesitate to open conversations about our job responsibilities?
- How can we design hiring and staffing processes that include regular and unprompted evaluations of our job descriptions and duties?
- How can we better document and inventory the inevitable "other duties as assigned" custom of TQ center(ed) diversity work?

Taxation of the Role and Burning Through

TQ center(ed) diversity workers are no strangers to the accumulating stack of *other duties as assigned*. Increases in responsibilities can come from filling gaps in staff within their departments, accepting new projects from leadership that extend beyond their written job descriptions, or unknowingly creating extra work for themselves as a byproduct of cultural and identity taxation (Hirshfield & Joseph, 2011; Padilla, 1994). At the same time, when a TQ center(ed) diversity worker does not receive the time, space, and opportunities to develop their capacities to take on new projects, then the results are feelings of pressure to seek out and rely on collaborators to get the job done (Broadhurst et al., 2018). These collaborators are typically students or other staff or faculty who are not TQ center employees but hold identities that are inextricably linked to the facilitation (and success) of this work on campus.

> **Tristan**: *I'm currently the single staff person for the LGBTQIA+ Student Services office at a small Lutheran University in the Midwest. This is my first job in higher education, my background is in electoral nonprofits and community organizing. I didn't necessarily intend to work in this setting, I was considering options for a potential career switch after feeling the burnout from political work and it was by complete happenstance that the position was open. This work has been incredibly rewarding, especially because I never made full use of the services that were available to me through the TQ center at the university I did my undergrad in. That being said, it is not a perfect work environment and there are challenges that I'm called to respond to on a daily basis.*

TQ center(ed) diversity workers' identities and cultural experiences have been proven to expand the workloads of faculty and staff of color (Padilla, 1994). Their identities also uniquely impact faculty and staff with other marginalized social identities such as gender, race, and sexual orientation (Hirshfield & Joseph, 2011). Because of this potential taxation, collaborators might be reluctant to express alignment with this work and choose to remain invisible (Lee, 2023). Along with increased workloads, those who work outside of formal TQ centers might experience demands for work that are beyond the scope of their role and/or capacity given their context (Kortegast & van der Toorn, 2018). This cultural and identity taxation has been linked to negative health consequences, immense emotional labor, and feelings of guilt (Hochschild, 1983; Joseph & Hirshfield, 2023). TQ center(ed) diversity workers apply for, accept, and show up every day for jobs under these conditions, which comes at a cost.

Burnout is a medically recognized form of exhaustion that results from immense feelings of overwhelm attributed to certain workplace experiences such as "unmanageable workloads," "not enough time to rest," and "confusing work responsibilities" (WebMD, 2024, para. 13). TQ center(ed) diversity workers are highly subject to experiences of burnout, compounded by personal experiences of cultural and identity taxation (Hirshfield & Joseph, 2011; Padilla, 1994), microaggressions (Cueva, 2014), queer and trans battle fatigue (Robinson, 2022), and institutional cisgenderism (Seelman, 2014; Venable et al., 2019). Anderson (2020) reframed burnout from the personal outcomes of being chronically overwhelmed in the workplace to burn-*through*. Anderson (2020) noted the taxation institutions place on oppressed communities and the staff tasked with leading cultural center spaces. Stephanie, one of Anderson's (2020) participants, noted, "I often say to colleagues or professionals of Color, that institutions literally burn through people of Color and queer and queer people of Color. It's not sustainable" (p. 359). We must challenge the passive role institutions are enabled to play and address "the underlying causes of diversity worker exhaustion" (Anderson, 2020, p. 360). In other words, no number of "work life balance" webinars will address the root causes of *burn-through*. TQ center(ed) diversity workers can adopt self-care and restorative practices *while also* expanding and refining our tactics and demands for enhanced and sustainable working conditions.

The effects of cultural and identity taxation and burn-through also extend to students, especially those engaged in diversity-related labor such as student leadership and activism, student internships, and on-campus employment (Rosales et al., 2022). The shared experiences of TQ center(ed) diversity workers, additional professional staff roles, and students doing TQ center(ed) diversity work on campus are a valuable connection point and can be used as a bridge between these groups.

There is a necessity to give attention to queer and trans workers (Griffiths, 2021):

> The skills to manage trans and queer existence on a social level lend themselves to exploitation as skilled labor in the spheres of social reproduction and hospitality. This view offers one possible explanation for the (otherwise paradoxical) fact that queer and trans people gravitate disproportionately to professions in which it is more difficult to be comfortably "out." ... Queers are often found in posts where it is more likely to result in abuse, stigma, dismissal, and blackmail when we are discovered: education, childcare, service labor, health care, and the Church. (p. 136)

In other words, queer and trans workers broadly are subject to exploitation for that which makes us discernibly queer and trans in society—our propensity for care work, our crafty solutions, our time assumed completely disposable if we choose not to raise children, etc. Given the realities of cultural taxation, burn through, and exploitation of our TQ identities, we ask:

- How can these unspoken side effects of doing TQ center(ed) diversity work be captured in something as simplified as a job description?
- How can we ensure institutions are accountable to the TQ center(ed) workers they recruit for these roles?

Recruitment and Retention of Staff: The Ultimate "Fit" Check

"Power concedes nothing without a demand."

—Frederick Douglass

Physical sites of TQ center(ed) diversity work on college campuses can attribute their origins to the work of campus activism (Self & Hudson, 2015). TQ center(ed) diversity worker positions and spaces as we know them today emerged out of Civil Rights era activism in the 1960s and 1970s (Marine, 2011). In 1971, the first TQ center(ed) space in higher education opened at the University of Michigan (Fine, 2012). Throughout the 1990s and 2000s, there was a steady expansion of TQ centers, student organizations, and staff positions at colleges and universities across the country (Marine, 2011) These positions and spaces are hard-won outcomes of bold efforts that demanded trans and queer people be represented, supported, and served on campuses traditionally not built for our communities.

> **R.B.:** *My role is housed within a larger office for diversity and inclusion, but I am the solitary staff person explicitly tasked with supporting queer and trans students. I am the second person ever to hold my position in its nearly 25 year history. My successor left in the aftermath of a discriminatory set of firings within our athletic department. I held a TQ center(ed) diversity role at my graduate institution as a 20-hour-a-week-on-paper graduate assistant in a student involvement and leadership department. I was the over-involved student leader trope in undergrad with a mile-long email signature, taking on roles in our LGBTQ+ student club, student newspaper, and coordinating the largest regional college conference in the country as a student planner. My roles have all taken place across the Midwest, which largely shapes and influences my experiences and perspectives in this work.*

As long as there have been TQ center(ed) diversity workers, there have been conceptual differences about the role, responsibilities, required training, and positionality of these roles. As mentioned in the previous section, institutional agents, TQ center(ed) diversity workers, students, and other stakeholders have varying perspectives on what these roles are expected to do and how their responsibilities are performed. This reveals another major pitfall experienced by TQ center(ed) diversity workers—the ways these varying perspectives manifest across hiring and staffing processes as miscommunications, risk of job actions, and insufficient training in TQ center(ed) diversity work (Oliveira et al., 2025). From the hiring committee to the supervision and staffing structures, TQ center(ed) diversity workers encounter mirrors that display to us what other institutional agents believe our roles to be—what we see in the mirror can offer both possibilities and challenges to our work on campus.

Internal structures and contradictions within organizational change processes can stifle TQ center(ed) diversity work. Who holds power and which influences carry more weight in decision-making processes can make it difficult for institutions to make sustainable organizational changes (Chan & Chou, 2020; Hoover & Harder, 2015). What institutional leaders say and/or do communicates the institution's commitment to its mission (Kruse et al., 2017) and their actions influence the buy-in and commitment to the mission from the rest of campus.

Smith et al. (2004) emphasized that engaging in behaviors, as an administrator, that strengthen institutional commitments is a beneficial strategy. This also applies to hiring and staffing of TQ center(ed) diversity work(ers). When administrators demonstrate a commitment to TQ center(ed) diversity work as part of the institution's mission, this can emphasize the importance of hiring TQ center(ed) diversity workers and supporting trans and queer communities on campus. However, these commitments often manifest in ways that perpetuate a "benign neglect," where support for TQ work remains superficial (Catalano et al., 2024).

Behaviors demonstrating this commitment should include ensuring that hiring committees are equipped to facilitate hiring and staffing processes, especially when TQ center(ed) diversity work(ers) are involved. These hiring committees must embrace practices that advance diversity (e.g., recruitment networks, creating a welcoming environment for candidates) to facilitate a more intentional hiring process (Griffin, 2020). Even if institutional leadership advocates for and allocates the necessary resources for diversifying the hiring and staffing of TQ center(ed) diversity worker positions, hiring committees do not always actualize these expectations (Kayes, 2006). The role of hiring committees can create barriers for TQ center(ed) diversity work in a variety of ways, and administrators must be mindful of how they are truly centering TQ experiences in their search processes.

Cavanaugh (2020) named a persistent issue wherein institutions often find that they must expend large amounts of time and effort to provide necessary training for search committees to adopt more diversity and inclusion-oriented policies. Identifying stakeholders who hold TQ center(ed) expertise is essential for ensuring hiring decisions are holistically made. Coordinating communication between several stakeholders is a difficult task that prolongs (and in other cases prevents) the implementation of these training programs. A stronger focus on this type of training is important because hiring and staffing decisions made by these committees can shape institutions for a number of years (Fraser & Hunt, 2011).

> **R.B.:** *My input as a stakeholder in who would become my supervisor didn't hold as much weight as I would have expected. In fact, I wasn't even invited to be on the hiring committee. I was scheduled to have lunch with the candidates during their daylong visits.*

Marine and Nicolazzo (2014) emphasized how there is tension related to staffing that reveals the complexity of whether employers view hiring a trans person for TQ center(ed) diversity work as an indication of their advocacy and support of trans communities. Targeted hiring of trans individuals for TQ center(ed) diversity worker roles can have a valuable impact and ensure the greatest possibility that the services and resources provided to trans students reflect a deeper understanding of their lived experiences (Hoffman & Pryor, 2023).

> **R.B.:** *I've never had a trans supervisor. In the eight years I've done TQ center(ed) work full-time, in the two years before that when I was a part-time graduate assistant, for the six weeks when I did a summer graduate assistantship, and when I was an undergraduate student intern for a semester, I never had a trans supervisor. In fact, I've never had a trans person in the reporting line or organizational chart "above" me in the time I've worked in TQ center(ed) diversity roles.*
>
> *I'll always carry with me the impact of having almost had a trans supervisor during my grad school assistantship. It was a learning moment in discovering what lengths a hiring manager might go to guarantee their choice came out on top. I remember hearing paltry excuses from my director about how one of the trans candidates wouldn't be likely to accept an offer. I remember telling my director some concerns about another candidate after having been mispronouned as well as some weariness about programming ideas that had emerged from the interview process. I framed this as a safety concern for trans and nonbinary students in particular, and about my prospective experiences as the one who would be supervised by this incoming person.*
>
> *I've never had a trans supervisor.*

Insufficient training on diversity-oriented hiring practices inhibits hiring committees in properly addressing biases and personal or political preferences, attitudinal barriers that these committees then use to shape "ideal" candidates (Smith et al., 2004). These biases are often rooted in assumptions about workplace culture and who best "fits" into that culture (Venable et al.,

2019). For TQ center(ed) diversity workers, especially racialized workers, these assumptions also have roots in whiteness (Tatum, 2003). Hiring committees should be expected to adhere to clear and meaningful selection criteria and "if it is not part of the criteria, it shouldn't be considered" (Tatum, 2003, p. 114). TQ center(ed) diversity workers roles both include and require use of their identities to ostensibly function as educators (Oliveira et al., 2025), leaving them vulnerable to bias during questions of "fit." Thus, supervisors and hiring committees must address these biases during the hiring process.

The concept of "fit" is at play throughout the hiring and staffing process. It is present in the interviewing and selection, in which hiring committees and hiring managers may default to biased assumptions about fit to make selections or recommendations about a candidate. "Fit" is also present in the daily in-office experience of TQ center(ed) diversity workers, especially for racialized and trans and nonbinary workers. Supervisors and search committees must remain critical of how they perceive "fit," and rectify any bias that emerges during the search process. "Fit" holds many implications for the TQ center(ed) diversity worker, both during the hiring process as well as while navigating their TQ center(ed) role.

Venable et al. (2019) discussed how trans professionals' bodies "impacts our abilities to participate in higher education environments while expressing our authentic gender" (p. 167). In this way, TQ professionals find their bodies, identities, and thinking as ill-fitting at some institutions of higher education. At the same time, those who do TQ center(ed) work, such as facilitating Safe Zones, often choose to or feel compelled to use their experiences and bodies to educate others (Catalano & Wagner, 2024; Catalano et al., 2023). Venable et al. (2019) also described how institutional cisgenderism (Seelman, 2014) and trans oppression merge together to form patterns of administrative violence (Spade, 2015). Administrative violence results in trans and nonbinary individuals feeling as though their participation in the institution is impossible and that they do not belong. On top of all these common experiences, TQ center(ed) diversity workers are actively facing an additional challenge to the ways our work and our roles "fit" within higher education. The 2024 anti-DEI legislation poses widespread threats to our job security, threats that contradict the histories that formed and continue to inform our work. The elimination of TQ centers and positions requires those who do this work to make hard choices about their next job and career moves (Catalano et al., 2025). In the same year, there remain campuses where students, staff, and faculty have just begun or are still advocating for the creation and expansion of positions supporting TQ center(ed) diversity work.

The nature of TQ center(ed) work requires tools to combat oppressive and poorly written policies that are inadequate to protect TQ campus populations. TQ center(ed) diversity workers must directly engage with general counsel and risk management offices because those are the organizational spaces where policy interpretation and policy application occur in response to anti-DEI laws. Without someone at the table with both fluency in policy and liberatory practices, TQ center(ed) diversity workers will remain powerless to those whose job is to protect the institution, not campus constituents.

> **R.B.:** *A friend and colleague recently shared that in light of anti-DEI legislation in their state, they strongly advocated to fill a vacant role in their TQ center with a candidate who has a legal background. The idea that this TQ center(ed) diversity worker could share space with general counsel and risk management officers and poke holes in their interpretations of vague and poorly written policies struck me as a subtle, but powerful tactic for overcoming over-compliance by having someone in the room who "speaks" the same language as university legal, risk management, and compliance officers.*

Legislation Navigation

In states such as Alabama, Florida, and Texas, state legislatures have passed bills that ultimately prohibit TQ center(ed) diversity work at public institutions and state agencies. Of eight "divisive concepts" banned by the Alabama state government, one expressly prohibits public higher education institutions from sponsoring or maintaining a DEI program or office (Kirmani et al., 2024). After the Florida State Board of Education and State University System of Florida Board of Governors both voted to prohibit spending on DEI programs that impacted 40 public colleges statewide, the University of Florida closed offices, eliminated positions, and reallocated around $5 million originally intended for DEI work toward a faculty recruitment fund (Valbrun, 2024). In January 2024, the University of Texas-Austin Gender and Sexuality Center was reconfigured into the Women's Community Center to comply with a new Texas law prohibiting DEI practices at public colleges. Just three months later, after state leaders threatened universities with million-dollar losses in state funding if they did not do more to enforce the ban, UT-Austin administrators laid off more than 60 employees who had previously been doing DEI work (Field, 2024). In response to the merciless dismantling of DEI offices, some states that have yet to introduce or pass similar legislation chose to preemptively take measures to prevent attracting ire from state governments.

The unprompted gutting and restructuring of the TQ center at the University of Kansas (KU) and additional identity-based DEI centers is an explicit example of over-compliance. Student efforts at KU under the banner of a "Save Our Centers" coalition crafted a series of demands, including advocating for the immediate cessation of any and all plans to consolidate and dismantle the impacted centers (Save Our Centers KU Coalition, 2024). The coalition also demanded "a commitment by KU administration that any future project to change or alter the structure of [the impacted centers] only be undertaken after a transparent process of democratic deliberation involving students, center staff, faculty, and relevant community stakeholders" (Save Our Centers KU Coalition, 2024, para. 1).

> **R.B.:** *I visited my alma maters—KU and UMKC—in the process of writing this chapter. Hearing the testaments and sensing the despair of cherished colleagues at these institutions was heartbreaking and themes around lack of transparency, being told about decisions rather than consulted as folks with embodied knowledge, and rapid changes without communal input were common. On my way out of KU's Center for Sexuality and Gender Diversity, I found a little box of bright pink buttons that say "Don't let over-compliance kill the OMA/SGD" and I brought them home with me. As the founding graduate student in the Center, it is a huge loss to see the hard-fought space be dismantled in this way. I am more than just a disgruntled former employee, I am an alumnx of institutions that are sending a clear message that this work is not valuable or worth protecting. That queer and trans people are not worth protecting.*

These dynamics raise significant questions that TQ center(ed) workers must consider as their positions and centers shift into potentially unintelligible roles that in no way allow for the work they aspire to actualize on campus. Over-compliance is the institutional tool for gutting and undoing TQ center(ed) diversity work, and we must wrench this tool from our institutions' grips. We must critically ask ourselves:

- What strategies can we adapt from our TQ center(ed) diversity workers in legislative battleground states that help elevate our work as institutional and organizational imperatives?
- How do we hold space for the grief of lost centers and staff positions while being transparent with students and other potential collaborators about the impacts on TQ center(ed) diversity work in the current moment?

- How do we assert ourselves and insert our voices amidst rapid changes while navigating risk and uncertainty in our work environments?

Working Conditions are Learning Conditions

One of the greatest pitfalls experienced by TQ center(ed) diversity workers is *where* the work happens. Working environments that are unprepared or outwardly hostile to TQ center(ed) diversity work leave everyone ill-prepared to do the job and diminishes satisfaction in these roles. TQ center(ed) workers not only deal with demanding workloads that often exceed the scope outlined in job descriptions (Tillapaugh & Catalano, 2019), and face persistent issues of understaffing (lgbtcampus.org, 2024; Oliveira et al., 2025). As discussed earlier, these issues are further exacerbated when supervisors are not accountable for supporting TQ center(ed) diversity workers to build relevant competencies and skills in their roles. Leaders who provide oversight of these spaces must be prepared to support TQ center(ed) workers at all levels of entry, from early career to experienced TQ center(ed) employees (see Chapter 11 by Joshua Moon Jackson).

Because TQ centers provide spaces that combat the potential harms of the institution's campus climate to TQ students (Coleman, 2016; Fine, 2012; Self & Hudson, 2015), TQ center(ed) diversity workers who face barriers in developing the necessary competencies to manage these spaces have the potential to contribute to a negative campus climate. Campus climate is "the current perception and attitudes of faculty, staff, and students regarding issues of diversity on campus" (Rankin & Reason, 2005, p. 48) and plays a significant role in the satisfaction and retention of TQ students and other staff/faculty (Campbell-Whatley et al., 2015; Coley & Das, 2020; Jayakumar et al., 2009). Work environments with staffing and supervisory structures fail to provide opportunities for TQ center(ed) diversity workers to grow and develop in their role means they are less able to do the work necessary to impact campus climate in a positive way (e.g., maintaining spaces for TQ students, providing necessary interventions against harassment). When there is a negative campus climate for TQ students, staff, and faculty, then TQ center(ed) diversity workers likely experience an amplification of these dynamics in their efforts to transform places and spaces into more hospitable environments.

To support TQ center(ed) diversity workers on campus is to engage in a larger project of advancing institutional commitments to DEI and other justice-oriented work. For instance, non-discrimination policies communicate institutional values and should communicate an institution's efforts to provide support to minoritized communities. Yet those statements tend to only gesture at ideas of inclusion without efforts to bring such dynamics into effect (Ahmed, 2012). The failure to enact substantial protections for minoritized communities instead conveys how such policies are oppositional to the existence of TQ individuals (Pitcher et al., 2018). These policies must create means to actively combat the discrimination that TQ students, staff, and faculty face on campus, whether through diversity trainings, a response system for instances of bias and discrimination, or setting a standard for respecting the identities and experiences of TQ students. Policies that lack the comprehensive language necessary to ensure a positive campus climate only serve to create more barriers to the execution of meaningful TQ center(ed) diversity work. This burdens the TQ center(ed) diversity worker with more responsibility beyond their primary duties and perpetuates the conditions that cause cultural and identity taxation, burnout, and burn through discussed earlier in this chapter. Thus, their leaders, whether TQ center(ed) specific or upper administration, must be prepared to understand the nuances of roles and advocate for their daily work.

TQ center(ed) diversity workers often use campus climate survey data to advocate for better learning environments for students. We encourage readings to consider how they might leverage stories of negative campus experiences by all campus constituents to champion transformations on campus. Questions to consider:

- How might we work across campus to use campus climate data to contextualize harm and opportunities for change?
- What do we envision when we imagine more inclusive campuses and climates where TQ center(ed) diversity work happens in solidarity and collaboration with other minoritized communities to transform institutions?

Concluding Thoughts

In the Consortium of Higher Education LGBT Professional's (2024) Member Needs Assessment, data about compensation, union status (a majority of QT professionals who responded to the survey are not part of a union), and member satisfaction with their role (a large percentage of respondents indicated they had considered leaving their job within a year of taking the survey), paint a pretty clear picture that TQ center(ed) diversity workers are doing their jobs in precarious work environments. How can TQ center(ed) diversity workers move beyond campus data to advocate for better working conditions on their specific campus?

> **Tristan:** *COVID-19 impacted my campus in several ways. Namely, it served as the catalyst for the staff to re-engage in its effort to unionize. While similar efforts have occurred in the past, they always stopped short for one reason or another (all of which are unknown to me as they were before the start of my employment in this institution). This time around, a series of unexpected layoffs and furloughs motivated the staff to demand the protections they needed during a very uncertain time in higher education. The process was long and drawn out. Bargaining our first union contract took a little over two years (2020–2022). University leadership was unwilling to move, especially when it came to things like wage increases and better healthcare for staff. It was a significant drain on the staff, taking hours out of their day to sit at the bargaining table but still carving out time to provide necessary services to students. And maybe it was that continued support of our students that rallied them to the staff's cause. By the last month or so before our contract was ratified, students showed up to several actions the union put on. They spoke in support of our effort to ensure that we are offered and provided the resources we need to continue working at the University. It was incredibly empowering to see students leveraging their voices in this way. Over the period of time that this chapter was being written, we are in the midst of another contract negotiation. Several conditions remain the same: leadership is unwilling to move and are asking for more than they are willing to give. And just like it was the first time around, we are walking in solidarity with our students.*

As we close, we recall the role student activism has played in the foundation of TQ center(ed) diversity work in higher education (Marine, 2011), reminding us of our commitments to the work and the students we serve.

> **R.B.:** *"I don't wanna leave the students" feels like a sentiment I've both held and heard from colleagues when we've contended with the looming desire to leave our job. This idea has been affirmed and repeated to the point of enforcement in my ten years of TQ Centered diversity work. I remember visiting a campus in Michigan for a conference and overheard a large event in a neighboring room targeted to the campus's faculty and staff. I hovered by the entry long enough to hear someone confidently proclaim "I'm sure we all wake up each morning and even if we're not feeling our greatest, we're motivated to come to work because of our students." Maybe it's the burnout, maybe it's the subliminal messaging about sacrificing our own well-being—but this has become harder to hold as a truth for myself or for me to see as an appropriate philosophy to hold in this work.*

Collective calls for racial justice, ceasefires, divestments, and better working conditions showcase the interconnectedness of struggles on college campuses which serve as the primary arena for TQ center(ed) diversity work. Modern histories of campus activism, especially student-led efforts, show us that when students and workers mobilize, our voices are indiscernible from one another. In other words, what students are demanding from their learning environments is not starkly different from what employees are demanding from our working environments. We are hopeful that with critical questions and considerations for advancing TQ center(ed) work in higher education, TQ center(ed) workers and their administrators can lead us to resist burn through and imagine liberatory futures where TQ center(ed) spaces uphold the practices and values that advance equity for trans and queer communities in higher education.

References

Adhikari, E. R. (2015). Understanding nuances and commonalities of job descriptions. *Journal of Training and Development, 1*(1), 67–76. https://doi.org/10.3126/jtd.v1i0.13093.

Ahmed, S. (2012). *On Being Included: Racism and Diversity in Institutional Life*. Duke University Press.

Anderson, R. K. (2020). Burned out or burned through? The costs of student affairs diversity work. *Journal of Student Affairs Research and Practice, 58*(4), 359–371. https://doi.org/10.1080/19496591.2020.1822853

Bazarsky, D., Edwards, B. J., Jensen, L., Subbaraman, S., Sugiyama, B., & Travers, S. (2022). Standards of practice: Core competencies for LGBTQIA+ directors and professionals in higher education. *Journal of Diversity in Higher Education, 15*(2), 141–152. https://doi.org/10.1037/dhe0000282

Broadhurst, C., Martin, G., Hoffshire, M., & Takewell, W. (2018). "Bumpin' up against people and their beliefs": Narratives of student affairs administrators creating change for LGBTQ students in the south. *Journal of Diversity in Higher Education, 11*(4), 385–401. https://doi.org/10.1037/dhe0000036

Campbell-Whatley, G. D., Wang, C., Toms, O., & Williams, N. (2015). Factors affecting campus climate: Creating a welcoming environment. *New Waves Educational Research & Development, 18*(2), 40–52. https://files.eric.ed.gov/fulltext/EJ1211418.pdf

Catalano, D. C., & Tillapaugh, D. (2020). Identity, role, and oppression: Experiences of LGBTQ resource center graduate assistants. *Journal of Student Affairs Research and Practice, 57*(5), 519–531. https://doi.org/10.1080/19496591.2019.1699104

Catalano, D. C. J., Duran, A., Feldman, S., Gonzalez-Siegel, V., Jourian, T. J., Kannan, K., Oliveira, K., Pryor, J., & Woods, C. (2025). Hope amid restless challenges: Trans and queer center(ed) diversity workers navigating the U.S. sociopolitical context. *Journal of College and Character, 26*(1), 38–48.

Catalano, D. C. J., & Wagner, R. (2024). Gender as spectacle: Safe Zone facilitation experiences of non-binary/trans educators. *Journal of Women & Gender in Higher Education, 1*(1), 63–78. https://doi.org/10.1080/26379112.2024.2307482

Catalano, D. C. J., Wagner, R., McDevitt, M., & Barrientos, C. (2023). "This is the place for questions:" Social justice educational intervention facilitation descriptions. *Journal of Student Affairs Research & Practice*. Advance online publication. https://doi.org/10.1080/19496591.2023.2269117

Catalano, D. C. J., Tillapaugh, D., Christiaens, R., & Simms, S. (2024). "More than lip service": LGBTQ+ social justice educational interventions as institutional benign neglect. *The Review of Higher Education*, 47(3), 373–400. https://doi.org/10.1353/rhe.0.a913752

Cavanaugh, C., & Green, K. (2020). Training faculty search committees to improve racial and ethnic diversity in hiring. *Consulting Psychology Journal: Practice and Research*, 72(4), 263–274. https://doi.org/10.1037/cpb0000167

Chan, S. J., & Chou, C. (2020). Who influences higher education decision-making in Taiwan? An analysis of internal stakeholders. *Studies in Higher Education*, 45(10), 2101–2109. https://doi.org/10.1080/03075079.2020.1823646

Coleman, K. (2016). The difference safe spaces make: The obstacles and rewards of fostering support for the LGBT community at HBCUs. *SAGE Open*, 6(2). https://doi.org/10.1177/2158244016647423

Coley, J. S., & Das, D. (2020). Creating safe spaces: Opportunities, resources, and LGBTQ student groups at U.S. colleges and universities. *Socius: Sociological Research for a Dynamic World*, 6. https://doi.org/10.1177/2378023120971472

Consortium of Higher Education LGBT Professionals. (2024). 2024 member needs assessment report. *Chicago Legal Forum*, 1989(1), 139–167. https://lgbtcampus.memberclicks.net/assets/2024%20Consortium%20Member%20Needs%20Assessment%20Report.pdf

Cueva, B. M. (2014). Institutional academic violence: Racial and gendered microaggressions in higher education. *Chicana/Latina Studies*, 13(2), 142–168. https://www.jstor.org/stable/43941436

Ellingson, L. L. (2008). Embodied knowledge. In L. M. Given (Ed.), *The SAGE encyclopedia of qualitative research methods* (pp. 244–245). Sage.

Field, K. (2024, February 12). What's in a name? After Texas banned DEI, a campus space for LGBTQ students got an overhaul. *The Chronicle of Higher Education*. https://www.chronicle.com/article/the-misnomer

Fine, L. E. (2012). The context of creating space: Assessing the likelihood of college LGBT center presence. *Journal of College Student Development*, 53(2), 285–299. https://doi.org/10.1353/csd.2012.0017

Fraser, G. J., & Hunt, D. E. (2011). Faculty diversity and search committee training: Learning from a critical incident. *Journal of Diversity in Higher Education*, 4(3), 185–198. https://doi.org/10.1037/a0022248

Gaucher, D., Friesen, J., & Kay, A. C. (2011). Evidence that gendered wording in job advertisements exists and sustains gender inequality. *Journal of Personality and Social Psychology*, 101(1), 109–128. https://doi.org/10.1037/a0022530

Griffin, K. A. (2020). Institutional barriers, strategies, and benefits to increasing the representation of women and men of color in the professoriate: Looking beyond the pipeline. In L. W. Perna (Ed.), *Higher education: Handbook of theory and research* (Vol. 35, pp. 277–349). Springer.

Griffiths, K. D. (2021). Queer workerism against work: Strategizing transgender laborers, &. Social reproduction & class formation. in Gleeson, J. J., O'Rourke, E., Rosenberg, J. (Eds.). Transgender Marxism. p. 133–146. Pluto Press.

Hirshfield, L. E., & Joseph, T. D. (2011). 'We need a woman, we need a Black woman': Gender, race, and identity taxation in the academy. *Gender and Education, 24*(2), 213–227. https://doi.org/10.1080/09540253.2011.606208

Hochschild, A. R. (1983). *The managed heart: The commercialization of human feeling.* University of California Press.

Hoffman, G. D., & Pryor, J. T. (2023). Navigating identity and politics as trans gender and sexuality center professionals. *Journal of Diversity in Higher Education.* Advanced online publication. https://doi.org/10.1037/dhe0000472

Hoover, E., & Harder, M. K. (2015). What lies beneath the surface? The hidden complexities of organizational change for sustainability in higher education. *Journal of Cleaner Production, 106,* 175–188. https://doi.org/10.1016/j.jclepro.2014.01.081

Janosik, S. M., Creamer, D. G., Hirt, J. B., Winston, R. B., Saunders, S. A., & Cooper, D. L. (2004). *Supervising new professionals in student affairs: A guide for practitioners.* Routledge.

Jayakumar, U. M., Howard, T. C., Allen, W. R., & Han, J. C. (2009). Racial privilege in the professoriate: An exploration of campus climate, retention, and satisfaction. *The Journal of Higher Education, 80*(5), 538–563. http://www.jstor.org/stable/27750744

Joseph, T. D., & Hirshfield, L. E. (2023). Reexamining racism, sexism, and identity taxation in the academy. *Ethnic and Racial Studies, 46*(6), 1101–1108. https://doi.org/10.1080/01419870.2022.2143719

Kayes, P. E. (2006). New paradigms for diversifying faculty and staff in higher education: Uncovering cultural biases in the search and hiring process. *Multicultural Education, 14*(2), 65–69. https://eric.ed.gov/?id=EJ759654

Kirmani, S. M., Thomas, M. D., & Harris, D. B. (2024, April 3). New Alabama law limits public employers' DEI efforts. *JacksonLewis.* https://www.jacksonlewis.com/insights/new-alabama-law-limits-public-employers-dei-efforts

Kortegast, C. A., & van der Toorn, M. (2018). Other duties not assigned: experiences of lesbian and gay student affairs professionals at small colleges and universities. *Journal of Diversity in Higher Education, 11*(3), 268–278. https://doi.org/10.1037/dhe0000046

Kruse, S., Rakha, S., & Calderone, S. (2017). Developing cultural competency in higher education: An agenda for practice. *Teaching in Higher Education, 23*(6), 1–18. https://doi.org/10.1080/13562517.2017.1414790

Lee, C. (2023). Coming out in the university workplace: A case study of LGBTQ+ staff visibility. *Higher Education, 85*(5), 1181–1199. https://doi.org/10.1007/s10734-022-00884-y

Marine, S. B. (2011). *Stonewall's Legacy: Bisexual, gay, lesbian, and transgender students in higher education.* John Wiley & Sons.

Marine, S. B., & Nicolazzo, Z. (2014). Names that matter: Exploring the tensions of campus LGBTQ centers and trans* inclusion. *Journal of Diversity in Higher Education, 7*(4), 265–281. https://doi.org/10.1037/a0037990

Mehta, A. S., Chauhan, A. S., & Ivanovic, A. (2023). Supporting LGBTQ employees in the workplace: The role of HR policies and practices. *Reviews of Contemporary Business Analytics*, 6(1), 57–71. https://researchberg.com/index.php/rcba/article/view/117

Oliveira, K. A., González-Siegel, V. A., Feldman, S., Kannan, K., Woods, C., Pryor, J. T., Duran, A., Catalano, D. C. J., & Jourian, T. J. (2025). An autoethnographic exploration of the realities of engaging in trans and queer center(ed) diversity work. *Journal of Diversity in Higher Education*, 18(2), 111–122. https://doi.org/10.1037/dhe0000501

Padilla, A. (1994). Ethnic minority scholars, research, and mentoring: Current and future issues. *Educational Researcher*, 23(4), 24–27. https://www.jstor.org/stable/1176259

Pitcher, E. N., Camacho, T. P., Renn, K. A., & Woodford, M. R. (2018). Affirming policies, programs, and supportive services: Using an organizational perspective to understand LGBTQ+ college student success. *Journal of Diversity in Higher Education*, 11(2), 117–132. https://doi.org/10.1037/dhe0000048

Pitcher, E. N., & Simmons, S. L. (2020). Connectivity, community, and kinship as strategies to foster queer and trans student retention. *Journal of College Student Retention*, 21(4), 476-496. https://doi.org/10.1177/1521025119895514

Pryor, J. T., & Hoffman, G. D. (2021). "It feels like diversity as usual": Navigating institutional politics as LGBTQ+ professionals. *Journal of Student Affairs Research and Practice*, 58(1), 94–109. https://doi.org/10.1080/19496591.2020.1740717

Ramhit, K. S. (2019). The impact of job description and career prospect on job satisfaction: A quantitative study in Mauritius. *SA Journal of Human Resource*, 17, a1092. https://doi.org/10.4102/sajhrm.v17i0.1092

Rankin, S. R., & Reason, R. D. (2005). Differing perceptions: How students of color and white students perceive campus climate for underrepresented groups. *Journal of College Student Development*, 46(1), 43–61. https://doi.org/10.1353/csd.2005.0008

Robinson, S. (2022). Trans faculty and queer battle fatigue: Poetic (re)presentations of navigating identity politics in the academy. *International Journal of Qualitative Studies in Education*, 35(9), 911–927. https://doi.org/10.1080/09518398.2022.2035457

Rosales, O., Schell, E. P., Gutierrez, C., & Padilla, A. (2022). Cultural taxation or "tax credit"? Understanding the nuances of ethnoracially minoritized student labor in higher education. *Ethnic and Racial Studies*, 46(6), 1109–1131. https://doi.org/10.1080/01419870.2022.2143717

Save Our Centers KU Coalition. (2024, September 19). *We encourage these demands to be posted on stories, pages, and more* [photograph]. Instagram. https://www.instagram.com/p/DAG1CUEOBvP/?img_index=1

Seelman, K. L. (2014). Recommendations of transgender students, staff, and faculty in the USA for improving college campuses. *Gender and Education*, 26(6), 618–635. https://doi.org/10.1080/09540253.2014.935300

Self, J. M., & Hudson, K. D. (2015). Dangerous waters and brave space: A critical feminist inquiry of campus LGBTQ Centers. *Journal of Gay & Lesbian Social Services*, 27(2), 216–245. https://doi.org/10.1080/10538720.2015.1021985

Smith, D. G., Turner, C. S., Osei-Kofi, N., & Richards, S. (2004). Interrupting the usual: Successful strategies for hiring diverse faculty. *The Journal of Higher Education, 75*(2), 133–160. http://www.jstor.org/stable/3838827

Spade, D. (2015). *Normal life: Administrative violence, critical trans politics, and the limits of law.* Duke University Press.

Tatum, B. D. (2003). *"Why are all the Black kids sitting together in the cafeteria?": And other conversations about race.* Basic Books.

Tillapaugh, D., & Catalano, D. C. J. (2019). Critical influences affecting the experiences of public university LGBT services graduate assistants. *Journal of Diversity in Higher Education, 12*(2), 126–135. https://doi.org/10.1037/dhe0000079

Valbrun, M. (2024, March 4). U of Florida eliminates DEI positions, appointments and spending. *Inside HigherEd.* https://www.insidehighered.com/news/quick-takes/2024/03/04/university-florida-eliminates-dei-positions-appointments

Venable, C. J., Inselman, K., & Thuot, N. (2019). Negotiating fit while "misfit": Three ways trans professionals navigate student affairs. In B. J. Reece, V. T. Tran, E. N. DeVore, & G. Porcaro (Eds.). *Debunking the myth of job fit in higher education and student affairs* (pp. 167–192). Routledge.

WebMD. (2024, March 5). *Burnout: Symptoms and signs.* https://www.webmd.com/mental-health/burnout-symptoms-signs

· 7 ·

FROM "SAFE" TO LIBERATORY: A NEW APPROACH TO EDUCATING CAMPUS COMMUNITIES WITH TQ CENTER(ED) DIVERSITY WORKERS

Kalyani Kannan and D. Chase J. Catalano

Introduction

Trans and queer (TQ) center(ed) diversity work on campus often requires educational efforts to increase support for TQ populations on campus. These TQ-focused sessions—often referred to as Safe Zone or Ally—aim to develop heterosexual and cisgender allies (DeVita & Anders, 2018), raise awareness, and foster good intentions. Yet a common limitation of Safe Zones is the transactional dynamic of attendance for a sticker, the function of curricula as an assemblage of activities that lack cohesion, and the fostering passive or performative allyship. Our chapter will address how TQ center(ed) practitioners can reimagine educational workshops that engage attendees in critical self-awareness, analyses of power and oppression, actions for change, and establish accountability across and within communities. We begin with a literature review that builds a case for the limitations of current iterations. Then, we lean on our own critical reflections as current and former practitioners to dream about new approaches to educate campus communities.

Vignette

Working as a trans and queer (TQ) center director, the demands on Laverne's time are substantial. At first, they just had relatively pedestrian issues such as reviews of policies for trans inclusion, programmatic planning for TQ history month, advising TQ student organizations, and some generative meetings about a potential living and learning community. Laverne believed they had the time to finally update and maybe even reimagine the campus-based ally training. They decided they wanted to pull together campus partners to evaluate the training and then seek out a professional development opportunity for themself to learn about facilitation and design—something that was not a part of their graduate preparation program. And then, the semester began. Now, they must respond to media requests about the current legislation that might close their office. They must respond to the students who are understandably panicked about what this legislation means for their experience at the university. They must respond to the faculty and staff who seek to offer support and want direction on how to do responsible advocacy on the office's behalf. At this point, Laverne can barely get through their email inbox and facilitate ally training, let alone reconsider and reconceptualize the curriculum.

Introduction

We imagine that many TQ center(ed) diversity workers strongly resonate with the opening vignette of this chapter. Unfortunately, inadequate preparation, training, and onboarding is still the norm for many who do TQ center(ed) diversity work (Oliveira et al., 2025). The reality is that many TQ center(ed) diversity workers often find themselves characterized as an expert of all TQ communities and experiences without adequate support from campus leadership (Pryor & Hoffman, 2021). The passion and energy that TQ center(ed) diversity workers bring to their roles forces them to confront dynamics that include legislative attacks on diversity, equity, and inclusion work (The Chronicle of Higher Education, 2023) along with persistent understaffing and under-resourcing of these roles (Catalano, Tillapaugh, et al., 2024; Tillapaugh & Catalano, 2019; Ortiz & Mandala, 2021; Pryor, 2021). TQ center(ed) diversity workers often find themselves stretched to the ends of their capacities trying to offer much needed resources, services, outreach, and education, while also attending meetings where they advocate, cultivate coalitions, and develop policies to support TQ populations (Bazarsky et al., 2022; Beal, 2024; Catalano & Tillapaugh, 2020; Gilbert et al., 2021; Oliveira et al., 2025; Tillapaugh & Catalano, 2019).

As one current and one former TQ center(ed) diversity workers, we know those in these roles face difficult choices of how and where to expend their energy. One area where many higher education and student affairs graduate programs inadequately prepare students and where limited professional development opportunities exist are in the realm of TQ social justice educational interventions (SJEIs) development. Given the overwork of many TQ center(ed) workers, it is no wonder that many TQ SJEIs are designs passed down from prior staff as an assemblage of activities with an occasional minor update (Catalano & Nicolazzo, in press; Catalano & Simms, 2025). Our goal in this chapter is to provide some opportunities for learning and reflection on considerations for how to construct TQ SJEIs. We aim to provide a path for readers to conceptualize and create TQ SJEIs that meet the needs of their campus communities.

A Brief History of TQ SJEIs

Trans and queer center(ed) diversity work on campus often deploys educational efforts to increase support for TQ populations on campus (Oliveira et al., 2025). Practitioners have long relied on SJEIs aimed at creating "safe zones" to educate campus communities on the experiences of TQ communities (Draughn et al., 2002; Evans, 2002; Evans et al., 2004; Woodford et al., 2014). Approaches to these SJEIs typically aim to develop heterosexual and cisgender allies (DeVita & Anders, 2018), raise awareness, and foster good intentions (Finkel et al., 2003). Yet a common limitation of SJEIs is the transactional dynamic of attendance for a sticker (Catalano & Christiaens, 2022), the function of curricula as an assemblage of activities that lack cohesion (Catalano & Simms, 2025), and the fostering of passive or performative allyship (Ahmed, 2025; Catalano & Perez, 2023). Additionally, these SJEIs have historically focused on providing individual support to trans and queer people rather than critically examining institution-level structures that perpetuate bias against trans and queer campus communities (Catalano et al., 2024; Woodford et al., 2014).

In the 2020s, as in the early 2000s, the value of TQ SJEIs lies in awareness raising and good intentions (Catalano, 2024; Finkel et al., 2003), with little attention paid to impact on TQ students' experiences on campus or the broader systems responsible for campus disparities. As highlighted by Catalano and Christiaens (2022), conceptions of allies and allyship in these settings often focus on the presence or absence of privilege, erasing the complexities of solidarity and allyship among and across communities and at the intersections of different identities. TQ SJEIs often aim to build understanding for why and how to develop practical strategies for supporting TQ campus communities, yet few—if any—incorporate mechanisms for follow-up and accountability (Draughn et al., 2002). On assessment, participant feedback often centers the value of SJEIs facilitators who themselves hold TQ identities. This forces the title of "expert" on TQ people who may or may not be prepared to fill this role and ultimately puts the onus of TQ liberation back on TQ diversity workers themselves (Catalano, 2024; Catalano & Christiaens, 2022; Catalano & Wagner, 2024; Evans et al., 2004).

Facilitators of TQ SJEIs often have little to no institutional authority to enforce implementation of strategies developed in workshops (Catalano, Tillapaugh et al., 2024). Instead, TQ SJEIs focused on ally development enable institutions and participants to "tick the box" of completing an SJEI despite having no meaningful follow up or accountability, contributing to what Ahmed (2012) described as tick-box diversity. Even when participation in the SJEI is little more than a box to be ticked, any effort by TQ center(ed) diversity workers to encourage participation by their colleagues diminishes the perceived value of the intervention because it is then seen as a matter of compliance rather than commitment. This constrains the intervention as a tool for individual transformation, let alone institutional change. That is, participants are engaged in individual-level feel-good ally development, and those who feel empowered to advocate for system-level or institution-level change are left on their own to do so. Meanwhile, facilitators face the Sisyphean project of improving campus climate with no real mechanisms or authority for enforcement or accountability (Ahmed, 2012; Catalano & Perez, 2023). With all of this in mind, we now shift to address how TQ center(ed) diversity workers in higher education might reimagine educational workshops that engage attendees in critical self-awareness (Wagner & Catalano, 2021), then discuss approaches that will invite analyses of power and oppression, actions for change, and establish accountability across and within communities (Love, 2018).

A Review of TQ SJEI Designs

Research on TQ SJEIs revealed that few utilize a clear theoretical or conceptual framework to construct the design (Catalano & Simms, 2025). Instead, many TQ SJEIs function like an assemblage of activities instead of a cohesive or scaffolded learning experience for attendees (Catalano & Simms, 2025). Without the cohesion of an intentional design or curriculum, activities may not receive the scrutiny necessary to determine if they are appropriate for the goals of the TQ SJEI. For instance, a TQ SJEI may include an activity that inspired the curriculum designer's learning in their individual social justice journey, or what Shlasko (2015) termed as legacy activity. On the surface, such a choice seems reasonable given the activity's impact on the designer. However, the personal connection an individual holds to an activity may mean unquestioning whether such an activity advances attendee learning or is in alignment with the broader goals of the overall SJEI (Shlasko, 2015). Institutional (e.g., religious affiliated institutions, urban, rural) and regional contexts (e.g., cultural norms of communication) can also impact how activities resonate (or fall flat) with audiences. Additionally, the emotional connection an individual may have to an activity might be because it resonated with oppressive dynamics an individual experienced in their past and may not be transferable to participants who hold different privileges (Shlasko, 2015). In short, well-known activities that aim to draw attention to privilege problematically attempt to replicate oppression to ostensibly work to end oppression (Barrett-Fox, 2007; Catalano, Wagner, & Simms, 2024; Shlasko, 2015). For example, coming out stars is an activity that encourages perspective taking to imagine the impacts of revealing oneself as trans and/or queer to significant people in one's life and their reactions to such news[1]. The goal is for attendees to imagine the pernicious reactions of rejection, avoidance, and other kinds of harm. While well intended, these oppressive activities ultimately perpetuate harm toward TQ individuals, who are often the facilitator of these activities.

A focus on reproducing oppression through the activity means a disproportionate attention to the negative consequences, ignores experiences TQ attendees bring to the SJEI, and "fails to account for how other identities and oppressions intersect to amplify experiences of isolation, abandonment, and resource scarcity" (Catalano, Wagner, & Simms, 2024, p. 3). An alternative approach to a similar learning goal about privilege and oppression is to reimagine the activity into transformational educational experience using Love's (2018) liberatory consciousness framework (Catalano, Wagner, & Simms, 2024, p. 3). A liberatory consciousness framework uses four non-linear components of awareness, analysis, action, and accountability as ways for individuals to develop in their allyship; these four elements are useful in consideration of every event or situation where we witness or experience oppression (Love, 2018). For example, if someone seeks to work to eliminate heterosexism and trans oppression, she/he/they must consider to whom she/he/they are accountable or what accountability for social change looks like, what actions she/he/they can take to interrupt or draw attention to problematic policies and practices, deepen their thinking about how she/he/they make sense of the information she/he/they have access to, and what forms of new information she/he/they must seek out or generate (Love, 2018). However, any analysis of TQ SJEI curriculum or designs must begin with attention to the often-forgotten role of designer and facilitator.

Focus on the Designer and Facilitator

We believe it is crucial for designers and facilitators of TQ SJEIs to engage in a process of critical self-awareness (Wagner & Catalano, 2021) to orient themselves towards emancipatory futures that include their own development and approaches. In general, the work of design and facilitation of the TQ SJEI tends to be an outward process, with the attention on attendees' learning, growth, and development. We applaud this desire to engage with and support the development of others. At the same time, those responsible for the education of others (facilitators and designers) must also recognize how her/his/their life experiences, identities, and values influence their approach to work with others and influence how she/he/they see the educational environment (Adams, 2016; Bell & Goodman, 2023; Bell et al., 2023; Wagner & Catalano, 2021). For instance, TQ center(ed) workers might want to reflect on what she/he/they believe and how she/he/they came to know their identities, as well as their beliefs about liberation, ethics, and principles (Wagner & Catalano, 2021). In the context of TQ SJEIs, topical prompts to consider are facilitator/designer ideas of allyship (what does that mean), engagement (how does that manifest), outcomes (what will attendees learn), and audience (who will attend).

The roots of social justice education pedagogy (Adams, 2016) include self-awareness that influences choices made about the design and facilitation of a TQ SJEI (Bell & Goodman, 2023; Bell et al., 2023). In this way, critical self-awareness is a continuous lifetime process that encompasses actively working to explore our relationship to power, privilege, people, institutions, and systems (Wagner & Catalano, 2021). "Components of critical self-awareness requires reflection (reconsidering events, interactions, programs), reflexivity (analyzing the role of power), and feedback (self-monitoring and dialogue with trusted others)" (Wagner & Catalano, 2021, p. 11). Because TQ SJEIs require attention to dynamics and manifestations of privilege and oppression, facilitators must be aware of their responses to triggers. A trigger, defined by Obear (2013), is "any stimulus through which facilitators experience an unexpected, intense emotional reaction that seems disproportionate to the original stimulus" (p. 152). In the context of an TQ SJEI, facilitators might imagine some of the worst case scenarios and possibly reacting poorly to that situation, such as an attendee who is aggressively resistant to learning and the facilitator responding with hostility. Certainly, volatile incidents could occur. However, we suspect it is more likely that a facilitator might experience a more subtle form of resistance that functions as a trigger such as a participant who never looks up from her/his/their phone or a participant verbally taking up a lot of room to share a response to each scenario/topic. In that case, the facilitator might feel intense emotional reaction to that behavior and be distracted by a desire to respond or actually respond in a way that distracts the entire group from the TQ SJEI.

Construction of TQ SJEIs must begin with individuals taking inventory of her/his/their own life experiences, an understanding of how she/he/they experience privilege and oppression, and how her/his/their multiple identities mediate their experiences of power and powerlessness (Adams, 2016; Bell & Goodman, 2023; Bell et al., 2023; Young, 1990). Using a critical self-awareness framework begins with a disposition towards a liberatory consciousness framework (Love, 2018). Love (2018) described a liberatory consciousness as consisting of four nonlinear components: awareness, analysis, action, and accountability. Wagner and Catalano (2021) used those components to structure student affairs practitioners' considerations of how to develop their own advising and supporting skills that comes from a place of liberation. We highlight how those components will offer TQ SJEI designers and facilitators new ways to consider their approach to campus-based education. For instance, for many TQ SJEIs, there is an emphasis on attendee awareness in the form of content acquisition (Catalano & Simms, 2025). In fact, facilitators of TQ SJEIs struggled to communicate to attendees that these SJEIs are the beginning of a learning experience, not the end (Catalano, 2024). Additionally, many attendees become overly focused on the transactional dynamic of getting a credential for attendance instead of considering their responsibility (accountability) to others to engage in thoughtful and sustained actions (Catalano & Christiaens, 2022). To address how we envision a liberatory consciousness could reframe designer and facilitator approaches to TQ SJEIs and other educational workshops on social justice issues, we offer provocative questions along with some of our reflections and insights.

Question 1: Intentions

We recognize that readers may find the following question overly simplistic *and* we think it is necessary to ask: **What is the outcome you want for attendees of your educational session/intervention?** This question must move beyond a superficial or generic response of ally development. We say this not because that answer is wrong, but because it is probably insufficient to address campus-based needs for students, staff, and faculty, as well as surrounding communities. Challenges constructing a TQ SJEI include how to balance content of community and campus-based resources, language, history and process of attendee engagement, reflection, and connection (and loads of other topics). The learning outcomes or goals of the TQ SJEI are important considerations for the design and activity choice. We also recognize—because so many people are now in the room—the desire to do all the things in a single TQ SJEI such as end all heterosexism and trans oppression on campus. At the same time, we encourage TQ center(ed) workers to consider how to scaffold goals and expectations to create communities of accountability instead of transactional educational experiences (Catalano & Christiaens, 2022).

Kalyani's response: When facilitating TQ SJEIs, I noticed participants usually fit into one of two groups: (a) TQ folks seeking to deepen their understanding of community history and solidarity, and (b) self-described allies seeking a sticker to put on their office door to signal to students that they were a "safe" person. Not wanting folks to attend just for the sake of attending, I built more checkpoints into my sessions to encourage reflection. While obviously not a perfect solution, I did find that it helped participants take a more active role in co-creating meaning with one another rather than simply receiving information to act on independently.

Chase's response: When we reworked our training, one thing that motivated our changes was the feeling that we were not meeting the needs. Honestly, I think I felt like we were failing to do any social justice work. Part of this came from the misuse of the word safe in Safe Zone. Why have a training where we promised something we could never deliver? Safety is contextual and up to the individual to determine. We needed to honor that and that was why we shifted our language from safe to *safer*. Our responses reflect the specific campus dynamics we faced in consideration of designing and facilitating SJEIs. We struggled with what it means when we perceive individuals who attend SJEIs as a form of moral grandstanding (Tosi & Warmke, 2016) where the priority is to have others perceive them as an ally. Instead, an ideal participant are those Kalyani described—those who seek "to deepen their understanding of community history and solidarity." The latter group are those who desire to develop a liberatory consciousness (Love, 2018). To be fair, there is value in both groups, although they have different impacts on facilitators and result in varying perceptions of the intention of SJEIs. The risk in offering any kind of SJEI is the absence of control, of how an individual makes meaning of the experience. Put simply, we cannot force anyone to learn, neither can we nor should we provide a simple tick-box of what a person needs to do to be a "good" ally or accomplice (Ahmed, 2012; Squire, 2019). It is therefore important to keep focus on intended outcome(s), and not get lost in what is "enough" in the context of allyship. Social justice work requires learning content and engagement in processes that seek transformations that are far more nuanced than a simple inventory of behaviors (or we would not be facing the complexities of a world riddled with oppression). We encourage designers to consider the long term results and liberatory future and try to design SJEIs backwards from there. After all, if we cannot envision liberation in the future, then what is the value in the work of survival now?

Question 2: Liberation

We can imagine that readers may wonder about this lofty idea of liberation, which seems a bit too fantasy and not practical enough. Leading to this question: **How do I break that down into more bite-sized actions?**

Kalyani's response: As a facilitator for TQ SJEIs, finding a balance between dreaming big about liberation and thinking critically about practical actions was an ongoing challenge. I would often open the session by asking folks to think about why they were in the room, encouraging them to reflect back to it when they felt discouraged about the seemingly endless road to liberation. From there, we'd spend time examining different bite-sized actions they could take and discussing the ways power and privilege might impact the actions that felt realistic for each individual to engage in. The session would conclude with participants writing down a statement of at least one action they would commit to moving forward. This was a way for folks to set goals and engage in conversation around the *how* of actualizing those goals. The unfortunate reality, however, was that there was no meaningful way to hold folks accountable to actually engage those commitments. I was often left wondering what—if anything—folks would actually engage in after the SJEI. For those tasked with developing and leading TQ SJEIs, I encourage you to consider how you might introduce to participants this balance of boldly dreaming of liberatory futures and pragmatically engaging what is actionable.

Chase's response: I know for myself, when I have the opportunity to develop any TQ SJEIs, I feel a compulsion to do all the things, cover all the topics, and engage the attendees in every way possible. I have to remind myself that attending a single TQ SJEI will never be a sufficient solution to ending trans and queer oppression. At the same time, that does not mean that I abandon liberatory thinking and I need not equate a limited amount of time with simplicity. In fact, I think there might be misconceptions that equate liberation with complexity and content acquisition with simplicity. Instead, let us use whatever time we have with attendees to try to imagine the world we want to create. Few people receive invitations or opportunities to dream of the futures they want because they spend so much of their time responding to and dealing with the manifestations of oppression. My suggestion is to allow attendees time and space to consider what liberation looks, tastes, and feels like. If I can imagine how my life or the lives of others would be improved through an emancipatory future, then I can begin to create plans for how to achieve that future. In their recent article making a case for liberation as an approach to housing and residence life, Catalano, Wagner, and Marine (2024) recognized that many professionals do not have the luxury of flight of fancy thinking. Much of student affairs and higher education administration work is "same day" and reactionary, where an email inbox and/or a crisis can overrun a day that began with very different intentions. Think back to our colleague Laverne: Laverne set out to gather colleagues for an educational intervention about supporting TQ students. As the day evolved, it became clear that they not only needed additional professional development to feel prepared to lead the SJEI, but their work on this was routinely interrupted by media requests, student drop-ins, and the never-ending stream of emails that has become standard in higher education.

At the same time, we must invite ourselves (and others) into the world of envisioning emancipatory possibilities of flourishing (Catalano, Wagner, & Marine, 2024; Kaba, 2021). We must imagine futures that allow us to delight in how our efforts are transformational on a small and large scale (brown, 2017). In practice, this means constructing SJEIs as opportunities for small wins that go beyond counting how many people attend. We imagine TQ center(ed) diversity workers scaffolding approaches to TQ SJEI outcomes that are both measurable and realistic given limitations to their time and capacity. For instance, instead of a TQ SJEI that attends to all the intersections of identities and manifestations of oppression, how might TQ center(ed) diversity workers develop SJEIs that fit with SJEIs offered by other offices/centers? How might an array of SJEIs across multiple offices work like an educational mosaic of ideas that deepen analysis, devise multiple actions, and ensure accountability? Are there ways to scaffold expectations across a series of SJEIs, potentially intersecting with different offices/centers, to allow building of knowledge, deepening analysis, devising actions, and ensuring accountability? How do you recalibrate expectations (as a designer/facilitator) that not everyone who leaves an SJEI is ready to do social justice work? We *know* this is true, and while we should not expect SJEIs to have zero impact, we do need to develop ways to cope with disappointment when former attendees make mistakes (say offensive things, engage in offensive behaviors, resist accountability, fail to consider alternative perspectives). While there may be opportunities to call former attendees back into conversation around their behaviors, it is also vitally important that TQ center(ed) diversity workers have access to networks where they can share experiences, offer support, and build solidarity. In addition, anticipating these potential challenges post-SJEI for attendees is another reason to include accountability expectations in the design (see Question 4).

Question 3: Collaboration

Now that we have set intentions and envisioned liberatory possibilities, we can begin to wonder about who is or ought to be involved in this work with us. Perhaps we're optimistic about engaged and enthusiastic co-conspirators, or perhaps we're preparing more realistically (or even with a dash of pessimism) to work with whoever shows up, no matter how apathetic. This leads us to the question: **How do I get those who feel uninterested in attending to come? When you consider your audience, what if we focused on who we want to be there or should be there rather than focusing on who is missing?**

Kalyani's response: In a previous role, I took stock of the existing relationships I had with colleagues in different units and considered who would (or could) be a champion for our TQ SJEsI. In some cases, that person would encourage their coworkers to join them in participating in an SJEI; in other cases, they'd take what they learned back to their workspaces to advocate for more inclusive practices. There was an entire department of coworkers who decided on their own that they wanted their department to have the highest rate of participation in TQ SJEIs on our campus. The outcome in that instance was a group in which some folks were deeply committed and engaged in reflection, continuing education, and action in support of TQ communities on campus and beyond. Conversely, there were also those within that unit who would participate in the TQ SJEI simply to help boost the department's numbers; a form of virtue signaling where their attendance was the sum total of their efforts. Attendance for most SJEIs is opt-in, which indicates those are individuals who (largely) seek new knowledge. The challenge with required or mandatory training is the level of resistance those attendees bring to the SJEI (Ahmed, 2012; Catalano, Tillapaugh et al., 2024). In some ways this is a good thing because the act of learning should not be a forced venture (Catalano, Wagner, & Simms, 2024, Girioux, 2020; hooks, 1994). At the same time, we recognize the reasonable frustration that it seems those who most often engage in harmful (in)actions are those who do not attend TQ SJEIs. This is another opportunity to intentionally engage with TQ "champions" as a mechanism of accountability; those already invested in developing a liberatory consciousness might need only a conversation to inspire them to take action to invite a coworker or colleague. We might also suggest a "think with us" meeting to provide opportunities for them to take action to advocate for change within and outside of their spheres of influence. Social media also provides some unique opportunities for micro-learning, especially on platforms where folks can re-share content and expand the reach of a post (Dolasinski & Reynolds, 2020). Student affairs professionals might be quite familiar with using social media as a publicity tool, and it is also a platform for sharing educational content (e.g., resources, media recommendations, and political action alerts).

Question 4: Accountability

One of the many challenges with liberation and allyship is that there is no "right way" to do it, yet there can be some truly problematic ways of enacting it (e.g., paternalistic approaches, replicating oppression to justify approaches to ending oppression). **How can we create opportunities for attendees to create plans of accountability?** Put another way, **how do TQ SJEIs potentially offer conceptual frameworks for participants in the hopes that it will guide their allyship moving forward, given that TQ center(ed) diversity workers rarely—if ever—have any means to enforce this.**

Kalyani's response: Let's be honest, even some folks with deep commitment to TQ liberation still want a sticker at the end of the SJEI. To help address this, my predecessor in a previous role added to the center's TQ SJEI a requirement that participants craft their own commitment to action, with an emphasis to focus on something they could consistently and sustainably do. That particular TQ SJEI also incorporated a number of "What would you do..." activities for participants to apply their learning to hypothetical scenarios, which we started in small groups before debriefing as a whole. This provided opportunities for participants to check themselves, discuss ideas with their peers, and hold each other accountable... at least, in the hypotheticals. With that said, I remain disappointed that regardless of participants' espoused commitment to action, there's no way to monitor — nor was I interested in policing — the follow-through of these individuals. This was particularly frustrating in instances where someone was engaging with the SJEI because they'd been "encouraged" to do so after saying or doing something harmful to TQ people (often students) within the university community. Those folks got to show up and engage with me (or not) for a couple of hours. Maybe they felt compelled to take action afterward, or maybe not, but either way there was not a structure in place that could support them in the follow-through, and no accountability if they turned right back around and continued harming TQ communities. Integral from the start of conceptualization of an SJEI is the notion of accountability. The design of your SJEI will provide the basis for how participants understand the importance of accountability and/or follow-through. Are there activities or opportunities for participants to apply their learning to their current work and/or lives? For attendees unfamiliar with the notion of accountability, what kind of opportunities for thinking about accountability (e.g., activities, resources, affinity spaces) does the SJEI offer? How do facilitators and/or TQ center(ed) workers inspire accountability (e.g., action plan development, creation of accountability partners)? How might the work of a TQ SJEI work in conjunction with other SJEIs on campus (e.g., race, disability, sexual violence prevention) to develop a more capacious view of accountability? If individuals feel invested in engagement to create more socially just campus and community spaces and places, then how can ideas of accountability inspire learning about the intersections of gender and sexuality with other minoritized identities and experiences? Consider how you might dovetail your design with other SJEIs at the institution and what it might mean to have a more extensive view of allyship beyond specific marginalized populations. Working with other cultural centers and DEI-focused individuals will invite intersectionality within the design and allyship as an expansive idea about relationships to power.

We mentioned throughout this chapter facilitation and design as significant to this work. A few resources worth exploring to broaden thinking about social justice education, facilitation for social justice, and design are Adams et al. (2022), Landreman (2013), and Maxwell et al. (2011).

When we think about what it means to develop a design that centers liberation, then we return to Love's (2018) liberatory consciousness framework. We envision that designers might want to consider activities and discussion topics that address awareness, analysis, action, and accountability, remembering that this is not a linear progression and they should overlap. For instance, there should be elements of content acquisition (awareness) and discussion about that knowledge (analysis), or there could also be case studies (action and analysis); a single activity might address all four components. Yet, all of those activities need to have a cohesion in what they build toward: opportunities to imagine a world where TQ people thrive.

Conclusion

As with any intervention, TQ SJEIs run the gamut from engaging and empowering, to performative and superficial. This is as true from the perspective of participants as it is for facilitators, who are often TQ-identified people and educate from their own experiences (Catalano et al., 2023). In addition, facilitators rarely receive adequate institutional support for this work nor financial resources to (re)imagine designs. It is our hope that this review of existing approaches, excerpts from our own experiences, and opportunities for your reflection support your future engagement with TQ SJEIs, whether as participant or facilitator. From framing out goals and intentions to identifying a target audience, and approaching the development of TQ SJEIs strategically as an avenue for critical reflection rather than assemblages of activities, we look forward to seeing and engaging with the evolution of TQ SJEIs as sites for collective and individual work rooted in liberatory consciousness.

Note

1 See The Trevor Project for an activity description: https://www.thetrevorproject.org/wp-content/uploads/2017/08/75ea657f061737b608_6pm6ivozp.pdf

References

Adams, M. (2016). Pedagogical foundations for social justice education. In M. Adams & L. A. Bell (Eds.), *Teaching for diversity and social justice* (3rd ed., pp. 27–53). Routledge.

Adams, M., Bell, L. A., Goodman, D. J., Shlasko, D., Briggs, R. R., & Pacheco, R. (2022). *Teaching for diversity and social justice* (4th ed.). Routledge.

Ahmed, S. (2012). *On being included: Racism and diversity in institutional life*. Duke University Press.

Bell, L. A., & Goodman, D. J. (2023). Design and facilitation. In M. Adams, L. A. Bell, D. J. Goodman, & D. Shlasko (Eds.), *Teaching for diversity and social justice* (4th ed., pp. 57–96). Routledge.

Bell, L. A., Goodman, D. J., & Vaghese, R. (2023). Critical self-knowledge for social justice education. In M. Adams, L. A. Bell, D. J. Goodman, & D. Shlasko (Eds.), *Teaching for diversity and social justice* (4th ed., pp. 409–432). Routledge.

Barrett-Fox, R. (2007). Tunnel of reification: How the tunnel of oppression reaffirms righteousness for members of dominant groups. *The Radical Teacher, 80*, 24–29. https://www.jstor.org/stable/20710423

Bazarsky, D., Edwards, B. J., Jensen, L., Subbaraman, S., Sugiyama, B., & Travers, S. (2022). Standards of practice: Core competencies for LGBTQIA+ directors and professionals in higher education. *Journal of Diversity in Higher Education, 15*(2), 141–152. https://doi.org/10.1037/dhe0000282

Beal, J. (2024). A place for us: Exploring gender and sexuality resource centers within the postsecondary orgscape. In K. Prieto & A. Herridge (Eds.), *LGBTQIA students in higher education: Approaches to student identity and policy* (pp. 198–211). IGI Global.

brown, a. m. (2017). *Emergent strategy: Shaping change, changing worlds*. AK Press.

Catalano, D. C. J. (2024). The paradoxes of social justice education: Experiences of LGBTQ+ social justice educational intervention Facilitators. *Journal of Diversity in Higher Education. 17*(4), 518–256. https://doi.org/10.1037/dhe0000436

Catalano, D. C. J., & Nicolazzo, Z. (in press). Responding to queer subordination: LGBTQ+ social justice educational interventions on campus. *Journal of College Student Development*.

Catalano, D. C. J., & Christiaens, R. (2022). Reimagining allyship: Commodification resistance and liberatory potentials. *College Student Affairs Journal, 40*(2), 87–99. https://doi.org/10.1353/csj.2022.0017

Catalano, D. C. J., & Perez, M.-V. (2023). Making a case for general qualitative descriptive: Revealing cisgender and heterosexual fragilities. *Departures in Critical Qualitative Research, 12*(4), 29–52. https://doi.org/10.1525/dcqr.2023.12.4.29

Catalano, D. C. J., & Simms, S. (2025). Troubling the basics: Types, components, and approaches to LGBTQ+ trainings. *Critical Questions in Education, 16*(1), 67–86.

Catalano, D. C. J., & Tillapaugh, D. (2020). Identity, role, and oppression: Experiences of LGBTQ resource center graduate assistants. *Journal of Student Affairs Research & Practice, 57*(5), 519–531. https://doi.org/10.1080/19496591.2019.1699104

Catalano, D. C. J., Tillapaugh, D., Christiaens, & Simms, S. (2024). "More than lip service:" LGBTQ+ social justice educational interventions as institutional benign neglect. *The Review of Higher Education, 47*(3), 373–400. https://doi.org/10.1353/rhe.2024.a921607

Catalano, D. C. J., Wagner, R., & Marine, S. M. (2024). Why should housing and residence life professionals care about liberation? *Talking Stick Magazine.* https://ts.acuho-i.org/may_2024/why_care_about_liberation.html#

Catalano, D. C. J., Wagner, R., & Simms, S. (2024). Toward liberation, not oppression: Reconsidering coming out stars. *Journal of Diversity in Higher Education.* Advance online publication. https://doi.org/10.1037/dhe0000565

DeVita, J., & Anders, A. (2018). LGTQ faculty and professionals in higher education: Defining allies, identifying support. *College Student Affairs Journal, 36*(2), 63–80. https://doi.org/10.1353/csj.2018.0016

Dolasinski, M. J., & Reynolds, J. (2020). Microlearning: A new learning model. *Journal of Hospitality & Tourism Research, 44*(3), 551–561. https://doi.org/10.1177/1096348020901579

Draughn, T., Elkins, B., & Roy, R. (2002). Allies in the struggle. *Journal of Lesbian Studies, 6*(3–4), 9–29. https://doi.org/10.1300/J155v06n03_02

Evans, N. J. (2002). The impact of an LGBT safe zone on campus climate. *Journal of College Student Development, 43*(4), 522–539.

Evans, N. J., Broido, E. M., & Wall, V. A. (2004). Educating student affairs professionals about gay, lesbian, and bisexual issues: An evaluation of an intervention. *College Student Affairs Journal, 24*(1), 20–31. http://files.eric.ed.gov/fulltext/EJ956991.pdf

Finkel, M. J., Storaasli, R. D., Bandele, A., & Schaefer, V. (2003). Diversity training in graduate school: An exploratory evaluation of the Safe Zone Project. *Professional Psychology: Research and Practice, 34*(5), 555–561. https://psycnet.apa.org/doi/10.1037/0735-7028.34.5.555

Gilbert, C., Siepser, C., Fink, A. E., & Johnson, N. L. (2021). Why LGBTQ+ campus resource centers are essential. *Psychology of Sexual Orientation and Gender Diversity, 8*(2), 245–249. https://doi.org/10.1037/sgd0000451

Giroux, H. A. (2020). *On critical pedagogy* (2nd ed.). Bloomsbury.

hooks, b. (1994). *Teaching to transgress: Education as the practice of freedom.* Routledge.

Kaba, M. (2021). *We do this til we free us.* Haymarket Press.

Landreman, L. M. (2013). *The art of effective facilitation: Reflections from social justice educators.* Routledge.

Love, B. (2018). Developing a liberatory consciousness. In M. Adams, W. J. Blumenfeld, D. C. J. Catalano, K. DeJong, H. W. Hackman, L. E. Hopkins, B. J. Love, M. L. Peters, D. Shlasko, & X. Zúñiga (Eds.), *Readings for diversity and social justice* (4th ed, pp. 610–615). Routledge.

Maxwell, K. E., Nagda, B. R., & Thompson, M. C. (2011). *Facilitating intergroup dialogues: Bridging differences, catalyzing change.* Routledge.

Obear, K. (2013). Navigating triggering events: Critical competencies for social justice educators. In *The art of effective facilitation* (1st ed., pp. 151–172). Routledge.

Oliveira, K. A., Gonzalez-Siegel, V. A., Feldman, S., Kannan, K., Woods, C., Pryor, J. T., Duran, A., Catalano, D. C. J., & Jourian, T.J. (2025). An autoethnographic exploration of the realities of engaging in TQ center(ed) diversity work. *Journal of Diversity in Higher Education, 18*(2), 111–122. https://doi.org/10.1037/dhe0000501

Ortiz, S. M., & Mandala, C. R. (2021). "There is queer inequity, but I pick to be happy": Racialized feeling rules and diversity regimes in university LGBTQ resource centers. *DuBois Review*, *18*(2), 347–364. https://doi.org/10.1017/S1742058X21000096

Pryor, J. T. (2021). Queer activist leadership: An exploration of queer leadership in higher education. *Journal of Diversity in Higher Education*, *14*(3), 305–315. https://doi.org/10.1037/dhe0000160

Pryor, J. T., & Hoffman, G. D. (2021). "It feels like diversity as usual": Navigating institutional politics as LGBTQ+ professionals. *Journal of Student Affairs Research and Practice*, *58*(1), 94–109. https://doi.org/10.1080/19496591.2020.1740717

Shlasko, D. (2015). Using the five faces of oppression to teach about interlocking systems of oppression. *Equity & Excellence in Education*, *48*(3), 349–360. https://doi.org/10.1080/10665684.2015.1057061

Squire, D. D. (2019). Ending allies through the eradication of the ally (industrial) complex. In E. M. Zamani-Gallaher, D. D. Choudhuri, & J. L. Taylor (Eds.)., *Rethinking LGBTQIA students and collegiate contexts: Identity, policies, and campus climate* (pp. 187–203). Routledge.

The Chronicle of Higher Education. (2023, July 14). *DEI legislation tracker*. https://www.chronicle.com/article/here-are-the-states-where-lawmakers-are-seeking-to-ban-colleges-dei-efforts?sra=true

Tillapaugh, D., & Catalano, D. C. J. (2019). Critical influences affecting the experiences of public university LGBT services graduate assistants. *Journal of Diversity in Higher Education*, *12*(2), 126–135. https://doi.org/10.1037/dhe0000079

Tosi, J., & Warmke, B. (2016). Moral grandstanding. *Philosophy & Public Affairs*, *44*(3), 197–217. https://doi.org/https://doi.org/10.1111/papa.12075

Wagner, R., & Catalano, C. J. (2021). A reflexive self-awareness framework for advising and supporting. In R. Wagner & C. Catalano (Eds.). *Advising and supporting in student affairs* (pp. 3–16). Charles C. Thomas Publisher.

Woodford, M. R., Kolb, C. L., Durocher-Radeka, G., Javier, G. (2014). Lesbian, gay, bisexual, and transgender ally training programs on campus: Current variations and future directions. *Journal of College Student Development*, *55*(3), 317–322. https://doi.org/10.1353/csd.2014.0022

Young, I. M. (1990). *Justice and the politics of difference*. Princeton University Press.

· 8 ·

SERVING TRANS STUDENTS AND ADDRESSING TRANS OPPRESSION WITHIN TQ CENTER(ED) DIVERSITY WORK

Alex C. Lange

Introduction

College and university educators have increasingly paid attention to trans identities and communities. This attention has been both positive and challenging, with many on campus seeking to support these students while others have continued to circulate trans oppression through their (in)actions. This chapter unfolds across four major sections. First, I detail my standpoint as a practitioner and scholar who works with and alongside transgender students. Second, I define and review trans oppression, detailing its three major levels: interpersonal, institutional, and cultural. The two remaining sections review the literature about transgender student experiences confronting oppression at interpersonal and institutional levels, given the power practitioners and researchers have to affect change at these levels in the college environment. I will conclude the chapter with reflective questions for practitioners and administrators to address trans oppression on campus. These questions will be for both those in trans and queer diversity work and those in other organizational contexts. Higher education institutions—long heralded as bastions of progressive thought and social advancement (Brint, 2018)—have begun to take important steps to ensure transgender students feel meaningfully included on campus. From the establishment of gender-inclusive housing options (Garvey et al.,

2018) to the implementation of policies that respect students' pronouns and chosen names (Goldberg et al., 2019a), many colleges and universities are working diligently to create environments where transgender students can thrive academically, socially, and personally (Beemyn, 2016; Catalano et al., 2020). However, despite this progress, the fight for transgender inclusion and equity on college campuses is far from over.

In recent years, a troubling wave of culturally conservative forces has influenced or entered state legislatures promoting anti-trans laws (Rogers & Radcliffe, 2023). This legislation has restricted access to gender-affirming healthcare, banned transgender athletes from competing in sports aligned with their gender identity, and curtailed the discussion of LGBTQ+ topics; such efforts are a stark reminder of the persistent and pervasive nature of transgender oppression. Importantly, these efforts are connected to waves of opposition to the teaching of critical race theory and broader programs that support diversity, equity, and inclusion outcomes in education (Confessore, 2024; Lange & Lee, 2024; Murib, 2023; Pendharkar, 2022). Though the specific anti-trans bills appeared to decrease in spring of 2024 due to the efforts of activists and advocacy organizations (Rubin, 2024), broader anti-DEI efforts that have taken hold and those still on the horizon jeopardize the well-being and safety of minoritized students broadly and transgender students specifically. Additionally, these bills have shifted the public discourse on inclusion and equity, weaponizing trans people's visibility to curtail their lives and livability. These moves also challenge the fundamental values of diversity and inclusion that higher education institutions aim to meet and uphold.

In the face of these efforts, it is crucial to understand the ways transgender oppression manifests on college campuses and affects the experiences of transgender college students at multiple levels, from the interpersonal to the systemic. From microaggressions and misgendering to systemic barriers and discriminatory policies, transgender students face unique challenges that demand our attention and action as educators. By recognizing and addressing these issues, administrators and advocates can foster a more inclusive and equitable environment that supports the success and well-being of all students. This chapter aims to shed light on transgender students, their needs, and their confrontations with trans oppression. Focusing on transgender oppression in this chapter is meant to illuminate the challenges trans students face on campus but is not meant to define them solely as a student population. As Nicolazzo (2021) argued, "trans* people may be from oppression, but we ourselves are not of oppression" (p. 517). Said otherwise, trans people continue to succeed, persist, and thrive despite the oppression they encounter on and off campus. This chapter brings attention to these oppressive forces so those who wish to better trans college students' lives might have directions and avenues to do so.

I organized this chapter into four major sections. First, I detail my standpoint. Second, I define trans oppression and its particular forms of manifestation. This section details the three significant levels of trans oppression: interpersonal, institutional, and cultural. Third, I organize the scholarship about trans students and trans oppression using interpersonal and institutional levels. Higher education practitioners and scholars can most influence these two levels in their work. I do not address the cultural forms of oppression given practitioners' limited abilities to affect change at this level, though addressing practices at the interpersonal and institutional levels may trickle up to change cultural-level forces. Finally, I conclude with questions and reflections for those seeking to make anti-oppressive environments for transgender college students. My hope is this chapter gives colleges and universities—and those who work within and around them—ways of thinking about supporting transgender students' thriving while challenging trans oppression.

Positionality

I have worked with and alongside queer and trans youth for over a decade in both community and college settings. I began working with queer and trans youth in an LGBT community center in Palm Beach County, Florida, first as an intern and then as a part-time staff member in youth and family programs while in college; these initiatives supported those as young as 13 and as old as 30. After earning my master's degree, I worked for a few years in Michigan State University's then-LBGT Resource Center, supporting trans and queer communities through programming, student organizations, and policy advocacy. Since then, I have studied the experiences of queer and trans students in higher education settings more formally as a transfeminine scholar, positioning me well to understand the needs of transgender students and the ways trans oppression manifests on campus. These experiences helped me organize this chapter and positioned me to offer recommendations and reflections to those interested in combating trans oppression and uplifting trans students.

Trans Oppression

Trans oppression refers to the discrimination, marginalization, and mistreatment of those whose gender identity differs from the sex they were assigned at birth (Catalano & Griffin, 2016). These forces manifest in economic, legal, and social domains, impacting the lives, livelihoods, and life chances of transgender people. This form of oppression emerges from broader social attitudes and systemic structures that prioritize binary and cisnormative understandings of gender. Trans oppression specifically encompasses ideologies of biological determinism, the idea that one's genes or physiological makeup determine how a person behaves and acts (Catalano & Griffin, 2016), and genderism, the system of power that utilizes biological determinism's creation of a cisgender binary to enforce expectations of gender performance, presentation, and norms on people societally (Bilodeau, 2009). In higher education, such manifestations look like inequitable facilities access (e.g., locker rooms, bathrooms), rigid name and gender marker systems, insurance coverage, harassment, discriminatory policies, and a lack of competent and relevant support services. The manifestations represent essentialist beliefs grounded in cisgenderism where access to services is mediated through gender binaries (e.g., Dirks, 2016).

Like all forms of oppression (Hardiman et al., 2013), trans oppression manifests at individual, institutional, and cultural levels. The individual level of trans oppression brings individual attitudes and behaviors—intentional or unintentional—into focus, with particular attention to bias, prejudice, and stereotypes between individuals. An example of individual-level trans oppression looks like microaggressions or overt discrimination by individuals in higher education. Importantly, microaggressions can include experiencing transphobic language or the endorsement of gender normative behaviors at the individual level; scholars have examined how microaggressions are also products of wider systems of oppression (Nadal et al., 2012; Woodford et al., 2017). The institutional level accounts for the policies, practices, and processes that maintain and produce trans oppression at the organizational level. Specific to college campuses, this includes the ways individual colleges and universities address issues of policy, climate, and normative institutional practices that affect transgender students. Health insurance policy—negotiated and set by college and university administrators—that do not cover gender-affirming care and procedures is an example of institutional trans oppression. Finally, the cultural level of oppression highlights how "social systems and cultural norms convey messages about what is correct and expected by the larger society" (Adams & Zúñiga, 2016, p. 103). At the cultural level, trans oppression looks like widespread societal norms, values, and ideologies that devalue or erase transgender identities. This includes media representation (or lack thereof), cultural stigmatization of gender nonconformity, and societal beliefs that reinforce the gender binary.

Importantly, trans oppression is a multidimensional and intersectional concept. Transgender people hold multiple racial, gender, sexual, and dis/ability identities that inform how they can move through the world. In this way, trans oppression understands that violence, barriers, marginalization, and impacts differ from one trans person to the next based on one's location in larger social structures (Nicolazzo, 2021). For instance, transgender women and femmes of color often report higher rates of experiencing violence, harassment, and hate crimes compared to other trans people (Gossett et al., 2017). This does not happen in a vacuum; rather, transgender women and femmes of color experience more violence precisely because of the unique combination of racism, sexism, and cisheterogenderism that creates these conditions on multiple levels. That said, as Nicolazzo (2021) pointed out, transgender people might be *from* oppression but are not *of* oppression; said otherwise, transgender people are not solely defined by the oppression they face. Instead, trans people have incredible stories of thriving and mundanity like other communities. Below, I interrogate the oppression trans students face on college campuses and highlight instances where they develop practices of resilience and thriving.

Encountering Oppression at the Individual Level

The individual level encompasses trans students' applying to college, experiences of major selection, identity exploration, developing interpersonal relationships, and financial management. When applying to colleges, transgender students are often guided by financial burdens and inclusion efforts on campus, often determined through proxies like the Campus Pride Index (CPI; Garvey et al., 2017; Lange et al., 2022). While many college students consider the cost of attendance when selecting a postsecondary institution to attend, transgender students often look for policy commitments and programmatic support for their identity (Lange et al., 2022). After students spend some time on campus, they frequently question the accuracy of the CPI in assessing their individual institutions' climates.

Regarding their academic majors, transgender and gender diverse college students are more likely to enroll in arts and humanities majors while being less likely to pick business, science, and technology related fields (White et al., 2023). This is not accidental; transgender students often report experiences of discrimination and exclusion in STEM disciplines while finding greater refuge in social science disciplines (Friedensen et al., 2021; Linley et al., 2018; Rankin et al., 2019). Even though trans students may enroll in arts and humanities fields at greater rates, these fields are not in and of themselves inclusive (Zalman & McHenry-Sorber, 2023). Researchers found that creative arts spaces are not consistently inclusive and supportive for transgender, nonbinary, and androgynous college students; these students faced a range of barriers—like exclusionary social norms—that hindered their experiences in these majors. To navigate these environments, Gutzwa (2021) found that transgender students often use their funds of identity—"the lessons individuals internalize from family resources that help them make meaning of the world and of themselves" (p. 305)—to navigate academic environments and demonstrate resilience. College instructors might take such an approach to build more inclusive classrooms for transgender students and help provide spaces for students to build community with one another.

Attending college can prompt one to (further) explore their multiple identities (Jones & Abes, 2013), including their gender identity and expression (Dolan & Garvey, 2024; Lange, 2022). This exploration process is often cyclical during one's college experience. Trans students' experiences of catalysts and inhibitors on their identity exploration can affect their experiences of gender dysphoria and decisions about gender-affirming processes (Lange, 2022). Online communities and other trans college peers help to influence this exploration process (Jourian, 2017; Lange, 2022; Simms et al., 2023). Trans and nonbinary students also wrestle with being visibly trans while valuing their privacy on campus (Dolan, 2023; Goldberg & Kuvalanka, 2018; Nicolazzo, 2016). These identity explorations can differ by one's specific experience of transness. For instance, trans men often wrestle with their simultaneous visibility as men but invisibility as trans (Catalano, 2015b). Transmasculine individuals conceptualize masculinity in complex ways informed by their intersecting identities, often disputing any single way of being trans or masculine (Jourian, 2017); for instance, Jourian and McCloud (2020) found that Black transmasculine college students often created and negotiated new ways of embodying and doing Black masculinity across Black and queer spaces. Collectively, this research points to the ways college provides trans students with an opportunity to explore their identities while simultaneously navigating processes of disclosure and privacy.

A common way trans students find support in higher education is through building kinship networks with other trans students and people (Duran & Nicolazzo, 2017; Nicolazzo et al., 2018; Pitcher & Simmons, 2020). Often, colleges and universities do not provide space for trans students to connect with one another and do not prioritize the emotional wellbeing of this student community; this is another manifestation of the various forms of oppression these students face. In this way, trans students often feel compelled to build kinship and community with others to resist the oppression they experience. Nicolazzo and colleagues (2017) found that trans students form kinship networks across material, virtual, and affective domains. Material domains are those physical points of gathering on and off campus, including student organizations and queer and trans conferences. Without a hospitable in-person climate, trans students often turned to online platforms and digital domains to build relationships, create networks, and access resources (Nicolazzo et al., 2023). Virtual domains for kinship building included social media and other networking sites. These locations often allowed trans students to connect and come out to others (Nicolazzo et al., 2018). These virtual spaces also have allowed trans students to learn about themselves and their communities while trying on different gender identities (Nicolazzo et al., 2023). This was especially true for trans students of color who struggled to find belonging on campus due to racism within queer and trans spaces (Simms et al., 2023). Unlike the two previous domains, trans students built kinship networks through the emotional work of the affective domain (Nicolazzo et al., 2018). This domain overlaps with the previous two and represents the ways trans students both received and gave support to one another. Whether institutional supports were present or not, trans students often forge their success through connecting with other trans students.

Transgender students also must navigate the material realities of attending college, including managing the cost of their college education. Transgender students apply for various forms of financial aid to cover the cost of their education (Stolzenberg & Hughes, 2017), facing barriers when applying for federal student aid due to potential data mismatch in the Free Application for Federal Student Aid given the way these systems have been set up to only understand sex and gender through binary categories (Lange, 2024; Prescott, 2017). Trans students often have to manage the disclosure of their identities to stay in college while weighing the costs of attending college against paying for gender-affirming biomedical support given potential and actual transphobia from parents and grandparents (Lange, 2024). Because of these issues, trans students report higher financial strain and lower financial optimism or self-efficacy, though not at levels vastly different than their cisgender peers (Rehr & Regan, 2022). A notable difference exists between cisgender and transgender and gender diverse students in post-graduation salary expectations: the latter group expects lower salaries upon graduation due to transphobia and trans antagonism (White et al., 2022). Taken together, these challenges make transgender students feel less likely to gain financial freedom, the sense of being free of anxiety and worry about financial decisions because of financial constraints.

Encountering Oppression at the Institutional Level

Institutional-level issues look at colleges and universities more holistically, understanding how their collective and sub-units' work affects trans students' experiences. In this section, I describe campus climate, LGBTQ+ resource centers, housing and residence life, and health services. Additionally, I discuss some of the initial research on trans student experiences at various institutional types.

Trans students' perceptions of campus climate have improved over time (Garvey et al., 2019), yet that improvement has not meant *consistently positive* experiences in college. Catalano (2015a) found that trans students experienced significant challenges in college, including a lack of accessible restrooms and policies. Researchers find that trans and nonbinary students often have more negative views of campus climate, including classroom climate and curricular inclusivity (Garvey & Rankin, 2015a, 2015b). Nonbinary students also report feeling unsafe on campus due to trans-antagonistic forces (Dolan & Matsuno, 2023; Marx et al., 2024). Interestingly, students' involvement on campus may shape their views of climate: those involved with LGBTQ-related curricular experiences reported more positive perceptions of climate than those engaged in co-curricular experiences (Garvey et al., 2019). Academic discipline may also affect climate perceptions (Garvey et al., 2023). What is clear is that transgender students can see through token gestures of inclusion and do not see the absence of hostility as an automatic positive for climate (Catalano, 2015a). When college administrators, faculty, and staff take moves to implement meaningful, inclusive, and equitable policies that affect trans students, these students' perceptions and experiences of campus are more favorable (Gartner et al., 2023; Goldberg et al., 2019a). Said otherwise, when officials take tangible steps to improve climate through policy and practice, trans students feel a greater sense of belonging on campus. For instance, when discussing issues of how institutions handle sexual violence transgender students often call for greater accountability, increased education and programming around gender diverse identities, and their inclusion in systemic efforts to improve campus climate.

LGBTQ+ resource centers and organizations on campus often provide broad support and advocacy for queer and trans students (Lange, 2019); institutions often rely on these organizational units and their staff members to try and address the larger institutional structures of trans oppression. Over time, these centers have moved from being inattentive to trans student communities (Duran & Nicolazzo, 2017; Marine & Nicolazzo, 2014) to providing more support (Goldberg & Kuvalanka, 2018). Pitcher et al. (2018) found that LGBTQ+ students broadly found these units and organizations as essential sources of support. And yet, room remains for further promotion of and inclusive practice within LGBTQ+ campus resources, particularly for transgender, nonbinary, and gender nonconforming students of color who often feel marginalized in such spaces due to racism, even when they recognize the totality of resources for their communities on campus (Day et al., 2024). There remains improvement for these offices and units to commit to an anti-racist practice in their service to trans students across racial groups, rather than simply defaulting to serving white trans students—a point that is captured in Chapter 9.

Gender-inclusive housing (GIH)—which is almost exclusively found on residential college campuses—is another institutional concern for trans students. GIH emerged as a response to housing assignments and residential buildings segregating students based on assigned sex. What once was a limited offering to a few campuses (Willoughby et al., 2012) has expanded to multiple residential campuses with various offerings (Marine et al., 2019; Taub et al., 2016). Trans students are often excluded in policy creation regulating GIH and must disclose their identities to benefit from such offerings (Nicolazzo & Marine, 2015). In this way, students have to out themselves as trans to residential life staff members in order to (potentially) qualify for such gender-affirming services. Students often express desires for apartment-style and self-contained single-housing units but are impeded by a lack of appropriate facilities and administrative support (Garvey et al., 2018; Krum et al., 2013; Taub et al., 2016). A tension often exists for administrators working to implement GIH between stakeholders and administrators who fear institutional- and political-level backlash and those who center trans students and their needs in making such decisions (Marine et al., 2019); the latter group is working to counteract trans-antagonistic forces that reify trans oppression on and through campus life. Though housing options have expanded, higher education staff must continue to advocate for the option by focusing on trans students in decision-making.

Another institutional concern for trans students is campus health services and benefits. This area is one where there has been improvement over time—particularly with access to hormone therapy and gender-affirming care—but more can be done (Beemyn, 2016). Trans students face a high amount of physical and mental health challenges because of fear of violence and lack of support on campus (Goldberg et al., 2019a). Denying these students access to gender-based facilities may heighten their risk of self-harm (Seelman, 2016). Trans youth also report greater access to gender-affirming medical care compared to nonbinary youth (Todd et al., 2019). Trans students have unique needs around physical, sexual, and mental health, requiring culturally competent providers (DeVita & Wesner, 2019). College campuses can provide important wellness programs to support trans students' thriving. That said, recent conservative legislative moves have sought to restrict or ban gender-affirming healthcare for trans people—particularly trans youth—in recent years. Institutional leaders have an obligation to resist these tactics by demonstrating the importance of such inclusive care for their students' wellness and success in postsecondary education.

Some research has explored trans students' experiences at differing institutional types. Students at women's colleges often report higher levels of support and more positive attitudes about gender identity (Freitas, 2017; Marine, 2011); however, trans and gender-expansive students report pressure to conform to binary gender norms (Farmer et al., 2020) with these organizations often constructing and regulating gender through campus policies (Nanney & Brunsma, 2017). Historically Black colleges and universities (HBCUs) have similarly regulated gender through policy design; these policies emerged from and are maintained by fears of femininity among men (Mobley & Johnson, 2019). HBCUs have worked to improve the experiences, retention, and success of queer and trans students (Mobley & Johnson, 2015), though much of this work can be attributed to the activism Black queer and trans students have undertaken to meet such aims (Mobley et al., 2021); these students are living up to the historical legacies of HBCU students who have fostered and advocated for social change. Conversely, queer and trans Latine students at emerging Hispanic-serving institutions perceived that their institutions were not ready to support Latine students with multiple marginalized identities, including supporting students' physical and mental health (Ortiz, 2024). Faculty and staff were often unequipped and unprepared to support trans students at best; at worst, they seemed to not care about supporting such students. Trans students also report that religiously-affiliated and two-year institutions were less inclusive compared to those attending other institutional types (Goldberg et al., 2019a). These institutional type differences highlight both the agency of transgender students who still work to carve out their own narratives and success in college while facing unique forces at various colleges and universities.

Pairing Reflection and Action to Support Trans Students and Challenge Trans Oppression

Trans college students deserve transformative educational experiences that help them learn new competencies, develop a positive sense of self, and engage in relationship building that lasts for life. As college student educators confront old and new challenges of trans-antagonism on and off campus, this call has never been more critical as trans students report leaving and dropping out of college due to gender-related stress (Goldberg et al., 2019b).

Regarding the individual level of trans oppression, educators and administrators have a plethora of opportunities to support these students. Administrators can ensure that trans students are aware of and can access appropriate financial aid that supports their college attendance. Relatedly, educators might be good company to trans students as they navigate unique financial challenges related to aid systems and affording gender-affirming care. Advisors and administrators can challenge students' assumptions of some academic majors are more friendly to trans students over others; they can also ensure this by providing training sessions and professional development for staff and faculty working closely with students. College administrators and educators should also take care to examine both the undergraduate *and* graduate experience for trans students, noting that the latter group often spends more time in their specific academic department and culture compared to the former who interact with campus more holistically. Those who work with trans students might also give them the space to explore and try on other forms of identity, especially for those who may not have had the support to do so prior to their college enrollment. It is also important to connect trans students with one another to build relationships and kinship networks through programs and events on campus and online.

Like the individual level, college administrators and educators can affect change at the institutional level to support trans students. This might look like developing trans-affirming campus policies and processes that help improve students' perceptions of campus climates and make colleges more livable for trans people. Those working with LGBTQ+ resource center can adopt intersectional framings of their work with, for, and alongside trans students from policy advocacy to belongingness. Administrators might partner with—and compensate—trans students in the development of specific campus policies, like gender-inclusive housing or preferred name systems. Administrators working in the nexus of campus health services should meet the physical, mental, and sexual health needs of trans students through competent and supportive providers and referrals. Lastly, administrators might take a closer look at the role organizational identity and institutional type play in efforts to help one's college or university be more affirming and anti-oppressive for trans students.

In this chapter, I outlined immediate actions educators and administrators might take at individual and institutional levels to support trans students and combat trans oppression. And yet, immediacy and recommendations are not enough. Instead, those wishing to improve trans students' lives in college need to take up a liberatory consciousness as outlined by Love (2018). Love's (2018) framework envisions ways for individuals to engage in equity and justice work through capacity-building efforts and actions; rather than seeing such work as a set of competencies to attain, a liberatory consciousness framework sees such labor as a continuous process of reflection, meaning making, and action (Love, 2018). There are four, non-linear components to the framework I apply specifically to the discussion of trans students and their experiences with trans oppression. *Awareness* denotes knowing about common manifestations of trans oppression. *Analysis* includes understanding how social, historical, and cultural factors of trans oppression play out on campus. *Action* requires the work to address, interrupt, and change trans-antagonistic policies and language. Finally, *accountability* includes supporting trans college students and identifies ways for individuals to own up to their own complicity with trans oppression. Guided by Love's (2018) liberatory consciousness framework, I close by offering readers four sets of questions to reflect upon as

Table 8.1. Reflection Questions Based on Love's (2018) Framework

Component of Love's (2018) Framework	Questions
Awareness	How do the issues raised in this chapter show up in my college or university? How am I uplifting trans college students in ways that grow and change over time? What are the experiences of the transgender students I work and interact with like?
Analysis	Why do particular issues related to trans oppression continue to pop up in my college or university? What other information do I need about trans students' experiences to address such issues? Who might I work with to address those issues?
Action	What actions can I take within my sphere of influence to address trans oppression? What actions can I take with others to combat such forces? What resources might I create or promote to help others take these actions?
Accountability	How do I center trans students and stay accountable to them while combatting trans oppression on campus? How do I stay in this work even when I make mistakes or mess up?

they (continue to) undertake this work in college and university settings (see Table 8.1).

References

Adams, M., & Zúñiga, X. (2016). Getting started: Core concepts for social justice education. In M. Adams, L. A. Bell, D. J. Goodman, & K. Y. Joshi (Eds.), *Teaching for diversity and social justice* (3rd ed., pp. 95–130). Routledge.

Beemyn, G. (2016). Transgender inclusion on college campuses. In A. E. Goldberg (Ed.), *The SAGE encyclopedia of LGBTQ studies* (pp. 1227–1230). SAGE Publications.

Bilodeau, B. (2009). *Genderism: Transgender students, binary systems, and higher education*. VDM Verlag.

Brint, S. (2018). *Two cheers for higher education: Why American universities are stronger than ever—and how to meet the challenges they face*. Princeton University Press.

Catalano, D. C. J. (2015a). Beyond virtual equality: Liberatory consciousness as a path to achieve trans* inclusion in higher education. *Equity & Excellence in Education*, 48(3), 418–435. https://doi.org/10.1080/10665684.2015.1056763

Catalano, D. C. J. (2015b). "Trans enough?": The pressures trans men negotiate in higher education. *Transgender Studies Quarterly*, 2(3), 411–430. https://doi.org/10.1215/23289252-2926399

Catalano, D. C. J., & Griffin, P. (2016). Sexism, heterosexism, and trans* oppression: An integrated perspective. In M. Adams, L. A. Bell, D. J. Goodman, & K. Y. Joshi (Eds.), *Teaching for diversity and social justice* (3rd ed., pp. 183–212). Routledge.

Catalano, D. C. J., Nicolazzo, Z., & Jourian, T.J. (2020). Engaging transgender students. In S. J. Quaye, S. R. Harper, & S. L. Pendakur (Eds.), *Student engagement in higher education: Theoretical perspectives and practical approaches for diverse populations* (3rd ed., pp. 179–195). Routledge.

Confessore, N. (2024, January 20). 'America is under attack': Inside the anti-D.E.I. crusade. *The New York Times*. https://www.nytimes.com/interactive/2024/01/20/us/dei-woke-claremont-institute.html

Day, J. K., Goldberg, A. E., Toomey, R. B., & Beemyn, G. (2024). Associations between trans-inclusive resources and feelings of inclusion in campus LGBTQ+ groups: Differences for trans students of color. *Psychology of Sexual Orientation and Gender Diversity*, 11(3), 458–470. https://doi.org/10.1037/sgd0000616

DeVita, J. M., & Wesner, K. A. (2019). An examination of trans college students' sexual health. In G. Beemyn (Ed.), *Trans people in higher education* (pp. 211–229). SUNY Press.

Dirks, D. A. (2016). Transgender people at four Big Ten campuses: A policy discourse analysis. *The Review of Higher Education*, 39(3), 371–393. https://doi.org/10.1353/rhe.2016.0020

Dolan, C. V. (2023). Mirrors and witnesses: Understanding nonbinary college students' sense of belonging. *Journal of College Student Development*, 64(1), 16–30. https://doi.org/10.1353/csd.2023.0012

Dolan, C. V., & Garvey, J. C. (2024). Dismantling gender binaries: An emergent model for nonbinary identity development. *Journal of Women and Gender in Higher Education*, 17(3), 167–185. https://doi.org/10.1080/26379112.2024.2306850

Dolan, C. V., & Matsuno, E. (2023). Safety strategies and the impact of misgendering among nonbinary college students: A minority stress perspective. *Journal of Diversity in Higher Education*. Advance online publication. https://doi.org/10.1037/dhe0000544

Duran, A., & Nicolazzo, Z. (2017). Exploring the ways trans* collegians navigate academic, romantic, and social relationships. *Journal of College Student Development*, 58(4), 526–544. https://doi.org/10.1353/csd.2017.0041

Farmer, L. B., Robbins, C. K., Keith, J. L., & Mabry, C. J. (2020). Transgender and gender-expansive students' experiences of genderism at women's colleges and universities. *Journal of Diversity in Higher Education*, 13(2), 146–157. https://doi.org/10.1037/dhe0000129

Freitas, A. (2017). Beyond acceptance: Serving the needs of transgender students at women's colleges. *Humboldt Journal of Social Relations*, 39(39), 294–314. http://www.jstor.org/stable/90007886

Friedensen, R. E., Kimball, E., Vaccaro, A., Miller, R. A., & Forester, R. (2021). Queer science: Temporality and futurity for queer students in STEM. *Time & Society, 30*(3), 332–354. https://doi.org/10.1177/0961463X211008138

Gartner, R. E., Ballard, A. J., Smith, E. K., Risser, L. R., Chugani, C. D., & Miller, E. (2023). "There's no safety in these systems": Centering trans and gender diverse students' campus climate experiences to prevent sexual violence. *Journal of Diversity in Higher Education*. Advance online publication. https://doi.org/10.1037/dhe0000512

Garvey, J. C., Chang, S. H., Nicolazzo, Z., & Jackson, R. (Eds.). (2018). *Trans* policies & experiences in housing & residence life*. Routledge.

Garvey, J. C., Niehaus, E., & Galbraith, M. C. (2023). LGBTQ students' campus climate perceptions across academic disciplines. *Journal of College Student Development, 64*(4), 485–490. https://doi.org/10.1353/csd.2023.a907344

Garvey, J. C., & Rankin, S. R. (2015a). The influence of campus experiences on the level of outness among trans-spectrum and queer-spectrum students. *Journal of Homosexuality, 62*(3), 374–393. https://doi.org/10.1080/00918369.2014.977113

Garvey, J. C., & Rankin, S. R. (2015b). Making the grade? Classroom climate for LGBTQ students across gender conformity. *Journal of Student Affairs Research and Practice, 52*(2), 190–203. https://doi.org/10.1080/19496591.2015.1019764

Garvey, J. C., Rankin, S., Beemyn, G., & Windmeyer, S. L. (2017). Improving the campus climate for LGBTQ students using the Campus Pride Index. *New Directions for Student Services, 2017*(159), 61–70. https://doi.org/10.1002/ss.20227

Garvey, J. C., Viray, S., Stango, K., Estep, C., & Jaeger, J. (2019). Emergence of third spaces: Exploring trans students' campus climate perceptions with collegiate environments. *Sociology of Education, 92*(3), 229–246. https://doi.org/10.1177/0038040719839100

Goldberg, A. E., & Kuvalanka, K. A. (2018). Navigating identity development and community belonging when "there are only two boxes to check": An exploratory study of nonbinary trans college students. *Journal of LGBT Youth, 15*(2), 106–131. https://doi.org/10.1080/19361653.2018.1429979

Goldberg, A. E., Beemyn, G., & Smith, J. Z. (2019a). What is needed, what is valued: Trans students' perspectives on trans-inclusive policies and practices in higher education. *Journal of Educational and Psychological Consultation, 29*(1), 27–67. https://doi.org/10.1080/10474412.2018.1480376

Goldberg, A. E., Kuvalanka, K., & Black, K. (2019b). Trans students who leave college: An exploratory study of their experiences of gender minority stress. *Journal of College Student Development, 60*(4), 381–400. https://doi.org/10.1353/csd.2019.0036

Goldberg, A. E., Kuvalanka, K., & Dickey, L. (2019c). Transgender graduate students' experiences in higher education: A mixed-methods exploratory study. *Journal of Diversity in Higher Education, 12*(1), 38–51. http://doi.org/10.1037/dhe0000074

Gossett, R., Stanley, E. A., & Burton, J. (Eds.). (2017). *Trap door: Trans cultural production and the politics of visibility*. MIT Press.

Gutzwa, J. A. (2021). "It's not worth me being who I am": Exploring how trans* collegians navigate classroom experiences through a funds of identity lens. *Journal of Women and Gender in Higher Education, 14*(3), 302–323. https://www.tandfonline.com/doi/epdf/10.1080/26379112.2021.1990077

Hardiman, R., Jackson, B. W., & Griffin, P. (2013). Conceptual foundations. In M. Adams, W. J. Blumenfeld, C. Castañeda, H. W. Hacksman, M. L. Peters, & X. Zúñiga (Eds.), *Readings for diversity and social justice* (3rd ed., pp. 26–35). Routledge.

Jones, S. R., & Abes, E. S. (2013). *Identity development of college students: Advancing frameworks for multiple dimensions of identity.* Jossey-Bass.

Jourian, T.J. (2017). Trans*forming college masculinities: Carving out trans*masculine pathways through the threshold of dominance. *International Journal of Qualitative Studies in Education, 30*(3), 245–265. https://doi.org/10.1080/09518398.2016.1257752

Jourian, T.J., & McCloud, L. (2020). "I don't know where I stand": Black trans masculine students' re/de/constructions of Black masculinity. *Journal of College Student Development, 61*(6), 733–749. https://doi.org/10.1353/csd.2020.0072

Krum, T. E., Davis, K. S., & Galupo, M. P. (2013). Gender-inclusive housing preferences: A survey of college-aged transgender students. *Journal of LGBT Youth, 10*(1–2), 64–82. https://doi.org/10.1080/19361653.2012.718523

Lange, A. C. (2019). Envisioning new praxis through gender & sexuality resource centers: Place-consciousness in postsecondary education. *Thresholds in Education, 42*(1), 59–73.

Lange, A. C. (2022). Transgender college students' identity exploration processes. *Journal of College Student Development, 63*(4), 351–367. https://doi.org/10.1353/csd.2022.0031

Lange, A. C. (2024). Transgender men and non-binary students managing their identities to pay for college. *The Review of Higher Education, 48*(1), 129–159. https://doi.org/10.1353/rhe.0.a925022

Lange, A. C., & Lee, J. A. (2024). Centering our humanity: Responding to anti-DEI efforts across higher education. *Journal of College Student Development, 65*(1), 113–116. https://doi.org/10.1353/csd.2024.a919356

Lange, A. C., Linley, J. L., & Kilgo, C. A. (2022). Trans students' college choice & journeys to undergraduate education. *Journal of Homosexuality, 69*(10), 1721–1742. https://doi.org/10.1080/00918369.2021.1921508

Linley, J. L., Renn, K. A., & Woodford, M. R. (2018). Examining the ecological systems of LGBTQ STEM majors. *Journal of Women and Minorities in Science and Engineering, 24*(1), 1–16. https://doi.org/10.1615/JWomenMinorScienEng.2017018836

Love, B. J. (2018). Developing a liberatory consciousness. In M. Adams, W. J. Blumenfeld, D. C. J. Catalano, K. DeJong, H. W. Hackman, L. E. Hopkins, B. J. Love, M. L. Peters, D. Shlasko, & X. Zúñiga (Eds.), *Readings for diversity and social justice* (4th ed., pp. 470–474). Routledge.

Marine, S. B. (2011). "Our college is changing": Women's college student affairs administrators and transgender students. *Journal of Homosexuality, 58*(9), 1165–1186. https://doi.org/10.1080/00918369.2011.605730

Marine, S. B., & Nicolazzo, Z. (2014). Names that matter: Exploring the tensions of campus LGBTQ centers and trans* inclusion. *Journal of Diversity in Higher Education, 7*(4), 265–281. https://doi.org/10.1037/a0037990

Marine, S. B., Wagner, R., & Nicolazzo, Z. (2019). Student affairs professionals' roles in advancing gender inclusive housing: Discourses of dominance and resistance. *Journal of Diversity in Higher Education, 12*(3), 219–229. https://doi.org/10.1037/dhe0000103

Marx, R. A., Maffini, C. S., & Peña, F. J. (2024). Understanding nonbinary college students' experiences on college campuses: An exploratory study of mental health, campus involvement, victimization, and safety. *Journal of Diversity in Higher Education, 17*(3), 330–345. https://doi.org/10.1037/dhe0000422

Mobley, S. D., Jr., & Johnson, J. M. (2015). The role of HBCUs in addressing the unique needs of LGBT students. In R. Palmer, R. Shorette, & M. Gasman (Eds.), *Exploring diversity at historically Black colleges and universities: Implications for policy and practice* (pp. 79–90). Jossey-Bass.

Mobley, S. D., Jr., & Johnson, J. M. (2019). "No pumps allowed": The "problem" with gender expression and the Morehouse College "appropriate attire policy." *Journal of Homosexuality, 66*(7), 867–895. https://doi.org/10.1080/00918369.2018.1486063

Mobley, S. D., Jr., Johnson, R. W., Sewell, C. J. P., Johnson, J. M., & Neely, A. J. (2021). "We are not victims": Unmasking Black queer and trans* student activism at HBCUs. *About Campus: Enriching the Student Learning Experience, 26*(3), 24–28. https://doi.org/10.1177/1086482220953221

Murib, Z. (2023, January 6). Expect more right-wing anti-trans, anti- "critical race theory" pushes in 2023—and 2024. *Teen Vogue.* https://www.teenvogue.com/story/more-trans-crt-push-murib

Nadal, K. L., Skolnik, A., & Wong, Y. (2012). Interpersonal and systemic microaggressions toward transgender people: Implications for counseling. *Journal of LGBT Issues in Counseling, 6*(1), 55–82. https://doi.org/10.1080/15538605.2012.648583

Nanney, M., & Brunsma, D. L. (2017). Moving beyond cis-terhood: Determining gender through transgender admittance policies at U.S. women's colleges. *Gender & Society, 31*(2), 145–170. https://doi.org/10.1177/0891243217690100

Nicolazzo, Z. (2016). 'It's a hard line to walk': Black non-binary trans* collegians' perspectives on passing, realness, and trans*-normativity. *International Journal of Qualitative Studies in Education, 29*(6), 1173–1188. https://doi.org/10.1080/09518398.2016.1201612

Nicolazzo, Z. (2021). Imagining what a trans* epistemology: What liberation thinks like in postsecondary education. *Urban Education, 56*(3), 511–536. https://doi.org/10.1177/0042085917697203

Nicolazzo, Z., & Marine, S. B. (2015). "It will change if people keep talking": Trans* students in college and university housing. *The Journal of College and University Student Housing, 42*(1), 160–177.

Nicolazzo, Z., Jones, A. C., & Simms, S. (2023). *Digital me: Trans students exploring future possible selves online.* Rutgers University Press.

Nicolazzo, Z., Marine, S. B., & Wagner, R. (2017). From best to intentional practices: Reimagining implementation of gender-inclusive housing. *Journal of Student Affairs Research and Practice, 55*(2), 225–236. https://doi.org/10.1080/19496591.2018.1399896

Nicolazzo, Z., Pitcher, E., Renn, K. A., & Woodford, M. (2017). An exploration of trans* kinship as a strategy for student success. *International Journal of Qualitative Studies in Education, 30*(3), 305–319. https://doi.org/10.1080/09518398.2016.1254300

Ortiz, G. C. (2024). Queering racialized designations: Centering queer and trans Latine students at an emerging Hispanic serving institution (eHSI). *Journal of LGBT Youth, 21*(2), 250–261. https://doi.org/10.1080/19361653.2024.2309509

Pendharkar, E. (2022, December 13). The evolution of the anti-CRT movement: A timeline. *Education Week*. https://www.edweek.org/leadership/the-evolution-of-the-anti-crt-movement-a-timeline/2022/12

Pitcher, E. N., Camacho, T. P., Renn, K. A., & Woodford, M. R. (2018). Affirming policies, programs, and supportive services: Using an organizational perspective to understand LGBTQ+ college student success. *Journal of Diversity in Higher Education, 11*(2), 117–132. https://doi.org/10.1037/dhe0000048

Pitcher, E. N., & Simmons, S. L. (2020). Connectivity, community, and kinship as strategies to foster queer and trans student retention. Journal of College Student Retention, 21(4), 476-496. https://doi.org/10.1177/1521025119895514

Prescott, S. (2017, July 25). Low-income transgender students face systematic barriers in applying for federal financial aid. *New America*. https://www.newamerica.org/education-policy/edcentral/low-income-transgender-students-face-systematic-barriers-applying-federal-aid/

Rankin, S., Garvey, J. C., & Duran, A. (2019). A retrospective of LGBT issues on US college campuses: 1990–2020. *International Sociology, 34*(4), 435–454. https://doi.org/10.1177/0268580919851429

Rehr, T. I., & Regan, E. P. (2022). An exploratory analysis of financial wellness of trans-spectrum college students. *Journal of LGBT Youth, 19*(1), 76–91. https://doi.org/10.1080/19361653.2020.1762147

Rogers, K., & Radcliffe, M. (2023, May 25). Over 100 anti-LGBTQ+ laws passed in the last five years—Half of them this year. *FiveThirtyEight*. https://fivethirtyeight.com/features/anti-lgbtq-laws-red-states/

Rubin, A. (2024, June 6). Exclusive: Anti-LGBTQ+ legislative agenda momentum slows in U.S. *Axios*. https://www.axios.com/2024/06/06/anti-lgbtq-bills-us-2015-2024

Seelman, K. L. (2016). Transgender adults' access to college bathrooms and housing and the relationship to suicidality. *Journal of Homosexuality, 63*(10), 1378–1399. https://doi.org/10.1080/00918369.2016.1157998

Simms, S., Nicolazzo, Z., & Jones, A. (2023). Don't say sorry, do better: Trans students of color, disidentification, and internet futures. *Journal of Diversity in Higher Education, 16*(3), 297–308. https://doi.org/10.1037/dhe0000337

Stolzenberg, E. B., & Hughes, B. (2017). The experiences of incoming transgender college students: New data on gender identity. *Liberal Education, 103*(2).

Taub, D. J., Johnson, R. B., & Reynolds, T. (2016). The implementation of gender-neutral housing: A mixed-methods study across ACUHO-I member institutions. *The Journal of College and University Student Housing, 42*(2), 76–93.

Todd, K., Peitzmeier, S. M., Kattari, S. K., Miller-Peruse, M., Sharma, A., & Stephenson, R. (2019). Demographic and behavioral profiles of nonbinary and binary transgender youth. *Transgender Health, 4*(1), 254–261. https://doi.org/10.1089/trgh.2018.0068

White, K. J., Love, K., McCoy, M., Reiter, M., Seponski, D. M., Koposko, J., & Regan, E. (2022). Factors associated with the financial strain of transgender and gender diverse college students. *The Journal of Consumer Affairs, 56*(4), 1617–1637. https://doi.org/10.1111/joca.12483

White, K. J., McCoy, M., & Love, K. (2023). The majors of transgender and gender diverse college students. *Journal of LGBT Youth*. Advance online publication. https://doi.org/10.1080/19361653.2023.2268605

Willoughby, B. J., Larsen, J. K., & Carroll, J. S. (2012). The emergence of gender-neutral housing on American university campuses. *Journal of Adolescent Research, 27*(6), 732–750. https://doi.org/10.1177/0743558412447852

Woodford, M. R., Joslin, J. Y., Pitcher, E. N., & Renn, K. A. (2017). A mixed-methods inquiry into trans* environmental microaggressions on college campuses: Experiences and outcomes. *Journal of Ethnic & Cultural Diversity in Social Work, 26*(1–2), 95–111. http://doi.org/10.1080/15313204.2016.1263817

Zalman, P., & McHenry-Sorber, E. (2023). The "traditional queer safe space" or "kinda, not really": Experiences of transgender, nonbinary, and androgynous college students in the creative arts. *Journal of Diversity in Higher Education*. Advance online publication. https://doi.org/10.1037/dhe0000533

· 9 ·

WHO SAID IT WAS SIMPLE?: REFRAMING DIFFICULTIES AND FAILURES OF SUPPORTING TRANS AND QUEER PEOPLE OF COLOR (TQPOC) STUDENTS IN TQ CENTER(ED) DIVERSITY WORK

Mycall Akeem Riley

Introduction

In her poem, "Who Said It Was Simple," Lorde succinctly highlighted some nuances of striving to build a liberated world—particularly, the ways race, gender and sexuality (and importantly, racism, sexism, and heterosexism) intersecting simply make this work harder. In this chapter, I will center how a deeper, more complex read of traditional supports for Black, Brown and Indigenous students are not as supportive, transformative, and affirming as originally thought; instead, many of TQ center(ed) diversity workers' tools reassert hegemonic systems we're dedicated to dismantling. With a more critical lens, unique theories and framing, and a reimagining of the possibilities and impossibilities of working within higher education containers, this chapter will detail how our equitable systems fail and how educators invested in liberation can strive, meet difficulties, fail, and move forward by imagining a better world.

My Scholarly Personal Narrative of Practices

It's taken me a lot of time and courage to put my fingers to these keys. To write so plainly that I/we, and the support we strive to provide Black, Brown, and Indigenous students who hold marginalized genders and sexualities isn't enough; it can feel heavy to know many of the tools I implement aren't sufficient, that I won't be able to shield them from systemic harm makes me want to scream, tearing down affirming posters, pronoun buttons, and safer sex supplies to the ground whilst setting these institutions on fire. But, I don't. Instead, I reposition myself in a space of striving for liberation. I revisit the words of Audre Lorde's 1973 poem, "Who Said It Be Simple." In this poem, Lorde highlighted the nuances of progress, white-passing women of color, the caught-in between-ness that many Black queer people may feel. The poems' title reminds me that liberation is not simple nor easily attained, and regardless of any misgiving I have and/or any negativity that impedes work we can do, and, again, no one said it would be simple. I know this to be true. However, current systems and models labeled diversity, equity, and inclusion (DEI) work have made it appear simple. Do the training, get the certificate, add the pronouns to your email signature, and voila, you have been transformed to the premier enemy to the hegemonic nation state.

Far too often, Black, Brown, and Indigenous students fail to enter the imaginary of those providing support for trans and queer (TQ) populations. The "assumed" TQ college student for many TQ center(ed) diversity workers are those that experience marginalization as a result of their marginalized genders and sexualities, but also one that benefits from privilege given their proximity to whiteness; the resulting consequence is that Black, Brown, and Indigenous individuals are frequently left unattended and further minoritized (Lange et al., 2022; McCoy, 2018). As queer of color scholars like Ferguson (2004, 2018) remind us, too often, ideals of liberalism frequently do not extend to those most minoritized—TQ people of color (TQPOC) And when TQ center(ed) diversity workers do seek to serve these students, the work of does not feel enough—either by virtue of the limited philosophies that the worker adopts (Duran & Jourian, 2023) or because of the ways that higher education institutions are not designed to support practices that center multiply minoritized people (Duran & Jourian, 2024). It is within these tensions that this chapter exists as I employ scholarly personal narratives (see Nash, 2004) to consider what it means to center TQPOC and how the work is not as simple as people may make it out to be.

Expectations of Whiteness

Chicago, 2017, in the pre-fall stinkiness of the last beats of summer, I labored within the upper floors of community cultural centers at a four-year private university. On the floor with me were four classrooms turned into resource centers—to the right was the Asian, Pacific Islander, Desi American (APIDA) Cultural Center, directly behind was the large-scale men's golf practice green. Opposite of the entryway is the Black Cultural Center, looping back was the Latinx Cultural center, and across the hall from where we began is the LGBTQIA+ Resource Center. These four centers—albeit archaically designed, financed, and envisions—were the last vestiges of the Center for Identity, Inclusion, and Social Change, an office once led by a queer woman of color who spoke up too often and too loudly that resulted in this "restructured" model. Many faculty and staff clamored for the center to stay. In the end, the change served as a reminder of who does and does not have power.

This was the beginning of the quarter. The four coordinators were expected to provide a bevy of welcome programs and to be the face of these identity-focused lounges. As the LGBT (QIA+ was added unofficially by our staff) Resource Center Coordinator, I was stationed at the doorway threshold. Surprisingly, two students were in the lounge; one student was scrolling aimlessly on their phone, and the other was the student staff member paid to be our lounges to respond to the needs of the communities on a more authentic level. In hindsight, this is a colossal task to ask of anyone let alone a full-time student and part time staff member working 10-12 hours weekly, but I digress. The non-binary, white student worker sat at the desk, waiting to greet our guest; the hope was students from these systematically marginalized communities would gleefully run into our centers, floating from space to space, joining listservs, building community and finding their sense of self. Instead, it was a trickle of one or two guests, all quietly looking into the four lounges. A collection of four Black students walked in. I internally beamed with excitement. As a Black queer person working in TQ center(ed) spaces in higher education, I'm keenly aware that whiteness that insidiously and parasitically positions itself as the focus in queer student support spaces. I have been struggling with this at every TQ center that I've worked at. Whiteness so pervasive that it hardly matters whether the senior leadership includes Black and Brown folks, because it infiltrates from the institutional roots (Stewart, 2020). Black, Brown, and Indigenous students continue to name TQ center(ed) spaces as uncomfortable, not for students of color, and full of too many white students. With this in mind, I greeted the students coming in. "Welcome to the LGBTQIA+ Center," I said warmly.

Two Black students slowly entered the space. The mood lighting casts a calm glow (hopefully) transforming the makeshift center into something inviting. A framed Tarell Alvin McCraney's Moonlight poster stares intently at the students. No one speaks for a few seconds. One student moves towards the diner fry basket, repurposed to now to hold buttons and stickers. "Fuck yeah stickers!" one of the Black incoming students woops as a smile creep onto their face, and they forage through pronoun buttons and lavender-colored stickers.

The white students previously within the space do not interact with the newcomers. Good, I think internally. Let this space hold Black queer joy for once, even if only for a moment. The moment feels special. Sacred even. I want it to be cherished.

"Let's go, girl. You know this isn't for Black folk," another student says. The sacred image taking root in my mind is shattered. The two students walk out, swiftly moving towards the Black Cultural Center where more Black students are congregating. I stay on the threshold of the LGBTQIA+ Center. This interaction was less than five minutes total and still it continues to be so indicative of the failures of TQ center(ed) support spaces. To be clear, I did not fail per se, although internally I felt like I did. What was clear was how the nuance presented in our roles. It is a wonky, lofty goal of building a space for TQPOC students within the container of higher education institutions and practices, made worse given the vast possibilities that go unachieved. This interaction dismantled any ideas of optical progress the entrance of those students offered into this space. It is a call to me and other higher education practitioners, that if we are to engage in more liberatory practices, we must remember, it is not so simple as shallow facades.

This story illustrates how diversity work is an inherently constrained practice, given the realities of anti-Black racism and colonialism that is intricately interconnected with institutions (Wilder, 2013). These insidious roots of colleges and universities manifests in contemporary contradictions as leaders purport to want to address the needs of minoritized communities, while creating barriers and infrastructures that prevent such progress. The result is a diversity worker—in this case, a TQ center(ed) diversity worker—that is caught within an impossible position of trying to enact visions of liberation in a setting with people who actually do not want students to be free, despite any statements otherwise (Ahmed, 2012). The failure that I share above is exactly how institutional leaders harm TQ center(ed) diversity workers, as they make professionals believe that any lack of progress is a fault of the individual, rather than what it truly is: a burning through by an organization that does not create the conditions for them to succeed (Anderson, 2012). To advocate for TQPOC, as a result, feels like an impossible task, one that is much more complex than stickers in a repurposed diner fry basket.

What People Think They Are Going to Get When Hiring Me

I am aware the system is using me and tokenizing both my Blackness and queerness. Currently, Black, Brown and Indigenous TQ center directors are far and few between. However, there are insidious similarities present in the number. Many of the directors of these offices possess a charisma—what Gallop StrengthsQuest characterized as a woo, an acronym for winning others over—this skill resonates with whiteness; the woos are people exceptionally talented and love the challenge of meeting new people and winning them over. They derive satisfaction from breaking the ice and making a connection with someone. At the same time, this useful characteristic functions as a proponent of hegemony. This statement means, regardless of the radical and liberatory-minded frameworks these practitioners have, the insidiousness of dominant systems that perpetuate inequalities thwarts the change they seek to introduce time and time again. I suspect most, if not all of these practitioners are deeply aware of this.

Most of us have experience tokenization several times over. Similarly, higher education culture treats first year undergraduate students as a goldmine of diversity when they are recognizable as a person of color and queer, as they become the perfect ornament for institutions to display their progressive values. I, like many of my peers, were thirsty for a space to be whole. We found this in the corners of empty classrooms used as meeting places of social change organizations, in the hallways of resident halls synthesizing classes from the morning, in the words uttered from the few TQPOC faculty and staff who came before us. I will always honor that amidst the violent terrains of these institutions, there are small glimmers of potential for care to exist. As I grew older, I could clearly see, how the TQPOC faculty and staff who co-created those pillow-y fortresses of care continually faced violence in the forms of low pay, queer antagonism, and racism And yet, I still continued down the niche path of becoming a higher education practitioner. Amidst a potpourri of ten years of trauma and joy, several of which were in direct support to TQ populations, I eventually made it to a director-level role. I am proud of the work that I had the privilege to engage in. I no longer think that much of what I get to do is, in any sense, revolutionary, alternatively, on my good days, I think of myself as reluctant staff in what Lorde (1984) described as The Master's House. I desire to set free my activism and rabble-rousing inclinations. I play this role. I also play the role of informant, letting other activists know what door to the master's house never locks, what creaky stair to avoid as they maneuver in the master's home. In this way, I contribute to the destruction of the systems and dynamics that I resist and find myself in some ways complicit in upholding. And honestly, I am aware and comfortable that as others destroy the master's house that I may go down with it. Regardless of the marginalized identities I hold, I may be a casualty.

Laden in the scholarly personal above is the active recognition that TQ center(ed) diversity work—much like higher education institutions more broadly—is shaped by larger systems of whiteness and white supremacy (Lange et al., 2022). To think otherwise is to be complicit and contribute to said structures that prey upon TQPOC. And yet, to exist within this system and acknowledge for what it is also opens the door for dismantling these cultures. In fact, prominent queer of color theorists such as Muñoz (1999) have underscored how TQPOC survive by taking the norms of dominant cultures and turning them on their head, enacting subtle forms of agency that may not easily read unless people are looking for it. In doing so, TQ center(ed) diversity workers attempting to center TQPOC may resist the expectations of whiteness and cisnormativity, even while existing within this master's house (Lorde, 1984).

Reflecting on this Position Personally

The privilege of working in the TQ center roles at several different institutions left me clear-minded about how I often an embodiment of diversity. By this I mean, I exist in higher education but have minimal systemic power. When community members raise a concern, such as consistent misgendering, TQ center(ed) diversity workers (including me) lack the authority coupled with institutional support to admonish perpetrators (Catalano et al., 2024). Alternatively, offices such as Title XI response to precarious legal compliance issues that also lack the structural power to address student holistic care needs nor address intersectional issues such as racial or sexuality harms.

Being in these roles for closer to a decade has given me countless examples that highlight the complications as a Black queer director of a TQ center. Often, it feels like a mindfuck that my role is to support students at institutions and educational systems that were not built to do such. Take, for instance, the absence of adequate financial support. Even as numbers of TQ students nationally increase, I have yet to see any of the budgets allotted increase. Several years ago, at a private four-year institution in the Midwest became hyper-focused on capturing census-like data of the student body who hold marginalized genders and/or sexualities. When I shared why collecting this data was a misguided effort, many community members dismissed my words and concerns. Instead, these quantitative questions (mostly attendance reports) were a backwards approach to highlight how much impact our work had on students, and ostensibly make a case to increase our budget. Even though others were adamant demonstrating our tremendous output of programs and services that outpaced our staffing capacity would result in a budget increase, I was unsurprised by continued denial of resources and perpetual lack of systemic support.

Another contradiction that I feel is deeply present is the lack of structure in creating an intentional intra-racial community. As institutions of higher education are often mirrors of issues in the world, tensions between white and Black, Brown, and Indigenous communities we are asked to serve is arduous and fraught. I have no hopes that any of our TQ center(ed) spaces have figured out queer racial relations, nor do I expect them to. These tensions are the legacy of white supremacy and colonization that impact every aspect of our worlds. However, even broaching the subject seems impossible. When programs make efforts to address intra-racial dynamics, they receive support and attention because leadership pushed through an equality-that-cosplays-as-equity framework. By this, I mean they fail to address the disproportionate impacts of historical and contemporary racism. The result are programs that keep conversations superficial and sanitized, centering whiteness and end up negatively impacting the communities looking for TQPOC spaces. For example, leadership at my current institution required that our current suite of programs for TQPOC students (entitled QTPOC NOW) reframe our language so as to not exclude white queer students. What were initiatives to be for and center Black, Brown, and Indigenous queer students became about Black, Brown, and Indigenous students. The result was many TQPOC students chose to opt out of attending since their needs were decentered in response to whiteness and to appease white discomfort (Applebaum, 2017).

In the face of these challenges, and as I try to persist in these TQ center(ed) roles, I strive to do the best work that I can. I believe to create and sustain liberatory spaces for TQ students is paramount, which includes working against white supremacy, colonization, and the many other embodiments of racism. However, higher education organization structures and practices impede TQ center(ed) work fighting against oppression at the intersections and enables white supremacy to persist. As a result, I often feel simply ornamental. I am unable to impact how the systems of hegemony envelop TQ center(ed) spaces and places. I am unable to do much but add flash and pazazz no matter how invested I am. I am the embodiment of the language of appeasement (Stewart, 2017) or possibly a non-performative (Ahmed, 2012) where because I exist at the institution, the institution need not call into effect any substantial change to transform campus. Diversity without equity. Again, this is of no fault to the TQPOC leaders in these roles. I—and I don't want to speak for my peers but will—have already begrudgingly acquiesced at best, and agreed at worst, that this was the price for gaining this level of position at colleges and universities.

As the body of literature that uses critical thought to interrogate whiteness demonstrates, whiteness is the dominant norm that all systems operate within—including higher education (Gusa, 2010). Thus, even in efforts that strive to support TQPOC, TQ center(ed) diversity workers frequently have to acquiesce to the demands of whiteness. In choosing to neglect the need for spaces that are explicitly for Black, Brown, and indigenous queer students, leaders erase the legacies of racism and contemporary realities that these students are grappling with, demonstrating a white racial ignorance that has devastating consequences (Lee et al., 2022). Operating within these structures is defeating at times, but at the same time, recognizing the ways these setting operates leads to being able to do what one can for TQPOC even despite these climates.

Strategies That Get Us Closer to Liberation: Comfort in Failure

I continue to stay diligent to create a better world, because I have learned to get comfortable with failure. Not in the simple, not "enough" students showed up to my queer zine making night sort of failure but in a deeper sense of failure a sense that sits closer to my heart and clears my vision removing any rose-colored lenses I may have. In a post-The Transgender Tipping Point (Steinmetz, 2014) Time magazine cover world, one way institutions attempt to advertise their spaces are safe and progressive is to spotlight openly Trans individuals on campus. Trans faculty and staff are a great asset too; however, Trans students are the better beacon to signal achievement. To be clear, there have always been Trans and gender expansive folks on our campuses, and I will not flatten nor simplify Trans identities for, suffice to say, words and conceptualizations of identities are not capacious enough to recognize this history. Many Trans students are not interested in sharing their identities with us for valid reasons, whether because they had access to medical gender affirming care and/or they identify or others perceive them "fit" into the gender binary, and/or they do not feel comfortable sharing this part of them (due to fears, exhaustion, or some other reason). Others are vocal about their trans identity. In short, some trans students might describe institutions as welcoming places.

This is not to say that these individuals live in a utopic collegiate life as they might exist in trans-antagonistic hellscape, but possibly it does not show. As our world changes, these individuals are becoming more and more common in primary schools and in turn, in colleges too. However, there's still failure here. If we begin to unpack who often has access to the many steps access trans-affirming experiences (people and places of affirmation), this leaves out so members of the trans community. To say it plainly, whiteness constructs the systems of affirmation and access, which means trans people of color tend to experience exclusion and hostility; the financial lifting one must do to make themselves more legible and digestible is not available to many Black, Brown, and Indigenous people for a bevy of reasons. Simply having a countable number of trans students is not always indicative of an inclusive space. At no TQ center where I had the privilege to work was there virtually any Black, Brown, or Indigenous trans women engaging with the space, either as staff or as consistent visitors. Similar results are also in the staff and faculty realm. For example, I have served on many institution's Trans advocacy teams, groups that do the important work of bettering the insurance offerings to ensure ease in access to gender affirming care options for trans employees. Although important, this committee remains unable to answer where all the Black, Brown and Indigenous Trans folks are on our campus? And because of this, in many ways I again fail.

In this narrative, as well as throughout this entire chapter, I plainly engage with the concept of failure, which may seem surprising to some. And yet, failure is a common feature of the lives of TQ people in a world where they are destined to fail by the cisheterosexist structures that undergird our society (Halberstam, 2011). In many ways, reckoning with failure can be empowering as we as TQ center(ed) diversity workers will always be failures in an institution that wills it as so. So, what happens when a TQ center(ed) diversity worker comes to term with failure? In many ways, it feels like a devastating thought; in other ways, embracing failure can open a path moving forward to continue to do the work of addressing the needs of TQPOC. We will continue to fail in this mission. And yet, we persist.

Thinking About Intersectional Programming

What it means to engage in intersectional programming that serves the needs of students by tackling multiple forms of oppression. . . this feels like a failure of imagination and practice. Individuals within and beyond higher education institutions have deeply misunderstood term intersectionality, removed from its deeper analysis of systems of inequity and oppression (Collins & Bilge, 2016; Crenshaw, 1989,

1991; Harris & Patton, 2019). *Instead, many use intersectionality to simply mean the experience of multiple social identities.* In my practice, I work very hard to appropriately and intentionally use the concept, especially in my programming. Working at several universities, this was always a phenomenal entry point to introducing equity, critical thinking, and uplifting QTPOC scholars and movement makers. Ranging from queer Latinx bakers to Black Trans actresses have aided in bringing intersectionality alive. However, *there is a failure here.*

In 2017, I made a concerted effort to partner exclusively with Black, Brown, and Indigenous queer thinkers, creatives, and theorists. This way queer communities of color, who by and large were unable to access the same financial opportunities as white queers, had equitable access to those who look like and had experiences like them. Swiftly, my thoughts that I found the golden ticket to changing my office for the better were shattered when it came time to compensating them for their labor. I failed to realize the archaic and bureaucratic payment methods enact administrative violence (Spade, 2015). These systems move at a glacial pace, meaning these partners were paid for their services far later than 30 days after the event. Even the typical payment within 30 days timeline assumes an individual's livelihood will not be in jeopardy by waiting that long. Not to mention how this system of payments requires physical addresses and/or access to a bank account which many TQPOC, particularly trans and gender expansive folks, may not always have (again due to requirements of identity, underemployment, etc.). Even with workarounds and schemes I tried to use, these tactics are still insufficient to navigate systems that function exactly as they are supposed to perpetuate inequities.

As TQ center(ed) diversity workers continue to exist in institutions that have hindered progress to liberation and equity (Ahmed, 2012), a way forward is to critically and intentionally assert practices that are intended to acknowledge how systems of oppression overlap. Intersectionality is one such tool that can aid in this goal. And still, to employ an intersectional lens means seeing how marginalization is designed to remain in place by those in power. So, an intersectionally informed praxis suggests that the work will never be simple, because it was never meant to be.

Addressing This Impossible Task

No matter how difficult to reach, liberation is still the goal. We will not achieve liberation through a check list of best practices or even through a thoughtful consideration of tips and tricks. I do not think we will reach it through inter- and intragroup dialogue spaces, although useful. In fact, liberation may not even be something we can find within our institutions of higher education. And still, we can continue to seek out how TQ center(ed) diversity workers and spaces can best support Black, Brown, and Indigenous TQ communities by seeking out honest conversation with TQPOC students, faculty, and staff. My constant evaluation of what it means to engage in TQ center(ed) work through an equity mindset requires consideration of nuances too many to delineate in a neat list to follow. I continue to grapple with the tension between the liberatory futures I want to bring into effect and the complicity of working within institutions built to perpetuate hegemony that functions best in my absence. I hope that these words serve as a reminder we do not need to get it right in our initial ideas, the solutions to TQPOC exclusion are problems that will require more work than we currently put into them. And still, we can continue to strive for liberation. The answers on how to achieve liberation might remain unclear yet, it is still the goal.

References

Ahmed, S. (2012). *On being included: Racism and diversity in institutional life*. Duke University Press.

Applebaum, B. (2017). Comforting discomfort as complicity: White fragility and the pursuit of invulnerability. *Hypatia, 32*(4), 862–875. https://doi.org/10.1111/hypa.12352

Catalano, D. C. J., Tillapaugh, D., Christiaens, & Simms, S. (2024). 'More than lip service:' LGBTQ+ Social justice educational interventions as institutional benign neglect. *The Review of Higher Education, 47*(3), 373–400. https://doi.org/10.1353/rhe.0.a913752

Collins, P. H., & Bilge, S. (2016). *Intersectionality*. Polity Press.

Crenshaw, K. (1989). Demarginalizing the intersection of race and sex: A Black feminist critique of antidiscrimination doctrine, feminist theory, and antiracist politics. *University of Chicago Legal Forum, 8*(1), 139–167. http://chicagounbound.uchicago.edu/uclf/vol1989/iss1/8

Crenshaw, K. (1991). Mapping the margins: Intersectionality, identity politics, and violence against women of color. *Stanford Law Review, 43*(6), 1241–1299. https://doi.org/10.2307/1229039

Duran, A., & Jourian, T. J. (2023). A narrative inquiry study exploring LGBTQ+ center professionals' engagements with anti-racism. *The Journal of Higher Education, 94*(3), 333–356. https://doi.org/10.1080/00221546.2022.2093077

Duran, A., & Jourian, T. J. (2024). Gender and sexuality center professionals' narrative accounts of racialized institutional resistance in anti-racism work. *Review of Higher Education, 47*(4), 437–465. https://doi.org/10.1353/rhe.0.a914005

Ferguson, R. A. (2004). *Aberrations in Black: Toward a queer of color critique*. University of Minnesota Press.

Ferguson, R. A. (2018). *One-dimensional queer*. Polity Press.

Gusa, D. L. (2010). White institutional presence: The impact of whiteness on campus climate. *Harvard Educational Review*, 80(4), 464–489. https://doi.org/10.17763/haer.80.4.p5j483825u110002

Halberstam, J. (2011). *The queer art of failure*. Duke University Press.

Harris, J. C., & Patton, L. D. (2019). Un/doing intersectionality through higher education research. *The Journal of Higher Education*, 90(3), 347–372. https://doi.org/10.1080/00221546.2018.1536936

Lange, A. C., Duran, A., & Jackson, R. (2022). How whiteness werqs in LGBTQ centers. In Z. Foste & T. Tevis (Eds.), *Critical whiteness praxis in higher education & student affairs: Considerations for the pursuit of racial justice on campus* (pp. 155–171). Stylus.

Lee, D. H., Ash-Bald, E., Ward-Zanotto, A., Black, J., & Poon, O. A. (2022). Relinquishing white innocence: Slaying a defender of white supremacy. In Z. Foste & T. L. Tevis (Eds.), *Critical whiteness praxis in higher education: Considerations for the pursuit of racial justice on campus* (pp. 90–114). Stylus.

Lorde, A. (1984). The master's tools will never dismantle the master's house. In *Sister outsider: Essays and speeches* (pp. 110–114). Crossing Press.

McCoy, S. D. (2018). *Where is my place?: Queer and transgender students of color experiences in cultural centers at a predominantly white university* (Publication no. 0262B_15285) [Doctoral dissertation, The University of Wisconsin—Madison]. UW-Madison Dissertations and Theses. https://digital.library.wisc.edu/1711.dl/MFQM7PCOIOXYM85

Miller, R. A., & Dika, S. L. (2018). Perceptions of campus climate at the intersection of disability and LGBTQIA+ identities. In K. M. Soria (Ed.), *Evaluating campus climate at research universities: Opportunities for diversity and inclusion* (pp. 77-101). Palgrave Macmillan.

Muñoz, J. E. (1999). *Disidentifications: Queers of color and the performance of politics*. University of Minnesota Press.

Nash, R. J. (2004). *Liberating scholarly writing: The power of personal narrative*. Teachers College Press.

Spade, D. (2015). *Normal life: Administrative violence, critical trans politics, & the limits of law*. Duke University Press.

Steinmetz, K. (2014, May 29). The transgender tipping point. *Time*. https://time.com/135480/transgender-tipping-point/

Stewart, D.-L. (2017, March 29). Language of appeasement. *Inside Higher Ed*. https://www.insidehighered.com/views/2017/03/30/colleges-need-language-shift-not-one-you-think-essay

Stewart, D–L. (2020). Twisted at the root: The intransigence of inequality in U.S. higher education. *Change: The Magazine of Higher Learning*, 52(2), 13–16. https://doi.org/10.1080/00091383.2020.1732753

Wilder, C. S. (2013). *Ebony and ivy: Race, slavery, and the troubled history of America's university*. Bloomsbury Press.

· 1 0 ·

ATTENDING TO ABLEISM IN TRANS AND QUEER CENTER(ED) DIVERSITY WORK

Ryan A. Miller and Liz Elsen

Introduction

Disabled trans and queer people contend with multiple, overlapping forms of oppression, including (at minimum) ableism and heterosexism and/or genderism. These systems of oppression manifest in higher education as a lack of accessibility and inclusion, prejudice and harassment, invisibility in curricula, negative mental health outcomes, and single-identity approaches to resource provision that fail to consider intersectionality. Within trans and queer (TQ) center(ed) work in higher education, disability and ableism are often ignored or treated as an afterthought—at best rendering disability invisible (or potentially rendering people hyper-visible through tokenization) and at worst actively excluding disabled TQ people from physical and online spaces, programming, policies, and practices. Though scholarly attention to experiences of disabled TQ students has increased, more focused attention is needed on translating research findings to inform campus practice, particularly the work of TQ center(ed) diversity workers. This chapter draws from scholarly literature about disabled trans and queer collegians and findings from a qualitative study of disabled TQ students and their experiences with TQ center(ed) diversity work. The chapter will conclude with a discussion of how campus-based practitioners and policymakers can create anti-ableist environments for and with disabled TQ people and three case studies focusing on ableism in TQ center(ed) work.

At the time of this writing, a wide swath of diversity, equity, and inclusion (DEI) initiatives in higher education are under attack in U.S. higher education as part of a broader culture war (Harper et al., 2024; Lange & Lee, 2024). Several states, including Texas and Florida, have enacted anti-DEI legislation resulting in the closure of trans and queer (TQ) centers, as well as cultural centers and other DEI-focused offices (Chronicle of Higher Education, 2024). Though initiatives around disability are less explicitly targeted, this is likely due in part to obligations under federal law to provide access and accommodations to disabled students. In addition to accommodations-focused disability services offices, some campuses have created disability cultural centers that focus on cultural, political, and activist notions of disability identity and provide community-focused focused spaces with events to build networks of disabled students (Chiang, 2020), and these spaces have not been prime targets of anti-DEI legislation. Still, the closure of TQ and cultural centers cuts off life-affirming and life-saving spaces for students (Miller, 2024). This is particularly true for disabled trans and queer students (hereafter, disabled TQ students), who may find understaffed disability services offices that primarily focus on providing accommodations rather than support for identity exploration and community building. Similarly, other resources such as counseling centers may not have culturally competent staff ready to support students in all facets of their identities (Miller & Dika, 2018). Furthermore, disabled TQ students also come to college campuses with racialized, classed, religious, and other social identities; for disabled TQ students of color, for instance, the assault on DEI supports on campuses may cut off additional lifelines.

In this anti-DEI context, the need for anti-ableist TQ resources on college campuses is vital and urgent. Disabled trans and queer people contend with multiple, overlapping forms of oppression, including (at minimum) ableism and heterosexism and/or genderism (Abrams & Abes, 2021; Kimball et al., 2018; Miller, 2018). These systems of oppression manifest in higher education as a lack of accessibility and inclusion, prejudice and harassment, invisibility in curricula, negative mental health outcomes, and single-identity approaches to resource provision that fail to consider intersectionality (Miller, 2018; Shelton, 2022). Within trans and queer center(ed) work in higher education, disability and ableism may be ignored or treated as an afterthought—at best rendering disability invisible (or potentially rendering people hyper-visible through tokenization) and at worst actively excluding disabled TQ people from physical and online spaces, programming, policies, and practices. Yet, little has been written about anti-ableist efforts within TQ center(ed) diversity work and the experiences of disabled TQ students with TQ center(ed) diversity work. In this chapter, we begin to address this need by first reviewing published higher education scholarship about disabled TQ student experiences in higher education, then sharing examples of student experiences with TQ center(ed) diversity work from a qualitative study, followed by a discussion of promising practices and implications for TQ center(ed) diversity work. We conclude with three case studies for addressing ableism in TQ center(ed) work.

Before we proceed, we want to situate how our backgrounds as authors influence our perspectives. Ryan is a white, queer, nondisabled faculty member whose research about disabled TQ students is informed, in part, by his experience directing a TQ center. Liz is a white, queer, non-binary, disabled former LGBTQIA+ Center Director, who served on the advisory board for the Disability Cultural Center at a large public university in the south. Their center was recently impacted by the legislation discussed and subsequently dissolved. Both of us worked for much of our careers in states with passed or proposed anti-DEI and anti-LGBTQ legislation.

Disabled TQ Experiences in College

As early as the 1990s, scholars discussed disabled trans and queer students in higher education literature, largely focusing on the population's service needs such as accommodations and training in multiple identities for staff members (Harley et al., 2002; Underhile & Cowles, 1998). One of the first studies in this area discussed inadequate support services and discomfort in discussing sexuality with disability services staff, as reported by one gay man with cerebral palsy and learning disabilities (Henry et al., 2010). Research related to disabled TQ students has increased since 2015 and tends to aggregate both disabled students and TQ students as umbrella groups, an approach that may surface commonalities in student experiences with oppression but conceal differences between the experiences of students with particular identities (Miller et al., 2020; Price, 2011).

Much contemporary research related to disabled TQ students focuses on how they navigate higher education institutions, construct, name, and communicate their identities, and access resources and services. Miller (2018) identified five identity discourses students drew upon (intersectional, interactive, overlapping, parallel, oppositional) to describe the relationships (or lack thereof) among their disability, gender, and/or sexual identities. These discourses "demonstrated [students'] resilience, creativity, and a complex level of introspection, and became practical tools for navigating and resisting oppression" (p. 341). When navigating campuses, disabled TQ students must make continual decisions about whether and how to disclose one or more of their minoritized identities to be able to access resources, communicate their needs, connect with peers, become activists, and protect their safety (Denton & Abes, 2022; Kimball et al., 2018; Miller, 2015; Miller et al., 2017, 2019). Online venues, namely social media, are promising venues for students to explore their identities, connect with others who identify similarly, and launch their political involvement and activism, particularly when accessible, intersectional spaces offline are lacking; however, students may also experience bullying and racism, among other forms of oppression in online spaces (Miller, 2017).

Increasingly, higher education scholars use concepts from queer theory and crip theory (Kafer, 2013; McRuer, 2006; Sherry, 2004) to examine disabled TQ student experiences. For instance, several scholars deconstruct how performativity pervades students' experiences of naming, disclosing, and/or concealing their disability, gender, and/or sexual identities (Abrams & Abes, 2021; Miller, 2015; Kimball et al., 2018). Concepts of queer/crip time have been used to call attention to the ways that disabled TQ students may transgress normative institutional timelines in higher education (Miller, 2020). However, the use of queer theory and reclaimed terminology such as "crip" have also been critiqued as inaccessible and overly academic (Sherry, 2013).

Scholars have also focused on disabled TQ students' mental and physical health and well-being as they frequently face experiences of marginalization on campus and in society (Miller et al., 2021). A national survey found 11 % of disabled trans students in college have engaged in sex work; the survey also found students reported poor overall health and suicidal ideation (Coston et al., 2022). Within colleges and universities, disabled TQ students often experience ableist, cisnormative, and heterosexist microaggressions in classrooms (Miller, 2015; Miller & Downey, 2020) and on the broader campus (Miller & Smith, 2021). Researchers have also focused on mental health experiences and challenges faced by disabled TQ students and how interventions such as culturally competent counseling and support groups can be helpful (Miller et al., 2022). Overall, this growing body of research provided valuable insights on student experiences and how students navigate campuses and resist oppression. But, thus far, research related to disabled TQ student experiences within TQ center(ed) diversity work in higher education is sparse.

Disabled TQ Student Experiences with TQ Center(ed) Diversity Work

While little published work addressed disabled TQ student experiences in TQ center(ed) diversity work, some insights from a study of disabled TQ students are instructive. A qualitative situational analysis study (Clarke, 2005) explored the experiences and identities of 25 disabled TQ students at a large, predominantly white research university in the United States. The larger study from which these themes are drawn focused on how students conceptualize intersections of their disability and LGBTQ identities (Miller, 2018) and how students negotiate their identities in classrooms (Miller, 2015) and online spaces (Miller, 2017); for more information about the study, readers can access these publications.

Students in the study described experiences with psychological/psychiatric disabilities, as well as medical, physical, temporary, learning, visual, and auditory disabilities. Most students experienced multiple disabilities. Students identified as women and/or female, men and/or male, cisgender, trans*, nonbinary, and genderqueer; several students identified with more than one term to identify their gender and/or sex. In terms of sexuality, students identified as queer, gay, bisexual, asexual, lesbian, polyamorous, demisexual, panromantic, quoiromantic, and straight. Disabled TQ students in the study discussed their experiences with the campus TQ center and noted the helpful staff and resources, while also discussing occasional difficulty of engaging socially in the space and the desire for more staff representation and diversity.

Helpful Staff and Resources

Regardless of how often students used the TQ center, they expressed appreciation for its presence and felt validated that it existed; as Sandy described, "This place saved my life." She elaborated,

> After I got outed, I started spending most of my out of class time here in the [center]. You kind of get it thrown into the whole queer world when you get outed, and your family is not super supportive or really, anti-supportive.

Sandy's experience demonstrated how the center provided a safe space for her when she lacked family support. Another student, Ella, called the center her "home on campus," noting:

> I came to this campus a very young, not quite out to people yet, trans person, queer youngling, who had no notions about socializing or what being queer even meant, or anything. [The center] was the one place where I felt most accepted and ... like I wouldn't have to explain everything so that's been really great.

Several students, such as Shannon, pointed out the staff of the center (both full-time and student staff) as a key resource:

> They're definitely people that I feel comfortable talking with and I feel that they're impartial. I feel like they really do care about the students. They're also valuable because they can say, "You know what? I know what you're going through. I've been through this before." Or at the very least, they're very knowledgeable and can say, "You know what? You should talk to this person. I think this person would really be able to help you," or "Here's this group of people that I think would be beneficial for you to go meet these people or this organization."

Shannon viewed the center staff as connectors and knowledgeable resources for support. Even students who utilized the center less often, such as Zachary, found the resources helpful: "When I have been there, the programs they put on, I really enjoy that. I feel it's been a large part of me becoming comfortable with my queer identity because I've had so many resources here and community also." While students appreciated the presence of the center and their comfort within it, students did not generally comment on specific anti-ableist or disability-inclusive measures that supported their engagement.

Tensions in the Sociality of the Space

The most difficulty students described in accessing the TQ center was its interactive, social nature. Particularly for autistic students and students with mental health and psychological disabilities, interacting in the space could drain their energy. Marie reflected,

> I never really engaged in the [center] because you walk in and people are talking and you just slip in and are expected to join in on the fun but if that's not your thing, it's a really intimidating place. I don't know what the exact solution is but finding a way to engage those who aren't as social or who aren't as extroverted and make them feel like these resources are available for them too.

Marie's experience points to the need for resources and programming provided outside of the main drop-in space for the center, which tended to be overflowing with students who may already know each other or work together. Aurora frequented the center and appreciated that everyone would use their correct pronouns, but still said they needed an ample supply of energy to socialize in the space: "It depends on how many spoons I have if I go in there because I'll have to interact with people and stuff." Aurora also said the programming going on in the center might affect whether they would use the center; they gave the example of a suicide prevention training in the space being difficult to handle and opting to leave that day.

Will lamented the "drama" that can accompany intense discussion of social justice issues:

> Whenever I go to the [TQ center], maybe one in 10 times there's some little fight going on over there. About like, privilege or somebody said something racist and somebody overreacted or underreacted or whatever. And, there's just a whole lot of drama that, like, creates tension between the communities that it's supposed to help.

Will did not have the stamina or bandwidth to participate in the intense debates in the TQ center, describing similar experiences as Marie and Aurora. While students appreciated the presence of the center, they often found it difficult to access the main drop-in space if it was crowded and noisy.

(Lack of) Staff Representation

One area for improvement noted by several students was the diversity of the full-time and student staff in the TQ center, particularly along dimensions of race, gender, and disability. Aurora described a "cis gay man model" that previously pervaded the center:

> But it's getting better, I think. The people who are working in the [TQ center], like the student workers, are really diverse this semester. . . . I feel like there's been like a renewed commitment, toward figuring out what's best for students. I'm really hoping that it's going to become a more, and more accessible place to people from all walks of life.

Some students avoided the center altogether due to a lack of staff representation. Desi said he frequented the multicultural center instead, remarking, "The only space that I feel is really inclusive is the [multicultural center]. That's about it. I honestly don't include the [TQ center] there because it's still very white-dominated and very cliquey." Desi also said when they tried to engage with a center staff member, they felt dismissed:

> I turned around and said [to TQ center staff member], "Hi. I need help, trying to find ways to connect my major to helping underserved people." [Staff member] said, "You're obviously in the wrong major," and then left. I felt very much dismissed.

Staffing in TQ center(ed) diversity work is vital; even when such centers may only have one or a few full-time staff members, striving for representation is one way to attempt to serve a diversity of student populations. In addition to representation of identities, staff understanding of student needs and inclusivity can help ensure students feel welcomed in the space.

Implications for Creating Anti-Ableist Environments in TQ Center(ed) Work

With the research on disabled TQ students and the experiences shared above about their experiences in TQ center(ed) diversity work in mind, as well as based on the experiences of the authors, we offer several suggestions for working against ableism in TQ center(ed) work.

One baseline for anti-ableist environments is the physical accessibility of TQ center(ed) space. Though employees are likely unable to control the location of a center, they can still think about access implications stemming from the location of the center on campus (considering transportation and parking that is available) and whether it is on the ground floor or a higher floor (necessitating elevator access). In addition, a center should be accessible with features such as motorized door push buttons and have sufficient, flexible space. For instance, this might entail having sufficient pathways to and through the center, and space in staff members' offices and rooms within the center. Such physical resources will serve to welcome students who use wheelchairs or have other mobility needs. Centers can provide access notes on their websites about how to find the center and where to find transportation and accessible parking. Beyond physical access, center employees can work to provide explicit messages of inclusion and anti-ableism in the space through artwork, signage, and other physical artifacts. For instance, students might be interested to see Disability Ally placards (e.g., Cal Poly Pomona, 2024) displayed by staff members who have completed neurodiversity or disability justice ally training on campus (and it is important that receiving such training is ongoing). A fidget box of sensory toys might make students feel "safe to stim" in the space, and a quiet "stim" room or space might also be helpful.

Ideally, disability becomes an integral part of a center's ongoing education, programs, and events, avoiding the trap of only mentioning disability during a disability awareness week or day. The center's programming, both inside and outside of the space, should be accessible. For instance, publicity materials for all events should include how to make accommodations requests. Ideally, centers can move toward more universally designed (Burgstahler & Cory, 2010) events that would expect and welcome disabled people without necessitating accommodations. An example of this might be proactively having sign language interpretation for a large event such as Lavender Graduation. We recognize that limited budgets to provide accommodations might necessitate waiting until a request is made, but there is still an opportunity for staff members to advocate within the institution for funding of accommodation requests. It is also important to ask those who will be attending events about dietary restrictions and viewing this as an access need. Programmatic inclusion means recognizing, for example, a student might be on a low-Fodmap diet to address food triggers and note this in an accommodations request that can then be addressed by event organizers.

As noted by students who participated in the research previously discussed, the social accessibility of a center's space and programming is vital as well. Autistic students and students with mental health and psychological disabilities might navigate anxiety about entering the space or becoming overwhelmed or overstimulated while they are engaging the space or its programming. While the drop-in spaces that many centers have are often, by their nature, socially active spaces, center staff can also consider how to offer means of engagement beyond in-person drop-in spaces and events. Programs that offer one-on-one or small group connections that are less socially taxing, such as mentorship programs or facilitated small group discussions, might be valuable for students, as are online spaces to connect with others with similar identities and interests.

To extend the center's reach, staff can partner with disability services and disability cultural centers (where they exist) on their campuses and beyond. These partnerships might include working with a disability resource center or cultural center to co-advise a student organization for students who are queer and neurodiverse. The TQ center can have a presence at disability-focused events such as disability orientation/welcome and graduation programs on campus. Disability and TQ center(ed) diversity work can partner to host guest speakers (and share costs) and invite each other's staff to serve on search committees and ad hoc projects. We recognize that many disability services offices operate with medical and legal approaches to disability that are driven by the accommodations process and compliance with federal laws; this might differ from the cultural, social, political, or social justice models employed by disability cultural centers. Some disabled students may not feel aligned with an office's particular approach and may not find staff who represent their identities (in disability- or LGBTQ-focused spaces), so practitioners should not assume disabled students use particular resources on campus, such as a disability services office, or consider the resources to be welcoming and inclusive. Even with those caveats in mind, keeping lines of communication open between disability and TQ center staff can help facilitate connections and partnerships and address disabled TQ students' needs. Particularly in the anti-DEI legislative era, staff members in TQ center(ed) diversity work and other diversity-focused spaces may lose their jobs or be forced to "do more with less" as fewer institutional resources are devoted to their work, so creative partnerships and alliances across campus will be vital—and it will be unreasonable to expect disability and TQ center(ed) diversity work can be the only sources of support for disabled TQ students on campus. Further, it will be more important than ever for staff to seek innovative ways to garner student input and feedback to make sure that the university is creating an inclusive, anti-ableist environment.

Conclusion

Illustrating the limitations of single-identity focused spaces in higher education, Shelton (2022) remarked that colleges and universities:

> too often segment and compartmentalize identities to the point of fracturing the wholeness of people in academia (e.g., a pride center is structurally isolated from services for disabled people). . . . In disabled/crip spaces, I often find myself "straightening" up—putting on a performance of heterosexual masculinity that is neither authentic nor healthy. Pretending to be a cisgender, heterosexual person is detrimental to my bodymind: it quite literally disables me, both physically and mentally. . . . Conversely, masking my access needs to feel momentarily like I belong in queer and trans spaces is exhausting. (pp. 116–117)

Shelton highlighted how TQ disabled people may face intersectional erasure even in spaces designed to contest oppression, such as TQ center(ed) diversity work (Abes & Wallace, 2018; Crenshaw, 1989). With this perspective in mind, this chapter provides a foundation for greater attention to anti-ableism within TQ center(ed) work and for disabled TQ student experiences to be centered in this work. We hope that the literature, student perspectives, and implications for future work offer tangible ideas for higher education TQ center(ed) work and workers to contest the manifestations and overlaps of ableism, genderism, and heterosexism. We invite you to consider the following case studies to extend your exploration of attending to ableism in TQ center(ed) work.

Case Study #1: Ableism on Movie Night

Several students have gathered for an event at the center. They are hoping to watch a DVD of a movie about Black queer communities. The QTBIPOC-focused student group co-hosting the event is excited to watch the movie, because it's not streaming, but it's in the center's resource library. The flier was designed to say that the event is open to students at the university and to email the center with any accommodation requests and/or access needs.

About halfway through the movie—the campus is hard to navigate, has no free parking, and the center is not near a parking lot—a group of community members who are friends with one of the students in the organization arrive. One of the students is deaf, and requests that the subtitles be turned on for the movie.

The student organizer finds the remote and discovers that it's not working, and there is no way to access the menu that has subtitles without access to the remote. There are extra batteries in the storage room, but the student does not know that. The student organizer apologizes and tells the friend, who signs it to the community member, who is frustrated and starts to leave. The organizer asks the friend who signs if they could translate the movie, but the friend says their ASL isn't that good. There are 25 other students waiting to finish the movie, so the organizer starts the movie. The group that just arrived, all decide to leave, and they take their friend who is in the group with them.

You are the administrator of the space and hear about this happening the next day.

- What are the underlying issues in this case as they relate to ableism in QT spaces and how could these issues have been prevented?

- In what ways do the identities of the various participants impact how they experienced this interaction?
- How do you support the student leader, who is feeling guilty about the interaction? How do you support the students impacted?
- What do you do to ensure that this doesn't happen again? What resources could be helpful?

Case Study #2: Physical and Financial Barriers

A student who uses a wheelchair, asks you, the director of the TQ center for a meeting about getting an automatic door opener, because it is sometimes difficult for them and their friends to access space. You have asked the ADA office for this accommodation before and were told that the university will not pay for an accessible door opener despite repeated requests from students. The rationale for rejecting the request is the TQ center is not "zoned" for them to have to pay for the renovation. The center could pay for the renovation out of its own budget and was quoted $4,000 for the project, which was over half of the center's programming budget for the renovation.

You are about to meet with the student.

- What do you say to the student about your past request for the device?
- How much do you disclose about the center's budget and the administrative barriers to completion?
- How do you support the student leader, who is feeling frustrated that they have to ask for help or knock on the door to enter a space that their student fees pay for?
- How do you and the student strategize together? What resources could be helpful?

Case Study #3: Names and Accommodations

You work at a university that has a "preferred name policy" that allows transgender students to change their name on forms, websites, rosters, and their ID. The university has an accommodation process that automatically sends ADA accommodation letters to professors on campus. A transgender student you know enrolled in a course you will teach this semester, but the name on the accommodation letter does not match the student's name on the roster.

When you look the student up in the database, you discover the name on the accommodation is the student's "deadname" or legal name.

You reach out to the information technology (IT) office and the disability office to let them know and are told that these two systems are unable to "talk to each other," or, in other words, to automatically convey the student's correct name across systems. You realize that every trans student who uses accommodations will have a letter with their "deadname" sent to their professors, which will likely not match the name listed on their roster. This will leave many trans students feeling like they have to choose which of their identities to disclose. If they use their accommodations, their professors will know they are trans and may treat them differently. If they choose not to use their accommodations so their professor does not know their deadname, they will not have access to their accommodations. Other staff have known about the glitch for years and have not worked to fix it.

You are about to meet with the disability office, the head of IT, and the registrar.

- How do you explain the harm that can come from this problem?
- What steps do you recommend each office take?
- How do you advocate for trans students with disabilities?

References

Abes, E.S., & Wallace, M.M. (2018). "People see me, but they don't see me": An intersectional study of college students with physical disabilities. *Journal of College Student Development* 59(5), 545–562. https://dx.doi.org/10.1353/csd.2018.0052.

Abrams, E. J., & Abes, E. S. (2021). "It's finding peace in my body": Crip theory to understand authenticity for a queer, disabled college student. *Journal of College Student Development*, 62(3), 261–275. https://doi.org/10.1353/csd.2021.0021

Burgstahler, S. E., & Cory, R. C. (Eds.). (2010). *Universal design in higher education: From principles to practice.* Harvard Education Press.

Cal Poly Pomona. (2024). *Ability Ally program.* Author. https://www.cpp.edu/ada/ability-ally-training.shtml

Chiang, E. S. (2020). Disability cultural centers: How colleges can move beyond access to inclusion. *Disability & Society*, 35(7), 1183–1188. https://doi.org/10.1080/09687599.2019.1679536

Chronicle of Higher Education staff. (2024). DEI legislation tracker. *The Chronicle of Higher Education.* https://www.chronicle.com/article/here-are-the-states-where-lawmakers-are-seeking-to-ban-colleges-dei-efforts

Clarke, A. (2005). *Situational analysis: Grounded theory after the postmodern turn.* Sage.

Coston, B. E., Gaedecke, T., & Robinson, K. (2022). Disabled trans sex working college students: Results from the 2015 US Trans Survey. *Disability Studies Quarterly, 42*(2). https://dsq-sds.org/index.php/dsq/article/view/9134/7748

Crenshaw, K. (1989). Demarginalizing the intersection of race and sex: A Black feminist critique of antidiscrimination doctrine, feminist theory and antiracist politics. *University of Chicago Legal Forum, 1989*(1), 139–167. http://chicagounbound.uchicago.edu/uclf/vol1989/iss1/8

Denton, J. M., & Abes, E. S. (2022). The art of masked advocacy: The care of the self of gay college men living with HIV. *Journal of College Student Development, 63*(4), 383–398. https://doi.org/10.1353/csd.2022.0033

Harley, D. A., Nowak, T. M., Gassaway, L. J., & Savage, T. A. (2002). Lesbian, gay, bisexual and transgender college students with disabilities: A look at multiple cultural minorities. *Psychology in the Schools, 39*(5), 525–538. https://doi.org/10.1002/pits.10052

Harper, S., Chang, M. J., Cole, E. R., Patton Davis, L., Garces, L. M., Gayles, J. G., Jenkins, T. S., Kimbrough, W. M., Park, J. J., Saenz, V. B., Smith, S. M., & Wolf-Wendel, L. (2024). *Truths about DEI on college campuses: Evidence-based responses to politicized misinformation*. USC Race and Equity Center. https://race.usc.edu/wp-content/uploads/2024/03/Harper-and-Associates-DEI-Truths-Report.pdf

Henry, W. J., Fuerth, K., & Figliozzi, J. (2010). Gay with a disability: A college student's multiple cultural journey. *College Student Journal, 44*(2), 377–388.

Kafer, A. (2013). *Feminist, queer, crip*. Indiana University Press.

Kimball, E., Vaccaro, A., Tissi-Gassoway, N., Bobot, S. D., Newman, B. M., Moore, A., & Troiano, P. F. (2018). Gender, sexuality, & (dis) ability: Queer perspectives on the experiences of students with disabilities. *Disability Studies Quarterly, 38*(2). https://dsq-sds.org/index.php/dsq/article/view/5937/4907

Lange, A. C., & Lee, J. A. (2024). Centering our humanity: Responding to anti-DEI efforts across higher education. *Journal of College Student Development, 65*(1), 113–116. https://doi.org/10.1353/csd.2024.a919356

McRuer, R. (2006). *Crip theory: Cultural signs of queerness and disability*. New York University Press.

Miller, R. A. (2015). "Sometimes you feel invisible": Performing queer/disabled in the university classroom. *The Educational Forum, 79*(4), 377–393. https://doi.org/10.1080/00131725.2015.1068417

Miller, R. A. (2017). "My voice is definitely strongest in online communities": Students using social media for queer and disability identity-making. *Journal of College Student Development, 58*(4), 509–525. https://doi.org/10.1353/csd.2017.0040

Miller, R. A. (2018). Toward intersectional identity perspectives on disability and LGBTQ identities in higher education. *Journal of College Student Development, 59*(3), 327–346. https://doi.org/10.1353/csd.2018.0030

Miller, R. A. (2020). Out of (queer/disabled) time: Temporal experiences of disability and LGBTQ+ identities in US higher education. *Critical Education, 11*(16), 1–20. https://doi.org/10.14288/ce.v11i16.186495

Miller, R. A. (2024, April 5). DEI isn't scary; political purges are. *Inside Higher Ed.* https://www.insidehighered.com/opinion/views/2024/04/05/dei-isnt-scary-political-purges-are-opinion

Miller, R. A., & Downey, M. (2020). Examining the STEM climate for queer students with disabilities. *Journal of Postsecondary Education and Disability*, 33(2), 169–181.

Miller, R. A., & Smith, A. C. (2021). Microaggressions experienced by LGBTQ students with disabilities. *Journal of Student Affairs Research and Practice*, 58(5), 491–506. https://doi.org/10.1080/19496591.2020.1835669

Miller, R. A., Dika, S. L., Nguyen, D. J., Woodford, M., & Renn, K. A. (2021). LGBTQ+ college students with disabilities: Demographic profile and perceptions of well-being. *Journal of LGBT Youth*, 18(1), 60–77. https://doi.org/10.1080/19361653.2019.1706686

Miller, R. A., Friedensen, R. E., Vaccaro, A., & Kimball, E. W. (in press). The intersectionality of accessibility. In K. C. Aquino & A. Lalor (Eds.), *The new accessibility in higher education*. Oxford University Press.

Miller, R. A., Nachman, B. R., & Wynn, R. (2020). "I feel like they are all interconnected": Understanding the identity management narratives of autistic LGBTQ college students. *College Student Affairs Journal*, 38(1), 1–15. https://doi.org/10.1353/csj.2020.0000

Miller, R. A., Wynn, R. D., & Webb, K. W. (2017). Complicating "coming out": Disclosing disability, gender, and sexuality in higher education. In S. L. Kerschbaum, L. T. Eisenman, & J. M. Jones (Eds.), *Negotiating disability: Disclosure and higher education* (pp. 115–134). University of Michigan Press. https://doi.org/10.3998/mpub.9426902

Miller, R. A., Wynn, R. D., & Webb, K. W. (2019). "This really interesting juggling act": How university students manage disability/queer identity disclosure and visibility. *Journal of Diversity in Higher Education*, 12(4), 307–318. https://doi.org/10.1037/dhe0000083

Miller, R. A., Wynn, R. D., Stare, B. G., Williamson, J. N., & Guo, L. (2022). Mental health and resilience among LGBTQ+ college students with disabilities. *Currents: Journal of Diversity Scholarship for Social Change*, 2(1), 60–80. https://doi.org/10.3998/ncidcurrents.1779

Price, M. (2011). *Mad at school: Rhetorics of mental disability and academic life*. University of Michigan Press.

Shelton, S. Z. (2022). Cripping the insider/outsider paradox: The experiences of a disabled, queer, non-binary Educator. In A. Duran, R. A. Miller, T.J. Jourian, & J. Cisneros (Eds.), *Queerness as being in higher education: Narrating the insider/outsider paradox as LGBTQ+ scholars and practitioners* (pp. 112–120). Routledge.

Sherry, M. (2004). Overlaps and contradictions between queer theory and disability studies. *Disability & Society*, 19(7), 769–783. https://doi.org/10.1080/0968759042000284231

Sherry, M. (2013, November 23). Crip politics? Just... no. *The Feminist Wire*. https://thefeministwire.com/2013/11/crip-politics-just-no/

Underhile, R., & Cowles, J. R. (1998). Gay, lesbian, bisexual, and transgender students with disabilities: Implications for faculty and staff. In R. L. Sanlo (Ed.), *Working with lesbian, gay, bisexual, and transgender college students: A handbook for faculty and administrators* (pp. 267–276). Greenwood Press.

Part III
VISIONS FOR THE FUTURE

· 1 1 ·

SENIOR LEADERS AS TRANS AND QUEER ADVOCATES FOR TQ CENTER(ED) DIVERSITY WORK

Joshua Moon Johnson

Introduction

Informed by a career that involved TQ center(ed) diversity work and that has now reached the point of senior-level leadership, this chapter strives to share insights to senior leaders at higher education institutions on how to best support people in these roles. Specifically, the chapter begins with an examination of why assistance from senior-level administrators is necessary to sustain TQ center(ed) diversity work. Next, it details concrete actions that senior-level professionals can take to aim to engage, advocate, and support TQ efforts at their institutions.

In my nearly twenty-year career, my work in trans and queer (TQ) centers had some of the most impact on students than any other position I have held. My role as a director of an LGBT center was also the hardest job I have ever had. The actual duties in the job description were not the hardest parts. Still, it was the emotional work, the constant surroundings of trauma, and the environmental obstacles that constantly devalued my work and my identities. As a Provost & Vice President of Academic Affairs and previously as a Vice President of Student Affairs at one institution, and a Dean of Equity at another, I continue to stay engaged in TQ campus work, but from a different position, direction, and perspective. My support for TQ students was based on my dedication to justice and love and my reason for being here on Earth, rather than on my position or income. I reflect on my many years of TQ advocacy work in higher education and aim to share insights and perspectives with other senior leaders at higher education institutions.

The Need for Senior Leaders

Most TQ centers report to senior administrators who are often not a part of the trans and/or queer community, and many of those senior administrators have limited understanding of the research, theory, promising practices, or current events affecting TQ people in higher education (Oliveira et al., 2025). When senior leaders do not advocate, whether due to limited knowledge or skill or a lack of interest, there are clear consequences. Most TQ centers began from grassroots organizing, such as student demands, faculty petitions, or sadly, hate, crimes and incidents (Marine, 2011). It is rare that TQ centers begin with senior leaders initiating on their own (Johnson et al., 2022). TQ people at the student level or lower levels of the hierarchy often had to fight to get small centers and limited budgets that currently exist; TQ personnel are exhausted from fighting to exist. When there is no advocacy from senior leaders, the hard work of TQ professionals go unnoticed, dismissed, and devalued. There were many days when I struggled to find hope to continue in my role as an LGBT center director. When senior leaders acknowledge the tangible and emotional work TQ professionals contribute, it supports, encourages, and motivates.

When senior leaders do not understand or advocate for TQ professionals and their work, it contributes to challenges with funding, staffing, policy change, and high turnover rates. It is a challenge for senior leaders to be able to advocate if they do not know the details of the challenges, the goals of the center or program, or even the terms and identities of the students being discussed. Many TQ center's potential is limited because senior leaders do not understand enough to remove barriers, change policies, and transform institutions. A director of a TQ center is rarely at the table making major decisions that impact TQ people. LGBT centers have been around for over five decades now, but sadly, much of the conversation remains the same. Some amazing progress has been made, but there is so much further to go. Over the last decade, many smaller institutions and community colleges have added TQ centers, services, and programs (Johnson et al., 2022). Institutional and societal transformation is happening, but it can happen faster and with less negative impact on TQ professionals with the support and advocacy of senior leaders in higher education.

Senior leaders and supervisors of TQ center professionals often have limited knowledge and skills on how to support the whole person (Pryor & Hoffman, 2021; Catalano & Tillapaugh, 2020). Working in a TQ center and other identity-based centers is a job, but it is also deeply personal. The types of supervision needed are different than supervising a professional whose work is not directly connected to oppressed groups. TQ faculty and staff report experiencing microaggressions, tokenization, exclusive environments, and even harassment in their jobs (Aguilar & Johnson, 2017). Additionally, the UCLA Williams Institute found that 46 % of LGBT workers have experienced unfair treatment, and 38 % have reported harassment at work (Sears et al., 2021). Many senior leaders and supervisors are not prepared to address the impact it has on their employees, and institutions are often not set up with adequate responses to prevent and address hate and bias incidents impacting TQ employees. Justice work and efforts are frequently only seen at the macro-level, but with supervisory relationships, justice work should also happen at the micro-level (Brown et al., 2019).

Avoiding Identity-Neutral Approaches

As senior leaders engage in identity, equity, and justice work, we must be cognizant of all our identities, including sexual identities and gender identities. To engage in identity-conscious work, one must consider relationships with self and others (Brown et al., 2019). Senior leaders (e.g., deans, vice presidents, presidents, etc.) must be aware of their identities, specifically their privileged sexual identities, such as being heterosexual, and their privileged gender identities and expression, such as being cisgender and gender-conforming. My multiple identities continue to impact my role and experience as a senior leader. I am often quickly assessed and perceived to be queer and gender nonconforming on my campus, which then people may expect me to automatically aim to support the work of LGBTQ+ centers, committees, clubs, and/or task forces. I do continue to find ways to advocate and support LGBTQ+ communities at my institutions, even if, at times, it is tokenizing and additional labor. Nonetheless, I issue a challenge to senior leaders who do not identify within TQ communities: find methods to demonstrate, promote, and assist the TQ work being done at your organization. The majority of senior leaders are heterosexual and cisgender and must use their positionality and power to continue to transform their institutions.

Before any of us are our titled roles, we are individual people with complex identities, that come with a voice, power, decision-making abilities, trauma, marginality, exclusion, discrimination, and even at times hatred. For anyone, especially as a senior leader, to be an effective social justice change agent, engaging in social justice and equity work must be personal and include self-awareness and individual identity exploration. Engaging in equity work for one's community comes with its own set of challenges, such as tokenization, re-engaging in past trauma, feeling like you are not doing enough, and always being the spokesperson for a specific population(s). I also note that just because a senior leader is a part of the trans and queer community does not mean they have knowledge or skills to advocate. Engaging in equity work for a marginalized community also comes with challenges, such as limited knowledge of that population, no personal experience, and limited trust. When examining how senior leaders fit into the trans and queer community, it is critical to acknowledge the diversity and power-differentials within the community. Most senior leaders in higher education who are in the trans and queer community are White, non-disabled, cisgender, and gender-conforming, meaning there is limited personal experience advocating for transgender, gender non-conforming, BIPOC, disabled people in addition to other intersecting identities within the LGBTQ+ community.

Moving into Action

As senior leaders aim to engage, advocate, and support TQ efforts at their institutions, I share the following recommendations and requests:

Take an Intersectional Social Justice Approach

Advocating for TQ populations does not mean they should be prioritized over other marginalized populations. The goal should be to transform the institution to move it away from centering historically dominant populations, making it more accessible, welcoming, and affirming to TQ students, disabled students, BIPOC students, poor students, undocumented students, and others who have been historically excluded. There is much diversity of experience within TQ communities and there is not a monolithic experience or needs. TQ folks are often overrepresented in experiencing other forms of traumas, such as food and housing insecurity. According to Goldrick-Rab (2019) LGBTQ+ students need basic needs support at higher rates than cisgender and heterosexual students. Additionally, LGBTQ+ youth have far higher rates of being in the foster care system (Baams et al., 2019). Many senior leaders make personal efforts to advocate for populations they are a part of and ignore other marginalized populations. Senior leaders should ensure they question the motivation and goals for their advocacy work; they should ask themselves if they are advocating only due to personal attachment to a community or experience, or because the societal and institutional challenge is reinforcing inequities and injustices to a marginalized population. People in power advocating for their marginalized community may have the ultimate goal of that group having the same power as other dominant groups, so they can have the same power to dominate others. The level of advocacy extended to one's own marginalized communities must also extend to other groups one is not a part of. The goal is liberation and justice, not the ability to oppress others.

Respect Grassroots Efforts

Much of the foundation work that has occurred in higher education came out of grassroots movements where students and marginalized employees spent countless unpaid hours begging to be seen, supported, and protected. Many of the LGBTQ+ employees spent many unpaid hours comforting, listening, loving, and supporting TQ students to not only keep them enrolled in school but also to keep them alive. As senior leaders aim to join TQ institutional efforts, it must be done first with listening, learning, and in coalition with the community. As one who is at a table where decisions are being made, TQ issues should be named and included in decision-making. As policies are being crafted and resources are being allocated, trans and queer students should be named. As research about retention rates and sense of belonging are being discussed, trans and queer issues should be inserted and included in equity plans. As a senior leader, create a space for those who have been doing the grassroots work to have a seat at the table where decisions are being made.

Keep Learning

Senior leaders, within and outside of TQ communities, must commit to learning about trans and queer issues in higher education and focus on learning skills to put that learning into action. I fully appreciate cultural humility and acknowledging a lack of knowledge, but that does not mean it is acceptable to stay there. Action without knowledge can be harmful. Many senior leaders will engage in research and data involving TQ students, and I challenge senior leaders to also learn about TQ employee issues. TQ employees face microaggressions, limited support and mentorship, heteronormative and cisnormative environments, and high turnover (Aguilar & Johnson, 2017). Senior leaders and anyone supervising must learn how to support, hire, develop, and protect their TQ employees. Identity-conscious supervision is critical to support employee wholeness, well-being, and a positive work environment (Brown et al., 2019). Having more TQ employees benefit students as they have more educators who have an understanding of their identities and have shared lived experiences. TQ employees, as well as other marginalized employees, have developed skills and assets as they have successfully overcome obstacles in higher education and achieved. The goal is not to hire historically excluded employees to show diversity of employees, but because those employees bring additional strengths that others may not. Moreover, hire, support, develop, and mentor LGBTQ+ people. Ensure hiring practices include education about TQ employees and bias they often face in hiring processes. Create and provide resources to trans and queer prospective and current employees, such as how to change name and gender in institutional systems and the protection they should be receiving. Ensure there are spaces, such as employee resource groups, for trans and queer employees to find community and peer support. Finally, as a supervisor, learn the basics of their identities and be prepared to support, protect, and advocate for them. Even if the institution as a whole is unsafe for TQ employees, a knowledgable and supportive supervisor goes a long way.

Ask What Is Needed

Many times, new efforts to support marginalized populations begin because of demands, protests, and a crisis incident. Instead of waiting for TQ students or employee groups to demand visibility, services, support, protection, or a center, engage with them and ask them what they need to be supported and successful at the institution. Show up at their events and meetings—check first to ensure it is the right time and space—and begin to build trust. As groups know your intentions and motivations, pay attention to needs they are discussing and find ways to connect the groups to resources and decision makers. As you realize there are overlaps in needs related to institution wide efforts, share with trans and queer groups to ensure they are included. As diversity and inclusion efforts are occurring and data is being gathered, ask the TQ groups if they want to be a part of those efforts.

Broaden DEI Efforts and Plans

Many institutions now have diversity, equity, and inclusion plans, strategies, and efforts. Many times, these are also simply focused on race. Yes, racism is something that should be combatted, focused on, and even centered; however, TQ issues must also be included in institutional DEI efforts and budget allocations. DEI efforts should be encouraged to be collaborative and intersectional and avoid creating divisiveness and competition between marginalized communities.

Senior leaders can also be effective by supporting and initiating LGBTQ+ specific professional development. Push for other leaders at the institution to further their understanding of LGBTQ+ issues. Most senior leaders have teams of people reporting to them. Incorporate social justice and LGBTQ+ justice training into new employee onboarding and regular meetings and retreats.

In many parts of the U.S. and globally, DEI efforts and trans and queer issues continue to be opposed and, in some places, opposed with more intensity. Strategies often must shift; however, advocacy for justice does not have to shift. Senior leaders can still include various marginalized groups into conversations and plans related to retention efforts, mental health initiatives, basic needs efforts, and conversations around safety. As institutions discuss more politically neutral efforts, there can still be research, plans, and funding focused on populations that experience lower retention rates, higher mental health crises, and more violence in higher education.

Cross-Institution Connections

Many institutions have one or a few employees pushing for TQ advocacy. It is critical to continue to build broader networks of people doing TQ work in various roles. Senior leaders often have broader working relationships with people across the institution. Senior leaders can often be helpful with getting support from facilities, student conduct, counseling, IT, and other areas critical to shaping how TQ employees and students experience the institution.

Institutionalize

Senior leaders may move on quickly, but even if they are in a place for a few years, they can make long-term institutional changes. Grassroots efforts are necessary and have laid the foundation for much great work combating trans oppression and heterosexism or cisnormativity and heteronormativity, but institutionalizing budgets, policies, positions, spaces, scholarships, and others can be critical. As senior leaders, we are often at the tables and understand how to navigate complex higher education systems. One of the most significant acts can be institutionalizing a gender-inclusive bathroom policy, creating a new housing policy, or creating a comprehensive bias response protocol. Engage with the TQ professionals and groups and ask what initiatives might need support getting embedded into the institution's fabric, structure, and culture.

Some Personal Action

Beyond the institutional and structural actions senior leaders can take, there are some specific ways senior leaders can personally support TQ centered work.

Show Up

Being visible and attending events such as Lavender Graduation, orientation and welcome events, social and educational events, and meetings mean something. Even if a senior leader just has their lunch in the TQ Center once a month, it shows that one cares and is willing to be present. If the senior leader is not a part of the LGBTQ+ community, be mindful to check in with the staff and ensure it is not a closed-community event or space.

Take Risks

Be willing to take risks. Senior leaders who are typically at-will employees try to minimize risks and protect themselves; however, this also minimizes their ability to create change. I do not encourage anyone to take unnecessary risks or jeopardize their livelihoods, but seeking true change will come with risks. One risk that TQ senior leaders can take is being open about their gender and sexual identities. According to the UCLA Williams Institute, more than 50 % of LGBTQ+ employees are not out at work (Sears et al., 2021). When students and employees within the institution see a visible trans and/or queer community member in leadership, that creates a sense of visibility and can help others know that there are many possibilities for people with similar identities and lived experiences. Senior leaders can also model authenticity in their identities for their holistic identity wellness, but that also opens up space for students and other employees to embrace all of their identities in name, pronouns, clothing, hairstyle, partners, and other parts of their gender and sexual identities.

Senior leaders can also model what accountability looks like by challenging microaggressions, and non-inclusive policies, and publicly holding the institution accountable. It can be risky and even push someone to seem difficult to work with, but change rarely happens when no one holds people and organizations accountable. Also, if a senior leader makes a mistake in public by reinforcing cisnormativity and/or heteronormativity, they could model self-accountability and vulnerability by acknowledging the harm they did and correcting it moving forward.

Role Model

Senior leaders can use their platforms to model using pronouns, informing others why one uses pronouns, and even build pronoun usage into the institutional culture, such as putting them on business cards, email signatures, name tags, and websites, and using them in introductions. Senior leaders are often speaking at major events such as commencements, convocations, and awards ceremonies, and they can begin their introductions with their pronouns and include it in the programs and agendas.

Many institutions I have worked at did not include or welcome vulnerability, grace, and humility in the institutional culture. I hope that senior leaders could model when they make a mistake, exclude a community such as trans and queer people, or display a limitation in their knowledge. Senior leaders have opportunities to role model how to "mess up," acknowledge harm, learn and do better in the future. When senior leaders take the risk of role modeling lifelong learning, vulnerability, and humility, it shifts a culture and allows others space to engage in hard conversations and to grow.

Public Relations Champion

Senior leaders are often in spaces where they are visible and heard at much higher rates than others in the organization. These leaders can use their time to acknowledge the work and accomplishments of the TQ Center. TQ center work should be a part of updates, announcements, and annual reports. The senior leader must connect the work of the LGBTQ+ Center to institutional strategic efforts. Too often, DEI efforts and especially TQ work is seen as less relevant and tertiary to institutional strategic priorities. TQ work and work to support all marginalized communities should be centered in institutional re-designs and transformations.

Show Up with Love

Institutions often have vital metrics such as graduation rates, retention rates, and/or funds secured, which are all important. However, in the end, TQ advocacy is an act of love, and as people, community members, educators, and leaders, this work must be grounded in love. As leaders and institutions, we love our TQ students and employees as complete and whole people, and we love them enough to protect them, celebrate, and support them. Loving our TQ community members means we want them to feel that the institution is their home and the space where they belong.

As a senior leader who has been in various roles, including working full-time in a trans and queer center, the challenge of transforming an institution and including many marginalized communities is hard work. One of the primary reasons I chose to seek senior administrator roles is to have the ability to advocate for marginalized communities and to transform educational systems to be more justice focused. When I am in positions to take risks and create change, I remind myself why I wanted a seat at the table. Taking risk in the name of love and justice must be at the center every day. If I am granted the power to make decisions that impact others' lives, I must be prepared to understand marginalized communities needs and experiences, in this case trans and queer peoples', and I must be prepared to do something. Even if I cannot sustain a title or my own well-being for a lengthy tenure, I aim to leave an institution in a better place than I found it. Senior leaders must continue to learn about TQ students, employees, and the institutional work that is being done or should be done. I challenge all senior leaders in higher education, to continue to learn, listen, act and love.

References

Aguilar, D., & Moon Johnson, J. (2017). Queer faculty and staff of color: Experiences and expectations. In J. Moon Johnson & G. Javier (Eds.), *Queer people of color in higher education* (pp. 59–73). Information Age Publishing.

Baams, L., Wilson, B. D., & Russell, S. T. (2019). LGBTQ youth in unstable housing and foster care. *Pediatrics, 143*(3), e20174211. https://doi.org/10.1542/peds.2017-4211

Brown, R., Desai, S., & Elliott, C. (2019). *Identity-conscious supervision in student affairs: Building relationships and transforming systems* (1st ed.). Routledge.

Catalano, D. C. J., & Tillapaugh, D. (2020). Identity, role, and oppression: Experiences of LGBTQ resource center graduate assistants. *Journal of Student Affairs Research & Practice, 57*(5), 519–531. https://doi.org/10.1080/19496591.2019.1699104

Goldrick-Rab, S., Baker-Smith, C., Coca, V., & Looker, E. (2019, March). *Realcollege-cccco-report*. https://www.evc.edu/sites/default/files/2022-04/RealCollege-CCCCO-Report.pdf

Marine, S. B. (2011). *Stonewall's legacy: Bisexual, gay, lesbian, and transgender students in higher education*. John Wiley & Sons.

Moon Johnson, J., Mitchell, E., & Watson, L. M. (2022). *Queer & trans advocacy in the community college*. Information Age Publishing.

Oliveira, K. A., González-Siegel, V. A., Feldman, S., Kannan, K., Woods, C., Pryor, J. T., Duran, A., Catalano, D. C. J., & Jourian, T. J. (2025). An autoethnographic exploration of the realities of engaging trans and queer center(ed) diversity work. *Journal of Diversity in Higher Education, 18*(2), 111–122. https://doi.org/10.1037/dhe0000501

Pryor, J. T., & Hoffman, G. D. (2021). "It feels like diversity as usual": Navigating institutional politics as LGBTQ+ professionals. *Journal of Student Affairs Research and Practice, 58*(1), 94–109. https://doi.org/10.1080/19496591.2020.1740717

Sear, B., Mallory, C., Flores, A. R., & Flores, K. J. (2021, September). *LGBTQ people's experiences of workplace discrimination and harassment*. https://williamsinstitute.law.ucla.edu/publications/lgbt-workplace-discrimination/#:~:text=Out%20at%20work%3A%20Many%20LGBT,any%20of%20their%20co%2Dworkers

· 1 2 ·

TQ CENTER(ED) DIVERSITY WORK IN CHALLENGING SOCIOPOLITICAL ENVIRONMENTS

Kathleen Hobson and T.J. Jourian

Introduction

At a time when national and state legislatures and local school boards are wreaking havoc in the lives and livelihoods of TQ people, especially trans people of color and youth, TQ center(ed) diversity work is ever more fundamental and urgent. Living and working in destabilizing conditions, the real-time impact on TQ center(ed) practitioners is still unfolding, leaving practitioners to wrestle with what role, if any, they want to continue to play in higher education. As they reevaluate principles and priorities, many are responding by leveraging existing networks to organize coalitions and build collective power to sustain each other professionally and personally. Contextualized in the current moment and informed through our collective histories, this chapter provides practical and strategic recommendations for TQ center(ed) diversity work in increasingly hostile sociopolitical landscapes. Propelled by critical hope (Duncan-Andrade, 2009), we seek to instill a queer futurity orientation (Muñoz, 2009) that helps us dream new worlds into being.

> The idea that hope alone will transform the world, and action undertaken in that kind of naïveté, is an excellent route to hopelessness, pessimism, and fatalism. But the attempt to do without hope, in the struggle to improve the world, as if that struggle could be reduced to calculated acts alone, or a purely scientific approach, is a frivolous illusion. (Freire, 1997, p. 8)

At a time when national and state legislatures and local school boards are wreaking havoc in the lives and livelihoods of TQ people, especially trans people of color and youth, TQ center(ed) diversity work is ever more fundamental and urgent. Living and working in destabilizing conditions, the real-time impact on TQ center(ed) practitioners is still unfolding, leaving them to wrestle with what role, if any, they want to continue to play in higher education. As TQ center(ed) practitioners reevaluate principles and priorities, many are responding by leveraging existing networks to organize coalitions and build collective power to sustain each other professionally and personally.

It is in this volatile and constantly shifting context that we offer this chapter as a proposal for critical hope (Duncan-Andrade, 2009), a concept built on Freire's (1997) pedagogy of hope, as exemplified in our opening quote. We situate critical hope within "queerness [as] essentially a rejection of the here and now and an insistence on potentiality for another world" (Muñoz, 1999/2009, p. 1). While we feel the harrowing and grave nature of the world(s) we live and work in, we also know and have experienced the resolve of diversity workers to transform institutions, or at least a corner of them. "But we still have to survive the institutions we are trying to transform" (Ahmed, 2019, p. 189), and thus we embed the collective survival of trans and queer people within resistance strategies.

After explicating our framework, we take a snapshot of the current sociocultural and sociopolitical moment, knowing that by the time this lands with readers, much has likely changed. Then, we summarize the ways administrations have responded/reacted thus far to legislation targeting diversity, equity, and inclusion (DEI) initiatives broadly and gender and sexuality matters specifically, as well as the impact on TQ center(ed) diversity workers navigating increasingly hostile sociopolitical landscapes. With critical hope and queer futurity informing our approach, we provide resistance strategies TQ center(ed) diversity workers may consider.

Framework

Propelling Duncan-Andrade's (2009) concept of critical hope, we seek to instill a queer futurity orientation to help us dream new worlds into being (Muñoz, 1999/2009). Critical hope is particularly apt, as Duncan-Andrade (2009) conceived it through the narratives of educators in underserved and marginalized communities. These educators nurtured the moral outrage of the youth they worked with into "actions that relieve the undeserved suffering in their communities" and by developing "a transgenerational capacity for long-term, sustainable, critical hope" (p. 182).

Critical hope is a potent alternative to both the despair of hopelessness and the deactivating nature of what Duncan-Andrade (2009) deemed as false hope. He described false hope as hokey, mythical, and deferred. False hope propagates assimilation to injustice and the myth of meritocracy, is "profoundly ahistorical and depoliticized" (p. 184), and does not manifest transformative action or projects.

In comparison, critical hope demands a committed and active struggle against personal despair and for collective liberation. Based on Tupac Shakur's (1999) metaphor of "the rose that grew from concrete" (p. 3), three elements comprise Duncan-Andrade's (2009) critical hope. *Material hope* tempers the realities of oppression by acknowledging that "there are always cracks in the concrete" (p. 186), such as resources and networks, giving marginalized people agency. Through trusting relationships and risk-taking, *Socratic hope* is "the courage to pursue the painful path of bursting through those jagged cracks in the concrete" (p. 186). Centering solidarity with the oppressed, *audacious hope* "defies the dominant ideology of defense, entitlement, and preservation of privileged bodies at the expense of the policing, disposal, and dispossession of marginalized 'others'" (p. 190).

Hope is central to Muñoz's (1999/2009) methodology of queer futurity as "a backward glance that enacts a future vision" (p. 4). Resisting either romanticizing the past or using it as a doomsday prognosticator, he offers "a theory of queer futurity that is attentive to the past for the purposes of critiquing a present" (p. 18). Hope also allows us "to know our queerness as a belonging in a particularity that is not dictated or organized around the spirit of political impasse that characterizes the present" (p. 28). Acknowledging that it can be hard to envision that which we have never seen, Muñoz reminds us that "to access queer visuality we may need to squint, to strain our vision and force it to see otherwise, beyond the limited vista of the here and now" (p. 22). Not to be satisfied by "mere inclusion in a corrupt and bankrupt social order" through assimilationist and homonormative politics, Muñoz (1999/2009) insists on "an understanding of queerness as collectivity" (p. 11) and positions "queer feminist and queer of color critiques [as] the powerful counterweight to the antirelational" (p. 17).

The Political Landscape

To enact a critically hopeful queer future, we must understand the present political landscape. With the end of quarantining in fall 2021, practitioners returned to a higher education landscape that the murder of George Floyd and the subsequent nationwide protests had galvanized. In response, university leaders disseminated statements, espousing institutional commitments to diversity and anti-racism (Connors & McCoy, 2022). There was a renewed energy in DEI programs and training, and administrations created councils and task forces to help embed DEI into both academic and co-curricular education (Pride, 2022). Despite rolling out robust DEI agendas, campuses started hemorrhaging practitioners (Morales, 2022). "While navigating the COVID-19 pandemic, some leaders...placed political ideology and enrollment numbers ahead of the health and welfare of those working on campus, and faculty and staff [were] fed up" (Ellis, 2021, as cited in Morales, 2022, par. 4). The pandemic forced practitioners to reevaluate priorities and examine their value in the estimation of their institution. Some left for the competitive pay that their campuses could not match, others for the accessibility and flexibility that working from home provided. Those engaging in DEI work had to weigh continuing to put in substantially more than 40-hour work weeks and relatively little work-life balance against these alternatives.

A nationwide, higher education focus on DEI was in stark contrast to the rise in campus hate speech and acts, explicitly far-right events such as the Unite the Right Rally at the University of Virginia in Charlottesville that occurred pre-pandemic (Kirk & Lepadatu, 2023). The DEI momentum caught the attention of conservative politicians at state and federal levels, who interpreted DEI as an attack on the foothold that the alt-right started to gain with Donald Trump's election. The once theoretical legislation that threatened the diversity work of TQ centers, started to take root and become a reality. Colleges and universities, in addition to K-12 schools, faced an explosion of proposed bills that targeted critical race theory, all-gender bathrooms, drag shows and performers, trans athletes, and ultimately, any identity-related work (ACLU, 2024; UCLA School of Law Critical Race Studies Program, 2024). The higher education-specific legislation targeted DEI practitioners and most doggedly pursued the elimination of offices and positions that educated and advocated for equity around race ethnicity, gender identity, and sexuality.

In 2023, as anti-DEI legislation gained traction, there was a shift away from the staunch commitment to DEI administrators had championed less than two years earlier. Collusion with anti-DEI legislators became evident as administrators downplayed the impacts that anti-DEI legislation would have on their campuses (McGee, 2023). Prioritizing funding over advocating for their students, administrators "tried to toe the political line between the competing visions for higher education among state leaders" (McGee, 2023, para. 37). With post-quarantine campus climates already proving difficult to navigate, TQ center(ed) practitioners had to reflect on the risks of staying in these vulnerable positions. Though TQ centers across the country felt the sting of proposed legislation, by early 2024, North Carolina, North Dakota, Tennessee, and Utah each had one anti-DEI bill signed into law, while Texas and Florida had multiple (Chronicle Staff, 2024).

Institutional Responses

Texas' Senate Bill 17 (SB 17) and Florida's Senate Bill 266 (SB 266) shared many of the same restrictions for public universities, including but not limited to the elimination of DEI offices, administrative positions and appointments, programs, mandatory training, and required candidate statements during hiring (Feder, 2024). Following their passage, public universities' general counsels and upper level administrators set about interpreting the implications of these bills. Practitioners responsible for doing DEI work had little, if any, input or control in this process or the subsequent decisions about the work moving forward. Although general counsels and administrators at different institutions conferred with each other, each campus was ultimately on their own in interpreting and enforcing the bills. A lack of understanding in how to interpret the policies led to a lack of consistency in the application of bills, even within the same state (Lu, 2023).

On some campuses, fear of non-compliance led to overcompliance and an unwillingness to explore how to support students' identities with the spirit of affirmation and visibility they had before (Hicks, 2024). Some campuses acted prematurely, eliminating offices months in advance of the required compliance date and laying off staff without attempting to transition them to new roles. For example, the University of Missouri at Columbia, dissolved the Division for Inclusion, Diversity and Equity and removed its vice chancellor, to pre-empt any legislative actions and convince conservative legislators to preserve institutional funding (Knox, 2024). Others allowed offices, staff, and programming to continue until laws went into effect, creating a false sense of hope that DEI offices would somehow emerge unscathed. Whether laid off or moved into different spaces, TQ center(ed) diversity workers received news about center shut-downs and employment changes only hours before the rest of the campus and without guidance on how to respond to the campus community's questions. Practitioners were expected to continue to support students and provide stability, while often receiving little transparency and support themselves.

Some campuses explored new ways to package student support, while staying in compliance, many leaning into name changes that included innocuous words like "engagement," "belonging," "excellence," "support," and "community" (Alonso, 2024). Practitioners had to determine how to generate programming that helped create a sense of belonging, while avoiding identity and not duplicating programming that existed elsewhere on campus. Despite legislation banning programming based on race, ethnicity, gender identity, and sexuality, some general counsels established that the new student support centers were allowed to focus on federally recognized history and heritage months, such as Black History Month, Asian Pacific American Heritage Month, and Hispanic Heritage Month. However, not all campuses included Pride Month, also federally recognized, in their identity-based recognition months, leaving students without university-sponsored TQ focused programming (Lu, 2023). University-recognized, identity-based student organizations were allowed to take on programming formerly done by staff. While this theoretically allowed for important TQ programming, it also pressured students and staff to provide unpaid labor to fundraise, plan, and execute these events.

Personal Impacts and Navigating the Landscape

More often than not, TQ center(ed) diversity workers get into the work because of the connection to their identities, their passion for serving trans and queer students, and their intentions to improve equity and inclusion for those students (Lamb, 2021). TQ center(ed) diversity workers have a chance to pay it forward, to provide the same affirming experiences they had, or create spaces and communities they never had access to. Dr. Gisela Vega, director at the University of Miami LGBTQ Center, expressed that her "...mission is to help students not only get involved but to experience belonging. As someone who was ostracized for my own sexual identity, I work to ensure other students do not feel like that" (Edmead, 2022, para. 9). TQ center(ed) diversity workers understand the excitement and fear in unearthing identity, the magic of wearing a dress or a binder for the first time, and the beauty of chosen family. They understand what an honor and a gift it is to travel beside a student on their path of discovery, and support and guide along the way. Their drive and dedication to working long hours and occasionally making personal sacrifices, are rewarded by the connections they form with students and the life-changing, sometimes life-saving, impacts they witness. TQ centered(ed) diversity workers recognize that "...the ability to play a part in that is not something everyone gets to do in the course of their life" (untunion, 2023, para. 5).

When rumors began circulating regarding bills that threatened TQ centers and support roles, it seemed unlikely that they would survive floor debates and votes. Conservative politicians often threaten extreme legislation against TQ people and spaces, much of which does not come to fruition. Conservative states had seen movement on legislation regarding trans minors and K-12 education, but it seemed improbable that these new bills would hold up in restricting funding, programming, offices, and jobs in higher education. It was hard to imagine a collegiate landscape in which such a substantial step backward could be taken. When the bills came to pass in multiple states, there was a crushing sense of shock and surreality. The delays in response and lack of preparation by campus administrations only added to the state of limbo in which TQ center(ed) practitioners found themselves.

Some TQ center(ed) practitioners left their roles soon before or after legislation passed, having to provide for family or tend to their own mental health, not having the option to exist in uncertainty. Others were fired and not given the chance to work in adjacent roles on campus. Regardless of whether they were fired immediately or several months down the line, a lack of reciprocal communication and care for the staff who had poured so much into their jobs and students, seemed to be a common thread across campuses. One laid-off practitioner stated, "What struck me was the audacity of the disrespect...Some people had been there for 20 years, and in 10 minutes they were gone" (Mangan, 2024, para. 7).

For Texas in particular, campuses had more than six months to prepare, from the moment SB-17 was signed into law, until the time it went into effect on January 1, 2024. Despite the time to plan, campus administrations seemed no better prepared on and after January 1, and "highly redacted correspondences among campus leaders obtained through open-records requests revealed a frantic attempt to shift gears" (Mangan, 2024, para. 9). At the University of Texas at Austin and the University of North Texas, communication to students about the upcoming changes was sparse and happened near or during finals week in December, when students were absorbed with exams or already off-campus, less likely to be checking their email (Alonso, 2023). At the University of North Texas, after being told in July that they would be included in the conversations about the transition of their offices, and that they should be grateful for such inclusion, employees at the Multicultural Center and Pride Alliance did not hear from administration again until December; at that point, employees were told the offices were closing and they would be demoted and moved to new offices (Alonso, 2023).

For the former TQ center(ed) staff members who were still employed in more generic titles and spaces, it became crucial to determine if they wanted to stay in their new roles, and if so, for how long. Though they still had jobs, the work looked nothing like what they signed up for. Florida State University "quietly dismantled its DEI office. The university changed title names and reclassified positions to give employees different roles...A position at FSU formerly titled Equity, Diversity and Inclusion Specialist has been repurposed and renamed as 'Compliance Specialist.' The position now focuses on compliance and engagement since the DEI duties have been removed" (Plaza & Barry, 2024, paras. 20–21). Former TQ center(ed) practitioners were asked to dismantle the spaces they helped build and that had been their passion, and for some, their life's work. They were asked to toe the company line and assure students that though the campus would comply with the laws, the administration cared about the students and they would still be committed to supporting them while the "restructuring" took place. That level of commitment and care translated to shoddily crafted titles and spaces, no clear communication to students, and little guidance on how staff were expected to comfort students, while receiving no support themselves and undergoing one of the hardest, if not *the* hardest and most taxing time of their professional careers.

The reason that TQ center(ed) practitioners are called to their roles, is the very reason the legislation was such a blow. The attacks on TQ spaces, programming, and funding are attacks on the existence of TQ students and educators. When one's identities are also their work, the pain, anger, grief, and despair cannot simply be left at the office for the evening and picked up the next day. In the midst of this fight, the personal cannot be separated from the professional. TQ center(ed) practitioners alongside students were... are, grieving immeasurable loss. They were placed in the impossible position of weighing self-preservation against staying to care for students, and determining if those two things could co-exist. Many found themselves asking this question: How do we move forward, how do we provide support to students, when simply existing feels like the hardest task we have the capacity to undertake?

Activism and Resistance Strategies

In the face of the aforementioned institutional responses, predominantly ranging from lukewarm to frigid, TQ center(ed) diversity workers are left to make sense of their more-unstable-than-usual realities and fend for themselves. They have not been entirely alone, as some students, faculty, professional associations, and community members are also responding to the legislative and institutional undoing of diversity work and spaces. In the case of students, the lack of communication from administrators and consistency across institutions has led to confusion on how to act and towards whom to direct the action. Additionally, often institutional leaders made final decisions behind closed doors without student input and put out announcements close to finals or while students were away to disempower student organizing.

Even so, it is important to highlight what students have done, such as Rice University students creating space for TQ University of Houston students after UH shuttered their LGBTQ+ Resource Center and Center for Diversity and Inclusion (Alonso, 2023; Ketterer, 2023), protesting (e.g., University of Texas at Arlington), publicly stating they will take their tuition dollars elsewhere (e.g., University of Central Florida), launching publications (e.g., Florida Atlantic University), and putting on regular programming with alternative titles (e.g., calling FAU's annual drag show "Owl Manor") (Pappano, 2024; Salinas, 2024).

Faculty have focused primarily on resisting the dismantling of academic freedom and the elimination of courses or entire academic programs, while some administrators are coordinating efforts. Delta College president Michael H. Gavin, who coalesced Education for All, a group of about 175 higher education leaders, found it imperative not to "get tricked into this notion that we have to somehow be quiet about things that are right in our domain" (Pappano, 2024, para. 26), like curriculum restrictions and book bans. The National Association of Diversity Officers in Higher Education (NADOHE, 2024) put out statements and resources supporting diversity workers. However, with few exceptions, the silence and complacency of many administrators and professional associations has been overwhelming (or rather underwhelming).

Staff often have less institutional power than students, faculty, and administrators to mount public expressions of dissent. Throughout the upheaval, staff at various institutions have remained anonymous in their commentary, due to fear of retaliation from administration (Alonso, 2023; Mangan, 2024). The lack of protections like tenure or unions, coupled with the prospect of financial precarity during a time of dramatically rising cost of living, make many unwilling and/or unable to be vocal. Others have left higher education entirely, opting for employment in nonprofits and the private sector, as well as self-employment and the gig economy[1]. That does not mean they are not resisting; rather, for many, their resistance has focused inward, networking and organizing within the community, as is known to the authors anecdotally. This has included:

- Building support systems with other TQ center(ed) diversity workers experiencing or anticipating similar impacts;
- Providing each other with emotional and strategic support, including sharing how offices at different campuses are managing forced restructuring and downsizing;
- Partnering with other identity-based centers and broader diversity and multicultural centers to work in solidarity; and
- Remembering that TQ people's existence on campuses did not start with TQ Centers, referencing histories of resistance and community-building, such as Stonewall (Baumann & White, 2019), ACT UP (Schulman, 2021), and ballroom (Tucker, 2022), all of which happened or originated during times of legislative, rhetorical, and institutional repression.

These efforts have been more possible and easier to access where coalitional and multi-identity work had already been done (within and across institutions) prior to legislative attacks. It is a reminder that TQ people, especially TQ people of color, have needed to stay vigilant and not allow institutionalization to presume permanence or stability. Furthermore, these strategies have included those engaging in TQ center(ed) diversity work outside of center spaces, including institutions already without centers, where the work continues to happen. The downside of under-the-radar organizing is that the narratives and perspectives of staff themselves are currently missing in the public domain.

In this section, we offer a variety of strategies that practitioners have and can adopt as they seek to navigate and/or resist their current realities. We do not presume to know which of these will be the right ones for different practitioners, as strategizing requires (1) evaluation of specific campus and state context, (2) reflecting on goals and objectives (in and outside of campus diversity work), (3) assessment of capacity and resources, including campus and community partners, and (4) ultimately making unenviable decisions about the best path forward. What we can do is offer options that we believe to be in the spirit of critical hope (Duncan-Andrade, 2009) and with an orientation towards queer futurity (Muñoz, 1999/2009). Additionally, we implore *all* TQ center(ed) diversity workers, regardless of geographic and political context, to consider these strategies proactively and prepare themselves for the possibility of facing similar legislative and institutional curtailments.

Queer Joy and Radical Rest as Fundamental

In an interview on Black queer joy, Ashon Crawley described joy as

> a disposition... a kind of mood that one must work daily to affirm and attempt to inhabit... [joy] is not an ephemeral feeling that is fleeting and goes away. It is actually a kind of fundamental recognition that the simplicity of our breath and our being and our becoming is itself celebratory. (Persaud & Crawley, 2022, par. 10)

Centering (collective) queer joy in moments of crisis is a kind of refusal to accept the "politics of violent visibility" that "reify the structures of power that created those material conditions [of trauma and violence] to begin with" (Tristano, 2022, p. 276). Black feminists like Audre Lorde (2006) have long pointed out how joy through pleasure is a source of power, resisting what systems of oppression seek to destroy. It is "energy for change" (pp. 87–88) that can disrupt, engage, instill critical hope, and center our collective and individual humanities. Joy can be a tool for solidarity and coalition building, as the "sharing of joy, whether physical, emotional, psychic, or intellectual, forms a bridge between the sharers which can be the basis for understanding much of what is not shared between them, and lessens the threat of their difference" (Lorde, 2006, p. 89). We offer some suggestions:

- In the maelstrom of legislation annexing our spaces, staying physically, emotionally, and virtually connected to our communities helps keep us

in joy and prevents us from being swallowed by queer despair (koalaty-girl, 2023).
- Pride celebrations in June have always been more than a party. TQ ancestors "demonstrated intersectional and insurgent planning wherein…queer people claimed agency through collectively expressing joy as an act of resistance" (Turesky & Crisman, 2023, p. 1). Temper the rainbow capitalism and dance, march, sing, chant.
- Co-create artistic expression honoring that "queers have [long] been using art to create their own temporal worlds that foster joy and belonging" (Keating, 2024, p. 1).
- Report on TQ people breaking barriers and experiencing wins, lest we focus only on news of devastation and hopelessness.

While joy energizes, rest slows us down to recharge. Capitalism and white supremacy, in their endless and urgent pursuit of productivity, underlie the myth that sleep deprivation and exhaustion are natural outcomes of activism and advocacy work (Hersey, 2022). Considering rest to be political work, Hersey (2022) implores us to "go slow and place intention at the forefront of this disruption" (p. 25). When our bodies are often themselves sites of oppression, particularly for trans and non-binary people, rest allows us to reclaim our bodies as sites of liberation instead. How can we slow down while staying committed to the struggle?

- Use sick days, vacation days, and comp time to focus on rest and recovery. Taking time away from work helps sustain the ability to show up for TQ communities (Johnson & McKenzie, 2022).
- Engage in rest-centered self-care activities, such as meditation, massage, gardening, breathwork, Reiki, yoga, and utilizing physical and mental healthcare when possible (Rest for Resistance, 2024).
- Make an intentional effort to protect your time and peace by setting boundaries with institutions, people, and social media (Shelton, 2024).

It might appear unorthodox or antithetical for us to start with joy and rest or to set them up as the foundation for these strategies. Yet, we contend that these *are* forms of resistance in worlds and circumstances that seek to rob us of both joy and rest. When TQ center(ed) diversity workers, as well as students, are in a constant mode of reaction and activation, they may sacrifice joy and rest to fight the good fight. Thus, creating space for joy and rest can be transformative and radical, even more so when that is co-created and/or adopted as collective practice. Employing an ethic of relationality, in essence centering relationships and kinships within these spaces, allows us to consider interconnectedness and responsibilities towards each other, towards all experiencing marginality/ies, as well as towards ourselves.

Community and Political Organizing

For some, the disappointment and sense of betrayal stemming from institutional responses, (mis)statements, and (in)actions may galvanize a desire to get (more) involved politically. Organizing is critical hope in action, as it requires understanding systemic and institutional oppression, as well as insisting that things can and should be different. Here, higher education and student affairs preparatory programs ought to rise to the occasion. Tragically, it is rare for those who come to diversity work through these programs to have learned how to engage in political analysis of higher education that goes beyond campus-based politics.

Part of political organizing is political education, the theory that informs the praxis. Political education develops an understanding of the dynamics of change and the underlying structural problems in political systems and institutions making some vulnerable to exploitation, dehumanization, and violence. An example are the Freedom Schools the civil rights movement spurred to organize Black people through education for social change (Hale, 2018). They inspired Atlanta's Freedom University (2021), which provides free college classes to undocumented youth. Through dialogue, participatory decision-making, and contextualizing individual immigrant narratives through history and broader systems, Freedom University spurs activism among its students and faculty.

Those who wish to organize ought to first take stock of the limitations that laws and policies impose on staff at their respective institutions. This is not to discourage organizing, rather to encourage an intentional and agentic approach, whether or not one decides to work within those limitations or push against/past them. Next, practitioners should identify those who could act as collaborators in organizing. Because TQ communities have a rich history of organizing and community-building as resistance, it is likely that TQ center(ed) diversity workers already have co-conspirators across campus and in the community with shared values. Seeking out statewide and regional coalitions with other TQ center(ed) diversity workers, as well as organizations like Lambda Legal and the American Civil Liberties Union (ACLU), can be sources for creativity and overcoming limitations, particularly for those with legal repercussions. Additionally, there are those unconfined by institutional restrictions and ever-shifting expectations, namely TQ and allied members of the community outside of campus walls. Many among them are also moved to act and may be looking for outlets or have resources and skills to offer. Regardless of who answers the call to join the fight, TQ center(ed) diversity workers must take care to move with a relational lens, prioritizing trust, shared community interests, and collective decision-making (Hurst et al., 2023).

Working with Students

In this current reality, it is hard to argue that doing diversity work on college campuses is *not* political. While some may have already approached this work through a politically-informed lens, working with TQ college students necessitates acknowledging that this too is a political choice.

At least some of the labor of TQ center(ed) diversity workers has begun to shift towards—or indeed back to—(mostly untrained) students, often those already engaged through TQ and other identity/justice-focused organizations. One University of North Texas student shared how "the dissolution of the Pride Alliance and Multicultural Center put a lot of pressure and strain on GLAD [a UNT TQ student organization]... We had to take on a lot more programs and responsibilities that originally would've been done by the Pride Alliance" (Duke, 2024, para. 17). Practitioners can help sustain the work by supporting and working directly with these students. Some of the parameters of this collaboration might be constrained by the specific ways that TQ center(ed) diversity workers' roles have changed and the level of support (or lack thereof) they can rely on from their own supervisors.

A critical point of collaboration is providing space for students, particularly multiply marginalized TQ people, to share grief. In addition to already contending with multiple and intersecting forms of violence and oppression, TQ students of color may also be feeling the impacts of anti-DEI legislation and rhetoric that often zero in on race, frequently steeped in anti-Blackness. These experiences of grief include the trauma that comes with the removal of life-saving spaces and resources, the dashing of dreams and possibilities those spaces allowed them to envision, and the questioning of their abilities to be unapologetically themselves in this climate. With administrators focused so heavily on "moving forward in a positive way" (as some have directed practitioners to do), it is essential to hold space for the reality of these losses. This is also an opportunity to collaborate with trauma-informed mental health practitioners who can responsibly unpack and process these griefs and traumas.

Other ways TQ center(ed) diversity workers can collaborate with students include:

- Providing opportunities for students to slow down and intentionally reflect on if and how they want to engage in this work based on their capacity, as well as academic and other commitments. Part of this necessitates the practitioner's own reflecting and boundary setting, both for self-sustenance and modeling purposes.
- Engaging students in conversation about what activism and resistance look like beyond demonstrations and beyond campus. Highlighting the multiplistic and creative ways that TQ people have historically resisted on and off college campuses as "a backward glance that enacts a future vision" (Muñoz, 1999/2009, p. 4).
- Discussing and modeling critical hope as a framework and practice for diversity work, such as through transparency about what is occurring and the impact on TQ center(ed) diversity workers. However, recognizing the power dynamics between students and staff, we caution against a complete unburdening of oneself onto students, who are already managing their own and their peers' emotions.
- Creating spaces for collective queer joy as previously described.

Pivots and Partnerships

Regardless of how TQ center(ed) diversity workers' roles and responsibilities have shifted, at minimum, practitioners will need to make decisions about how to maximize fewer resources. Prior to this era of legislative undoing of campus diversity work, TQ center(ed) diversity workers were already underresourced (Oliveira et al., 2025), and now the proverbial purse strings are even tighter. We offer the following as prompts towards those decisions:

- What is critical to hold onto and what can be let go of, at least temporarily?
- Where are alternative campus spaces or offices where some programs and/or initiatives can live?

- How can TQ identities still be highlighted outside of specific gender and sexuality programming?
- What campus and community-based partnerships are the most reliable?
- What resources and organizations exist outside of institutional bounds that can supplement or replace existing efforts?
- How can students be connected to possibility models both on and off campus?
- What opportunities exist to build regional and national coalitions?

Making these decisions is not only necessary for the present moment but also for future-proofing. Given how suddenly and repeatedly institutions are shifting in their (over)reactions to anti-DEI legislation, the immediate and long-term futures of TQ center(ed) diversity work and workers remain uncertain. Acknowledging that uncertainty means creating contingency plans both for the work (what can or should it look like if there is further restructuring and elimination of positions) and for the workers themselves. The latter ought to entail a self-inventorying of skills, networks, financial means and limitations, support systems, and possibilities beyond TQ work or higher education. As Dr. Joshua Hamilton, UNT's former director of the Multicultural Center, wrote in his open letter of care institutions are not in the business of caring for Black people, or for that matter, other marginalized students and diversity workers, including TQ and especially TQ people of color (Latinx Hispanic Student Union, 2024). It is OK—and some might argue necessary—not to care for institutions over caring for ourselves and each other.

Conclusion

While this "moment" might stand out for some as a particularly disorienting one, the reality is that TQ people, especially TQ people of color, immigrants, disabled people, and other multiply marginalized TQ people, have collectively resisted and survived lifetimes of these "moments" and continue to. Our histories and present are littered with all manners of violence—colonial, administrative, carceral, sexual, epistemic, physical, rhetorical, legislative—and yet, here we all are. And here we shall remain.

There is also opportunity here. Thinking of a queer future as not yet here (Muñoz, 2009) allows us to dream up new potentialities for what TQ center(ed) diversity work can look like and do, who it centers and serves, who and what it mobilizes, and even where it is done. It beckons a moving away from strictly pragmatic and identitarian politics that limit center work to "just" sexual orientation and gender identity, as if these things can exist outside of the domains of race, class, and disability. And it calls for us to think, and act collectively, in kinships across margins, to move together towards (more) collectivist futures.

Our resistance and survival have been contingent on our willingness to engage in a variety of forms of mutual aid and to abandon notions of institutional saviorism in favor of saving ourselves. Some—including our institutions, supervisors, and colleagues—might be seeking to cast us back into the shadows, but as trans feminine people's refusal to wilt away reminds us, "we also use the shadows as spaces to bloom with each other, to feel and be together" (Nicolazzo, 2021, p. 125). Much like the rose pushing out of concrete, we can face this moment—and the moment after that, and the moment after that—with critical hope and knowledge that it will not outlast us. We can choose to believe and act as if a different world is possible and dream intersectional collectivist queer futures into reality.

Note

1 A gig economy is "a labour market characterised by the prevalence of short-term contracts or freelance work, as opposed to permanent jobs" (Wilson, 2017, par. 2)

References

ACLU. (2024, September 5). *Mapping attacks on LGBTQ rights in U.S. legislatures in 2024*. American Civil Liberties Union. https://www.aclu.org/legislative-attacks-on-lgbtq-rights-2024

Ahmed, S. (2019). *What's the use? On the uses of use*. Duke University Press.

Alonso, J. (2023, August 24). U of Houston closes LGBTQ+ and DEI centers. *Inside Higher Ed*. https://www.insidehighered.com/news/quick-takes/2023/08/24/u-houston-closes-lgbtq-and-dei-centers

Alonso, J. (2023, December 19). Texas colleges prepare for the end of DEI. *Inside Higher Ed*. https://www.insidehighered.com/news/students/diversity/2023/12/19/texas-institutions-prepare-anti-dei-law-go-effect

Alonso, J. (2024, April 10). Are DEI name changes enough? *Inside Higher Ed*. https://www.insidehighered.com/news/government/state-policy/2024/04/10/diversity-office-name-changes-spark-concern-both-sides

Baumann, J., & White, E. (Eds.). (2019). *The stonewall reader*. Penguin Random House

Chronicle Staff. (2024, May 24). DEI legislation tracker: Explore where college diversity, equity, and inclusion efforts are under attack. *The Chronicle of Higher Education.* https://www.chronicle.com/article/here-are-the-states-where-lawmakers-are-seeking-to-ban-colleges-dei-efforts

Connors, I. C., & McCoy, H. (2022). Performing anti-racism: Universities respond to anti-Black violence. *Race and Justice, 12*(3). https://doi.org/10.1177/21533687221101787

Duke, D. (2024, June 4). Former director of multicultural center resigns, publishes open letter denouncing UNT administration. *North Texas Daily.* https://www.ntdaily.com/news/former-director-of-multicultural-center-resigns-publishes-open-letter-denouncing-unt-administration/article_38371a94-22b5-11ef-8251-6b40e9f7a93a.html

Duncan-Andrade, J. M. R. (2009). Note to educators: Hope required when growing roses in concrete. *Harvard Educational Review, 79*(2), 181–194.

Edmead, N. (2022, March 9). LGBTQ student center director continues a streak of excellence. *NEWS@TheU.* https://news.miami.edu/studentaffairs/stories/2022/03/lgbtq-student-center-director-continues-a-streak-of-excellence.html

Ellis, L. (2021, August 25). The great disillusionment: College workers are burning out just when they'll be needed most. *The Chronicle of Higher Education.* https://www.chronicle.com/article/the-great-disillusionment

Feder, T. (2024). State anti-DEI laws sow uncertainty in public colleges and universities. *Physics Today, 77*(4), 22–25. https://doi.org/10.1063/pt.xkpj.fvsv

Freedom University. (2021). *Mission.* https://www.freedom-university.org/mission/

Freire, P. (1997). *Pedagogy of hope.* Continuum.

Hale, J. N. (2018). *Freedom Schools: Student activists in the Mississippi civil rights movement.* Columbia University Press.

Hersey, T. (2022). *Rest is resistance: A manifesto.* Little, Brown Spark.

Hicks, M. (2024, June 21). The new anti-DEI bureaucracy. *The Chronicle of Higher Education.* https://www.chronicle.com/article/the-new-anti-dei-bureaucracy

Hurst, B., Johnston, K. A., & Lane, A. B. (2023). A relational approach to social impact: Moving beyond instrumental and consumer approaches. *Public Relations Review, 49*(1), 102–264. https://doi.org/10.1016/j.pubrev.2022.102264

Johnson, K., & McKenzie, R. (2022, March 25). *Rest as resistance.* National LGBTQ task force. https://www.thetaskforce.org/news/rest-as-resistance/

Keating, A. (2024). *Laughing [until/because] it hurts: Finding time for queer joy and belonging through art and aesthetics* (Publication no. 10309). [Doctoral dissertation, Western University]. Electronic Thesis and Dissertation Repository.

Ketterer, S. (2023, September 1). Rice University students open space to University of Houston LGBTQ population after anti-DEI Law. *Houston Chronicle.* https://www.houstonchronicle.com/news/houston-texas/education/article/rice-lgbtq-uh-anti-dei-law-18338437.php

koalatygirl. (2023, June 28). *Seeking queer joy in times of queer despair.* Word Press. https://alesbianandherlaptop.com/2023/06/28/queer-joy

Kirk, K., & Lepadatu, D. (2023). Campus hate crimes during the Trump era: The rhetoric of conflict during the 2017 unite the right rally at the University of Virginia in Charlottesville. In A. P. Lamberti & A. R. Richards (Eds.), *Academia in conflict: Engaging stakeholders through transformational crisis communication* (pp. 37–64). Palgrave Macmillan. https://doi.org/10.1007/978-3-031-35617-9_3

Knox, L. (2024, July 31). Mizzou dissolves DEI office. *Inside Higher Ed.* https://www.insidehighered.com/news/diversity/race-ethnicity/2024/07/31/u-missouri-axes-dei-office-pre-empt-state-mandate

Lamb, C. (2021). *Well decorated, but still a closet: The lived experiences of LGBT center professionals in higher education* [Doctoral dissertation, The University of Texas at Austin]. Texas ScholarWorks.

Latinx Hispanic Student Union [@untlhsu]. (2024, May 18). *Letter of care from former director of the Multicultural Center at UNT, LHSU & BSU advisor.* https://www.instagram.com/p/C7HmpyWLVGZ/

Lorde, A. (2006). The uses of the erotic: The erotic as power. In K. E. Lovaas & M. M. Jenkins (Eds.), *Sexualities and communication in everyday life: A reader* (pp. 87–91). Sage.

Lu, A. (2023, November 17). Are public colleges in Texas still allowed to celebrate Pride month? Depends on who you ask. *The Chronicle of Higher Education.* https://www.chronicle.com/article/are-public-colleges-in-texas-still-allowed-to-celebrate-pride-month-depends-who-you-ask

Mangan, K. (2024, June 27). "A slap in the face": How UT-Austin axed a DEI division. *The Chronicle of Higher Education.* https://www.chronicle.com/article/a-slap-in-the-face-how-ut-austin-axed-a-dei-division

Morales, A. (2022, June 17). *Take this job and (change) it: The great resignation in higher education.* NASPA. https://www.naspa.org/blog/take-this-job-and-change-it-the-great-resignation-in-higher-education

McGee, K. (2023, May 10). House signals readiness to fight Senate over bills to ban tenure, diversity efforts at Texas universities. *Texas Tribune.* https://www.texastribune.org/2023/05/10/texas-house-tenure-dei-bills/

Muñoz, J. E., with Chambers-Letson, J., Nyong'o, T., & Pellegrini, A. (2009). *Cruising Utopia: The then and there of queer futurity* (10th anniversary ed.). NYU Press. (Original work published 1999).

NADOHE. (2024). *Navigating barriers to equity: Resources for NADOHE members.* NADOHE. https://www.nadohe.org/stories/legislation-resources

Nicolazzo, Z. (2021). Ghost stories from the academy: A trans feminine reckoning. *Review of Higher Education, 45*(2), 125–148. https://doi.org/10.1353/rhe.2021.0018

Oliveira, K. A., Gonzalez-Siegel, V. A., Feldman, S., Kannan, K., Woods, C., Pryor, J. T., Duran, A., Catalano, D. C. J., & Jourian, T. J. (2025). An autoethnographic exploration of the realities of engaging in TQ center(ed) diversity work. *Journal of Diversity in Higher Education, 18*(2), 111–122. https://doi.org/10.1037/dhe0000501

Pappano, L. (2024, May 5). Meet the campus leaders fighting back against right-wing anti-DEI crackdowns. *Truthout.* https://truthout.org/articles/meet-the-campus-leaders-fighting-back-against-right-wing-anti-dei-crackdowns

Persaud, C. J., & Crawley, A. (2022). On Black queer joy and the digital. *Social Media + Society, 8*(2). https://doi.org/10.1177/20563051221107629

Plaza, B., & Barry, C. (2024, April 16). Florida universities are dismantling DEI offices in wake of conservative attacks. *Watermark*. https://watermarkonline.com/2024/04/16/florida-universities-are-dismantling-dei-offices-in-wake-of-conservative-attacks/

Pride, A. J. (2022). A world pandemic and a clarion call: The new push for DEI initiatives in higher education. In O. Noroozi & I. Sahin (Eds.), *Proceedings of IHSES 2022—International Conference on Humanities, Social and Education Sciences* (pp. 125–132). ISTES Organization.

Rest for Resistance. (2024). *Rest fest*. Rest for resistance. https://restforresistance.com/restfest

Salinas II, J. (2024, January 25). After UT Arlington quietly ends LGBTQ+ programs, students demand answers. *KERA News*. https://www.keranews.org/education/2024-01-25/ut-arlington-ends-lgbtq-programs-students-demand-answers

Schulman, S. (2021). *Let the record show: A political history of ACT UP New York, 1987–1993*. Macmillan.

Shakur, T. A. (1999). *The rose that grew from concrete*. MTV Books.

Shelton, T. (2024). *Protect your peace*. Hay House.

Tristano, M. (2022). Performing queer of color joy through collective crisis: Resistance, social science, and how I learned to dance again. *Cultural Studies ↔ Critical Methodologies*, 22(3), 276–281. https://doi.org/10.1177/15327086221087671

Tucker, R. (2022). *And the category is: Inside New York's vogue, house, and ballroom community*. Beacon Press.

Turesky, M., & Crisman, J. J. A. (2023). 50 years of Pride: Queer spatial joy as radical planning praxis. *Urban Planning*, 8(2), 262–276. https://doi.org/10.17645/up.v8i2.6373

UCLA School of Law Critical Race Studies Program. (2024). *CRT forward*. UCLA School of Law Critical Race Studies Program. https://crtforward.law.ucla.edu/

untunion. (2023, June 8). *Pride Alliance: Fostering inclusion and empowerment on campus*. WordPress. https://untunion.wordpress.com/2023/06/08/pride-alliance-fostering-inclusion-and-empowerment-on-campus/

Wilson, B. (2017, February 10). What is the "gig" economy? *BBC*. https://www.bbc.com/news/business-38930048

CONCLUSION: DREAMING OF LIBERATION & SOLIDARITY: NOTES FOR HOW WE KEEP GOING

D. Chase J. Catalano and T.J. Jourian

Introduction

In this conclusion chapter, we weave together the threads of ideas, insights, and possibilities for critical, intersectional, and liberatory TQ center(ed) diversity work in higher education. Drawing from the inspiration of the chapters within this volume, we offer questions for TQ center(ed) diversity work practitioners and scholars to consider in their approaches. We resist the expectation to provide "best practices" because institutions, practitioners, scholars, and communities are too capacious to prescribe any singular action to attend to our needs, desires, and dreams. We provide tools to help individuals and collectives imagine without boundaries and foster coalitional relationships that will sustain without becoming stagnant.

The preceding chapters provided provocative thinking through historical and contemporary experiences, frameworks, and practices. They engaged with policy, power, collaboration, staffing, programming, intersectional manifestations of oppression, leadership, and worldmaking. In its totality, we hope this collection of chapters validates invalidated experiences, challenges staid practices, and inspires new thinking. The contributors to this book offer a recognition of challenges, critical analysis of how TQ center(ed) diversity workers engage in their work, *and* liberatory possibilities for contemporary approaches that avoid or at least minimize trauma and imagine futures of joy. In short, we all—to a great deal of variability—must endure these systems of oppression, and we need not only imagine responses to oppression; we must practice liberatory thinking if we are to do more than survive *and* create new worlds where responses to oppression are less and less necessary. In this conclusion, we focus on how a liberatory consciousness framework can support our work to begin with liberation (Love, 2018). We do not provide answers because we do not believe there is "one right way" to do social justice work—although to be clear, we do believe it is imperative that we not further enact harm on others or ourselves. What we do provide are some examples of how we could think with a liberatory consciousness in our practice and questions for readers to consider.

A Liberatory Consciousness

A liberatory consciousness begins with recognition that we are all living with and under the conditions of oppression (Love, 2018). Dr. Barbara J. Love (2018) characterized liberation workers as those who have a commitment to changing systems and institutions to achieve greater equity and social justice. To develop a liberatory consciousness is to acknowledge that we must each endure oppressive environments and dynamics and still need not succumb to despair and hopelessness. Instead, as liberation workers we recognize how everyone plays a role in maintaining these systems without focusing on blame; we are all complicit *and* we are all responsible to cultivate intentional practices that aim to dismantle systems of oppression. There are four elements to a liberatory consciousness: awareness, analysis, action, and accountability (Love, 2018). These four elements are not linear, as this is not a developmental or stage model. These elements or components require continuous practice, "event by event, [and] each time we are faced with a situation in which oppression or internalized oppression is evident" (Love, 2018, p. 611). Anyone can become a liberation worker, and this is a lifetime of work.

The Four Components

Awareness is the act of noticing. Are you aware of what is happening around you, near you, before you arrived in a space, since you arrived? It requires us to notice words, ideas, behaviors that we witness and that we enact.

Awareness is noticing when no one greets a new person who enters an office, when someone's comment in a meeting is ignored, or when someone makes a comment that denigrates another. It is also noticing that which is not as easy to distill to individual behavior, such as when certain groups rarely show up in our applicant pool or when ostensibly-neutral policies impact some people more than others. Noticing requires that we do not shrug off our observation as a harmless or unimportant event. Analysis is how we make meaning of the world around us. It is the process of thinking about what we notice and wondering why this happened or why it continues to happen and considering what can be done about it. Analyses are opportunities to consider what actions might be possible in response to a situation and thinking through our choice of how to proceed. Action is how we take ideas and put them into practice. Action is how all of us engage in the project of liberation and is "the best possibility of gaining liberation for any of us" (Love, 2018, p. 613). Action can be individual or collective, large or small scale, taking on a task or drawing the attention of others to a task they can support. Accountability reminds us that we need not, nor should we, work in isolation. In fact, solidarity is a requirement for how we work across and within groups to achieve liberation for us all. "The accountability element of a liberatory consciousness is concerned with how we understand and manage this opportunity and possibility for perspective sharing and allyhip in the liberation work" (Love, 2018, p. 613). We are all responsible for our liberation because our liberation is bound up in each other. As those who work in higher education, we must remember that our TQ center(ed) work can be intersectional if we remember to communicate and think across and within identity groups; this is how we find common ground, engage in mutual aid, and form collectives. Taken together, awareness, analysis, action and accountability help us share knowledge and experience, think with each other, interrupt hegemonic norms, and develop new ways of thinking, learning, and being that bring about emancipatory futures.

In some ways, a liberatory consciousness seems too easy because those four elements are so accessible to understand. Does liberation need to be complicated? Why would it seem more plausible if we introduced a multi-stage model with complex terms and idiosyncrasies? At the same time, it might not be that simple when we consider this is a lifetime of work that is quite a bit harder in practice than in conceptualization. In the next section, we will provide some examples of what can get in the way of doing liberation work.

Starting with Liberation: We Can Expect More

To start with liberation is to push against most U.S. born individuals' educational experiences that function as compliance training (Freire, 2003; Giroux, 2020; hooks, 1994; Love, 2020). Educational practices train us to exist within these systems of oppression while learning to accept exploitation, marginalization, powerlessness, violence, and cultural imperialism (Young, 1990). We are so inured to how this socialization process occurs that it takes considerable effort to recognize our complicity and by the time we do, the task of responding likely feels overwhelming. At the same time, we must believe in the possibility of a different future or life experiences to participate in actions to transform it (Freire, 2021). If we do not believe liberation is possible, then what is the purpose of doing TQ center(ed) work to dismantle oppression (Catalano et al., 2024; Love, 2018; Shlasko, 2015)? Let us push back on thoughts that the goal of TQ center(ed) work is to make life a bit more bearable for people with marginalized identities within marginalizing institutions; we can want and expect more. Feelings of disempowerment when doing the work of liberation are inevitable, and TQ center(ed) work can sometimes feel like shouting at time itself with the expectation we can speed it up or slow it down. That exhaustion and those feelings of powerlessness are actually a function of oppression working as it is supposed to work (Young, 1990).

Feelings of powerlessness also stem from believing TQ center(ed) work does not lead to tangible, material, or documentable change. Educational efforts are not meant to be transactional, but transformational (Freire, 2021; hooks, 1994), which means the impact may happen in an instant and/or take years to manifest. The demand to prove the results of TQ center(ed) work functions to diminish hope by oversimplifying how oppression functions. Hope requires continuous practice (Hayes & Kaba, 2023). Higher education and other broader systems are too large to wrap our individual arms around *and* we can still contribute to transformation. "To practice active hope, we do not need to believe that everything will work out in the end. We need only decide who we are choosing to be and how we are choosing to function" (Hayes & Kaba, 2024, par. 6).

To develop a liberatory consciousness means to choose to question who benefits when we think our work does not result in change. It means interrupting our thinking to ask what we expect change to look like, feel like, smell like, sound like. We believe to start with liberation is to unlearn transactional thinking in favor of transformational approaches. It means choosing not to respond to a problem a student encounters with a shrug that communicates, "What are you going to do? This is how the world works." Instead, we recognize the shrug as insufficient and even harmful, as it normalizes oppression. A liberatory consciousness encourages us to recognize that how the world works is unacceptable and to imagine a different reality. Exclusion and inequity are problems that require solutions because of how systems and institutions work. Formal educational practices train students to solve problems and those tools have, at times, served us well to tweak and change things to make life more livable for some people. A liberatory consciousness reminds us that we were never trained in dreaming about liberation. For that, we need to work in and across communities to support each other, where we expand our awareness and thinking, and conceive of actions that serve to disrupt these systems of oppression.

Take, for instance, research on trans and nonbinary students in college. Catalano (2015) explored the experiences of trans men in college. One of the significant findings was how these students had low expectations for inclusion such as two of five friends using their correct pronouns or lack of physical violence as a sign of safety (Catalano, 2015). Some contemporary research on trans and nonbinary students examined how and why they might engage in activism even on campuses perceived as more inclusive (Goldberg et al., 2020), how they navigate the costs of higher education (Lange, 2024), and how they make meaning of institutional efforts for inclusion (Lange et al., 2022). This research demonstrated some progress towards more inclusive campus climates, policies, and practices. At the same time, what does progress mean in the face of the 2023, 2024, and 2025 legislative attacks on trans and nonbinary bodily autonomy and anti-diversity, equity, and inclusion (DEI) legislation? To juxtapose trans and nonbinary student experiences with political attacks reveals how campus transformations are fragile and easily erased. We argue that in some U.S. states, measures of TQ inclusion may have remained or will return to small measures of recognition and limited threats of physical harm. Instead, a liberatory consciousness framework inspires us to ask why we expect so little as signs of inclusion? TQ students' material, emotional, and other needs remain largely unmet, regardless of the progress since the first TQ center in the 1970s—yet institutions seem safe enough because some friends or faculty will respect their pronouns? We must dream more expansively if we are to achieve liberation. We must analyze what we think and ask why we think it. We must consider what others say and how that causes us to consider our actions and inactions. Liberation is the antidote to the shrug that says this is how it's always been and we can not change it. Teaching ourselves to think with a liberatory consciousness is how we do not become complacent and complicit when institutional leadership shrugs and tells us there is nothing they can do. We must relearn how to think and then endeavor to think capaciously if we want to create institutions where inclusion is more than an empty gesture at a policy without a practice (Ahmed, 2012).

We Cannot End Oppression by Replicating Oppression

TQ center(ed) work often involves educating others and it is easy to lament how one-time educational sessions are often ineffective. At the same time, given the anti-DEI legislation pervasive since 2023, these educational endeavors became illegal in some states and many misunderstand their good intentions to create more inclusive places and safer spaces. We do not believe diversity education sessions are a panacea that will save us all from oppression. However, liberation must begin with a willingness to engage; social justice and cultural transformation must begin with efforts to interrupt the status quo or to at least ask questions that cause us to question the things we take for granted as truths (Love, 2018). To that end, we must begin to examine what our goals are and to their end what activities we include in these workshops.

There are many different kinds of education and facilitation and design requires innovative approaches to engage learners, participants, or whoever is in the audience. As Kannan and Catalano wrote about in chapter seven, there is no one size fits all to activities that inspire attendees. However, there remain legacy activities (Shlasko, 2015) that often replicate oppression. Legacy activities come from a good place as they may have been activities a facilitator experienced as a participant that was quite powerful for them (Shlasko, 2015). To us, a legacy activity might also be one that we inherited in a design without ever having experienced them, and thus do not recognize how they might cause harm. These activities were so powerful, in fact, that the facilitator uses it over and over again to elicit the same emotional reaction in participants that occurred for the facilitator. Unfortunately, these legacy activities often "support linear, single-issue thinking, and largely fail to account for intersectionality" (Shlasko, 2015, p. 350). For instance, the coming out stars activity actually functions to replicate oppression as a way of ending oppression (Catalano et al., 2024). Briefly, the activity asks participants to write the names of people who are of importance to them (family, mentors, friends, etc.) on the arms of a five pointed star[1]. Then the facilitator reads a series of prompts that reveal as these people of significance learn of the person's sexual orientation, one or all of those people reject the individual; with each rejection, the individual tears off that person from the star. The facilitator then leads a discussion about how it felt to experience rejection or support, as well as how it felt to see others did not experience the same kind of rejection.

A liberatory consciousness framework reminds us that using tools of oppression, such as pity or shame to emotionally engage individuals instead of inviting them into uncomfortable conversations about power, privilege, and oppression, empowers those very tools (Lorde, 1984). A liberatory consciousness framework reminds us that evoking pity or shame uses tools of oppression to emotionally engage individuals instead of inviting them into uncomfortable conversations about power, privilege, and oppression. This is especially true if we want to name how power, privilege, and oppression are not discrete but overlapping and sometimes contradictory experiences based on our multiple social identities. Drawing attention to the manifestations of oppression need not require trauma bonding or personal vulnerability revelation to compel others to (re)consider ideas, meaning making, or action to recognize we are all accountable to each other to achieve collective liberation. Practices that encourage difficult dialogues (Nagda et al., 1999; Quaye & Johnson, 2016) do not force others to feel negative emotions as a way to empathize how marginalized groups experience oppression. Enacting activities that engender pain in others is a way of lashing out so that those individuals feel pain too. Those are tools of oppression, not liberation. Instead, we can increase each other's awareness and analysis through frameworks that inspire critical thinking. Let us imagine educational practices that lean on complementary approaches to interrupt oppression. Shlasko (2015) reworked the privilege walk using Young's (1990) five faces of oppression. Catalano et al. (2024) reimagined coming out stars using a liberatory conscious framework. Use that which speaks to you, such as brown's (2017) emergent strategy, underworlding (Gossett & Huxtable, 2017), or the Black radical imagination (Kelley, 2002). These approaches foster coalition building because oppression is not singular. Intersectionality teaches us that we must work to eliminate all oppressions because they are interrelated and support the existence of each other (Harris & Patton, 2019); they must all come down to achieve transformative change.

We live intersectional lives and must consider how we teach and engage with others through intersectional thinking towards liberatory possibilities.

The Fear of Making Mistakes

The thing about engaging in TQ center(ed) or any social justice work is that mistakes are inevitable. In fact, Love (2018) wrote, "As liberation workers, it is axiomatic that we will make mistakes" (p. 614). However, as brown (2020) so aptly described, our fears of making mistakes gets in the way of transformative justice. In fact, it is the fear of mistakes that might cause us to choose not to act because we fear the repercussions of getting it wrong. We understand this fear, as it has frozen us all at times (and will continue to). This caused us to wonder, instead of being afraid of mistakes, how can we build communities and coalitions that can hold us in loving accountability through our mistakes and even our gravest missteps (e.g., by using abolitionist transformative justice rather than carceral logics; Mingus, 2019)? Our communities of accountability can help us understand the implications of our mistakes, to help us consider opportunities to repair harm we caused, and to rethink and relearn ways to respond that offer repair, healing, and hope.

In our earnest desire to advocate on behalf of an individual or a group, especially in circumstances where we have privilege over that individual or group, we may overstep. We may try to influence them using normative ideas that undermine their approaches. Humility sounds good *and* is hard in practice. Do you know how to apologize? A real apology that is about an authentic appeal to repair harm caused, not a performance that recenters the person who enacted the harm? Do you know how to accept an apology? Are you willing to forgive harm done to you, to move forward with someone? This is not about us advocating that anyone should forgive all harm committed upon them. Every individual should have agency to choose or deny forgiveness. We mean, if we decide to work in collectives, how can we establish the kind of trust and communication that create opportunities for us to learn, change, and stay in the fold when we make mistakes? How do we determine boundaries and invitations that allow for sustained dialogue where we learn from each other, taking time to explore ideas that are unfamiliar and uncomfortable? With whom are we willing to be in conversation so we can ask questions that might seem intrusive or ignorant and to whom and when are we unwilling to go there? After all, to engage in liberation work is to take risks on allyship.

CONCLUSION

Where Do We Go from Here?

In our work to be advocates and accomplices with each other, where do we begin? Perhaps, we first need to be clear about what and who we care about and where we are willing to go to determine where we can start. Black queer feminist organizer and scholar, Charlene Carruthers (2018), offered the following questions to gain that clarity:

- Who am I?
- Who are my people?
- What do we want?
- What are we building?
- Are we ready to win?

Clarity about self allows us to approach this work with honesty—with ourselves and others—and intentionality, so we can hold ourselves and be held to account to align our intentions with our practice. As we believe in autonomy and choice, we further offer these questions aligned with a liberatory consciousness development:

- What do I/we need to know and understand?
- How will we think together?
- What actions and risks am I/we willing to take and able to take?
- How will I/we hold myself and each other in community in support and accountability?

Knowing there is no safe or simple path to liberation is not an excuse to opt out. Those of us who have chosen to take on TQ center(ed) roles cannot opt out of liberation work for fear we will cause harm otherwise we enable oppression through pinkwashing institutions (LGBTQ Nation, 2022). Nor is it a reason to be afraid to try. For us, a liberatory consciousness framework provides a way to move towards social justice and to transform the world around us. We are all both impacted and complicit in oppression, so we must remind ourselves that we all have a vested interest in liberation. We invite everyone to cultivate and imagine communities where we can experience joy, share pain, and find support. Liberation is about recognizing how our learned pathways of thinking are working against us and seeking out new information to think differently. Liberation is about a multitude of actions, many of them small and not insignificant. Liberation is caring for ourselves and caring for others. Imagining sustainable efforts that inspire others and most importantly, ourselves.

Note

1 See The Trevor Project for an activity description: https://www.thetrevorproject.org/wpcontent/uploads/2017/08/75ea657f061737b608_6pm6ivozp.pdf

References

Ahmed, S. (2012). *On being included: Racism and diversity in institutional life.* Duke University Press.
brown, a. m. (2017). *Emergent strategy: Shaping change, changing worlds.* AK Press.
brown, a. m. (2020). *We will not cancel us: And other dreams of transformative justice.* AK Press.
Carruthers, C. (2018). Unapologetic: A Black, queer, and feminist mandate for radical movements. Beacon Press.
Catalano, D. C. (2015). Beyond virtual equality: Liberatory consciousness as a path to achieve trans* inclusion in higher education. *Equity & Excellence in Education, 48*(3), 418–435. https://doi.org/10.1080/10665684.2015.1056763
Catalano, D. C. J., Wagner, R., & Simms, S. (2024). Toward liberation, not oppression: Reconsidering coming out stars. *Journal of Diversity in Higher Education.* Advanced online publication. https://dx.doi.org/10.1037/dhe0000565
Freire, P. (2003). *Pedagogy of the oppressed* (30th anniversary ed.). Continuum.
Freire, P. (2021). *Pedagogy of hope: Reliving pedagogy of the oppressed.* Bloomsbury.
Giroux, H. A. (2020) *On critical pedagogy.* Bloomsbury.
Goldberg, A. E., Smith, J. Z., & Beemyn, G. (2020). Trans activism and advocacy among transgender students in higher education: A mixed methods study. *Journal of Diversity in Higher Education, 13*(1), 66-84. https://doi.org/10.1037/dhe0000125
Gossett, C. & Huxtable, J. (2017). Existing in the world: Blackness at the edge of trans visibility. In R. Gossett, E. A. Stanley, & J. Burton (eds.), Trap door: Trans cultural production and the politics of visibility (pp. 39-56). MIT Press.
Harris, J. C., & Patton, L. D. (2019). Un/doing intersectionality through higher education research. *The Journal of Higher Education, 90*(3), 347–372. https://doi.org/10.1080/00221546.2018.1536936
Hayes, K., & Kaba, M. (2023). *Let this radicalize you: Organizing and the revolution of reciprocal care.* Haymarket Books.
Hayes, K., & Kaba, M. (2024, February 19). Hope is a practice and a discipline: Building a path to a counterculture of care. *Nonprofit Quarterly.* https://nonprofitquarterly.org/hope-is-a-practice-and-a-discipline-building-a-path-to-a-counterculture-of-care/
hooks, b. (1994). *Teaching to transgress: Education as the practice of freedom.* Routledge.
Kelley, R. D. G. (2002). *Freedom dreams: The Black radical imagination.* Beacon Press.

LGBTQ Nation. (2022, July 26). What is pinkwashing? *LGBTQ Nation.* https://www.lgbtqnation.com/2022/07/what-is-pinkwashing/

Lange, A. C. (2024). Transgender men and non-binary students managing their identities to pay for college. *The Review of Higher Education, 48*(1), 129–159. https://doi.org/10.1353/rhe.2024.a937146

Lange, A. C., Linley, J. L., & Kilgo, C. A. (2022). Trans students' college choice & journeys to undergraduate education. *Journal of Homosexuality, 69*(10), 1721–1742. https://doi.org/10.1080/00918369.2021.1921508

Lorde, A. (1984). *Sister outsider.* Penguin Random House.

Love, B. L. (2020). *We want to do more than survive: Abolitionist teaching and the pursuit of educational freedom.* Beacon Press.

Love, B. (2018). Developing a liberatory consciousness. In M. Adams, W. J. Blumenfeld, D. C. J. Catalano, K. DeJong, H. W. Hackman, L. E. Hopkins, B. J. Love, M. L. Peters, D. Shlasko, & X. Zúñiga (Eds.), *Readings for diversity and social justice* (4th ed, pp. 610–615). Routledge.

Mingus, M. (2019, January 11). *Transformative justice: A brief description.* TransformHarm.org. https://transformharm.org/tj_resource/transformative-justice-a-brief-description/

Nagda, B. A., Spearmon, M. L., Harding, S., Balassone, M. L., Moise-Swanson, D., & De Mello, S. (1999). Intergroup dialogues: An innovative approach to teaching about diversity and justice in social work programs. *Journal of Social Work Education, 35*(3), 433–449. https://www.jstor.org/stable/23043570

Quaye, S. J., & Johnson, M. R. (2016). How intergroup dialogue facilitators understand their role in promoting student development and learning. *Journal on Excellence in College Teaching, 27*(2), 29–55.

Shlasko, D. (2015). Using the five faces of oppression to teach about interlocking systems of oppression. *Equity & Excellence in Education, 48*(3), 349–360. https://doi.org/https://doi.org/10.1080/10665684.2015.1057061

Young, I. M. (1990). *Justice and the politics of difference.* Princeton University Press.

NOTES ON CONTRIBUTORS

R.B. Brooks (they/them) is an unabashedly queer educator, writer, and podcaster. They studied creating writing and journalism at the University of Missouri Kansas City (2014) and received their masters in higher education administration from the University of Kansas (2016). They are a founder of the Midwest Institute for Sexuality & Gender Diversity. They currently serve as program coordinator for Sexuality & Gender Equity Initiatives at the University of Minnesota Duluth.

D. Chase J. Catalano (he/him) is an associate professor of Higher Education at Virginia Tech. Chase's career in higher education began in student affairs and spanned numerous functional areas with his last role prior to faculty life as the Director of the LGBT Resources Center at Syracuse University. His research and scholarship address conceptual and applied knowledges about social justice education with a focus on trans(*)ness, queerness, social justice educational interventions, liberation, and pedagogies. He is a co-editor of *Readings for Diversity and Social Justice, 4th edition* (Routledge, 2018) and co-edited *Advising & Supporting in Student Affairs* (Charles C. Thomas Publisher, 2021) with Dr. Rachel Wagner. Beyond his various book chapters, he has published articles in *Equity & Excellence in Education*, *Transgender Studies Quarterly (TSQ)*, and *Journal for Diversity in Higher Education*.

Roman Christiaens (they/she) recently received their Ph.D. in Higher Education in the Center for the Study of Higher Education at the University of Arizona. Prior to their doctoral program, Roman served as the Assistant Director for Learning and Development at the University of Michigan's Spectrum Center for four years. Roman's professional experience of ten years in student affairs includes the areas of community engagement, student activities, multicultural affairs and orientation. Their research interests focus on diversity equity and inclusion (DEI) efforts in higher education by utilizing frameworks around critical whiteness, transfeminism and critical geography. Specifically, they are interested in how DEI educators and professionals navigate institutional contexts and various political climates. Roman received their M.Ed. in Higher Education and Student Affairs from the University of Vermont and their B.A. in English with a focus in Creative Writing from Seattle University.

Andy Cofino (he/him) is a passionate educator with over 15 years of experience in advancing diversity, inclusion, and belonging on college campuses across the U.S. He is currently the Assistant Vice President for Diversity, Belonging, and Well-being at Princeton University, where he oversees strategies, programs, and policies to create an inclusive campus environment. Previously, Cofino was the Director of the UCLA LGBTQ Campus Resource Center, leading advocacy efforts to improve policies and procedures impacting over 85,000 students and employees. Andy is a Co-Core Member for Trans Inclusion for the National Association of Student Personnel Administrators. He also runs a consultancy serving clients across industries as a strategist and facilitator on LGBTQ+ inclusion. Andy holds a B.A. in English and Women's and Gender Studies from Pace University; a M.A. in LGBTQ Studies, Social Justice, and Creative Writing from NYU; he is currently pursuing his MBA at UCLA Anderson School of Management.

Tristan Crowell (he/him) is a queer, Filipino Immigrant and educator. He studied Sociology and Political Science at the University of Minnesota-Twin Cities and received his master's in Social Work with a focus on anti-oppressive macro practice from Augsburg University. Tristan's background is in electoral politics and community organizing, engaging young people to actively participate in change-making work. He currently serves as the Program Manager for LGBTQIA+ Student Services with Augsburg University's Department of Multicultural Life.

Antonio Duran (he/él) is an associate professor and program co-coordinator of the higher and postsecondary education program at Arizona State University.

Antonio has developed a robust agenda in the field of higher and postsecondary education, including research on queer and trans students of color, Latinx/a/o communities, and in the areas of sorority and fraternity life. His work is in journals like *International Journal of Qualitative Studies in Education*, *International Journal of Qualitative Methods*, *Journal of Higher Education*, *Journal of College Student Development*, *Journal of Diversity in Higher Education*, among others. He has also published a text through Peter Lang on culturally based sororities and fraternities.

Liz Elsen (they/she) is the Director of Education and Training at The Center on Colfax in Denver, Colorado. Prior to working in non-profit spaces, they were the Director of The Gender and Sexuality Center at the University of Texas at Austin (before the center closed due to an "anti-DEI" law in 2024) & ran the "Intersections" Living and Learning Community at the University of Illinois Urbana-Champaign. They studied Creative Writing and Dramatic Art at The University of North Carolina at Chapel Hill & received a master's degree in College and University Student Personnel Administration from UT Austin. They are currently on the board of the Texas Exes Pride Alumni Network & were on the Advisory Board for the founding of the Disability Cultural Center at UT Austin.

Vanessa Aviva González-Siegel (she/her) is an intersectional speaker & educator, TQ center(ed) diversity worker, and a published researcher and scholar focused on TQ center(ed) diversity work and organizational development in higher education. She is a member of the National Advisory Council and QTPOC Caucus Co-Chair for the National Conference on Race & Ethnicity in Higher Education (NCORE) and serves as a member of the Board of Directors of the New York Transgender Advocacy Group, a transgender-led organization that advocates and creates gender-based policies that benefit transgender, non-binary, and gender non-conforming people in the State of New York. She currently works full-time engaged in TQ center(ed) diversity work at the University of California, Los Angeles. Vanessa holds Dual B.A.s in Women's, Gender, and Sexuality Studies and Social Justice Education from Rutgers University—New Brunswick and an M.A. in Higher & Postsecondary Education from Teachers College, Columbia University.

Justin A. Gutzwa (they/them) is an Assistant Professor of Higher, Adult, and Lifelong Education at Michigan State University. Shaped by their experiences as a queer, nonbinary, trans scholar, Justin employs critical theories and qualitative methods to dismantle deficit-based understandings of queer and trans communities in postsecondary education, particularly trans Communities of Color. Their research has also interrogated systemic minoritization in postsecondary STEM education spaces. Justin began their higher education work in student affairs, working both in undergraduate admissions and international student services before completing their Ph.D. in Higher Education & Organizational Change at the University of California, Los Angeles in 2022.

Kathleen Hobson (they/them) is an advocate, educator, and care worker and has done DEI-related work in higher education for 15 years. Originally from Ohio, Kathleen received their B.A. in Sociology from Ohio University and their M.A. in Higher Education Administration from the University of Akron. They moved to Denton in 2014 to open the University of North Texas Pride Alliance, where they served as director for 10 years. Kathleen is also a proud founding and executive board member of the non-profit, PRIDENTON. Their previous queer work includes ACPA's Coalition for Gender Identity & Sexuality, the Consortium of Higher Education LGBT Resource Professionals, OUTreach Denton, Texas Pride Impact Funds, and the (Dallas) Black Tie Board of Directors. Kathleen is currently pursuing their second master's degree in Clinical Mental Health Counseling at UNT and looks forward to supporting the mental health and healing of queer and trans clients.

Em C. Huang (they/them) has worked to advance queer and trans community, policy, and advocacy work in higher education through an intersectional lens over the past decade. Their experiences as a queer, trans, and nonbinary East & Southeast Asian American inform their passion for social justice education and advocacy. As the Director of LGBTQ+ Advancement & Equity at UC Berkeley, Em leads advocacy efforts to improve university and system-wide policies and practices that impact LGBTQ+ students, faculty, and staff, develops programming and initiatives to address community needs, and advises campus organizations, stakeholders, and individuals on issues of gender and sexuality. Em is a Co-Core Member for Trans Inclusion for the National Association of Student Personnel Administrators (NASPA). Em earned their B.A. in Sociology with minors in Gender Studies, Psychology, and Natural Science at the University of Southern California and their M.Ed in Higher Education and Student Affairs Administration at the University of Vermont.

T.J. Jourian (he/him/his) is an independent scholar, consultant, coach, and trainer with Trans*Formational Change. Previously, he has served as faculty at six institutions in their higher education and student affairs programs, as well as a student affairs practitioner in LGBTQI life, housing and residential life, women's center work, and multicultural affairs at a number of colleges and universities. T.J. earned his PhD in higher education at Loyola University Chicago, studying how diverse trans masculine college students conceptualize masculinity. Centering trans and queer people of color's experiences and epistemologies, his scholarship examines race, gender, and sexuality in higher education, with particular attention to campus gender and sexuality centers and practitioners; masculinity, transness, and racialization; and trans*ing constructs and methodologies. T.J. has published extensively in journals, books, monographs, and blogs, including the co-edited books *Queerness as Being in Higher Education:* and *Queerness as Doing in Higher Education: Narrating the insider/outsider paradox as LGBTQ+ scholars and practitioners.*

Kalyani Kannan (they/them) is an Associate Director for the Center for Women & Gender Equity at West Chester University of Pennsylvania. Their career in higher education has included work in new student programs, housing, student conduct, campus activities, and LGBTQ+ student support. As a scholar practitioner, Kalyani's scholarship focuses on the experiences of trans and queer professionals and students. Their work has been published in *Journal for Diversity in Higher Education* and *Journal of College and Character* and has presented at numerous regional and national conferences including NASPA, NCORE, and MBLGTACC.

Alex C. Lange (they/them) actively works for a more equitable form of higher education in the United States. They are currently an assistant professor of higher education at Colorado State University-Fort Collins, where they also coordinate the Higher Education Leadership Ph.D. program. Their research examines the learning and development of minoritized college students with emerging interests in graduate student learning. Before faculty life, Alex worked in various institutional functional areas, including division operations, LGBTQ student services, intercultural engagement, first-year and summer bridge programs, and leadership programs. In their own time, Alex loves spending time with the kiddos in their life, reading queer fiction, being near big bodies of water, and watching great movies and TV shows.

Ryan A. Miller (he/him) is Associate Professor of Higher Education and Bonnie E. Cone Early Career Professor in Teaching at the University of North Carolina at Charlotte, where he teaches courses on college student affairs administration and higher education leadership. His research focuses on the experiences of minoritized social groups in higher education (namely, disabled and LGBTQ people) and the institutionalization of diversity and equity initiatives within colleges and universities. Ryan has co-edited two books and published more than 50 journal articles and book chapters. Prior to becoming a faculty member, he worked in college student affairs for eight years, including a role directing the LGBT center at the University of North Florida. Ryan received graduate degrees in education from The University of Texas at Austin and Harvard University.

Chelsea E. Noble (she/her) is a scholar-practitioner committed to creating more equitable and just higher education institutions. Currently, she serves as a project director at the University Innovation Alliance. As a scholar, she is interested in students' experiences in postsecondary education, especially among students from marginalized backgrounds, as well as how institutions organize to support these students' success. Most recently, she explored how students experience campus an LGBTQ+ resource center and how these centers fit into student's ecosystems. Her professional experiences include work in LGBTQ+ resource centers, multi-institutional STEM innovation networks, admission, and medical school curriculum change. She holds a bachelor's degree in French from Bowdoin College, a master's degree in higher education from the University of Michigan, and a Ph.D. in higher, adult, and lifelong education from Michigan State University.

Jonathan T. Pryor (he/him) is an Associate Professor of Higher Education Administration and Leadership and serves as chair of the Department of Educational Leadership at California State University, Fresno. Prior to his appointment at Fresno State, he managed the University of Missouri-Kansas City's LGBTQIA Programs and Services for six years. In this capacity, his work consisted of advocating for trans and queer-centered policy and practice, including collaborating with colleagues across academic and student affairs units to advance trans and queer equity within policy, curriculum, and practice. His higher education student affairs experiences inform his scholarship, which primarily interrogates leadership and systemic higher education structures to advance LGBTQ+ equity within higher education. His work has specifically explored LGBTQ+ students and staff experiences working in and with college and university LGBTQ+ center spaces. His research has been published in the *Journal of Student Affairs Research and Practice, the Journal of Diversity in Higher Education, the Journal of LGBT Youth, Innovative Higher Education*, and *the Journal of College Student Development*.

Mycall Akeem Riley (any pronouns) is a liberatory-focused educator. Currently, Mycall is the Director of the Gender and Sexuality Center for Queer and Trans Life at the University of Minnesota Twin Cities. Mycall is also a founding member of the **Blaq Agenda: A Social Experiment Indexing Black Queer experiences.** Mycall is a graduate of Syracuse University's Cultural Foundation of Education master's program. Previously, Mycall was the inaugural coordinator for the LGBTQIA+ Resource Center at DePaul University, Social Justice Education Coordinator for the Center for Identity, Inclusion, and Social Change at DepPaul University, as well as the Assistant Director of the LGBT Resource Center at Syracuse University. Mycall has also had the privilege to teach several courses such as Queer Chicago and Introduction to LGBT Studies. Outside of the ivory tower, Mycall loves book clubs, using style as a personal tool of liberation, and imagining a better world.

J. Audra Williams (he/they) is a dedicated PhD student in Educational Policy and Evaluation at the Mary Lou Fulton Teachers College, Arizona State University. With over a decade of experience as a higher education practitioner, most recently serving as the Program Coordinator for the Office for Equity and Diversity's Education Program at the University of Minnesota. Their research interests broadly focus on topics related to diversity, equity, inclusion, and social justice in higher education, with an emphasis on queer and trans communities. They seek to transform the narrative surrounding these groups by centering conversations on joy. J. Audra earned their M.A. in Higher Education from the University of Minnesota-Twin Cities and their B.A. in Sociology from Luther College.

A BOOK SERIES FOR EQUITY SCHOLARS & ACTIVISTS

Dr. Elizabeth Powers, *General Editor*

Globalization increasingly challenges higher education researchers, administrators, faculty members, and graduate students to address urgent and complex issues of equitable policy design and implementation. This book series provides an inclusive platform for discourse about—though not limited to—diversity, social justice, administrative accountability, faculty accreditation, student recruitment, admissions, curriculum, pedagogy, online teaching and learning, completion rates, program evaluation, cross-cultural relationship-building, and community leadership at all levels of society. Ten broad themes lay the foundation for this series but potential editors and authors are invited to develop proposals that will broaden and deepen its power to transform higher education:

(1) Theoretical books that examine higher education policy implementation,
(2) Activist books that explore equity, diversity, and indigenous initiatives,
(3) Community-focused books that explore partnerships in higher education,
(4) Technological books that examine online programs in higher education,
(5) Financial books that focus on the economic challenges of higher education,
(6) Comparative books that contrast national perspectives on a common theme,
(7) Sector-specific books that examine higher education in the professions,
(8) Educator books that explore higher education curriculum and pedagogy,
(9) Implementation books for front line higher education administrators, and
(10) Historical books that trace changes in higher education theory, policy, and praxis.

Expressions of interest for authored or edited books will be considered on a first come basis. A Book Proposal Guideline is available on request. For individual or group inquiries please contact:

    editorial@peterlang.com.

To order other books in this series, please contact our Customer Service Department at:

    peterlang@presswarehouse.com (within the U.S.)
    orders@peterlang.com (outside the U.S.)

Or browse online by series at www.peterlang.com

www.ingramcontent.com/pod-product-compliance
Lightning Source LLC
Chambersburg PA
CBHW052016290426
44112CB00014B/2263